The Will to Do, the Soul to Dare

Hungarian Refugee Changes the Carbon Fiber World

by
Zsolt Rumy

The contents of this work, including, but not limited to, the accuracy of events, people, and places depicted; opinions expressed; permission to use previously published materials included; and any advice given or actions advocated are solely the responsibility of the author, who assumes all liability for said work and indemnifies the publisher against any claims stemming from publication of the work.

All Rights Reserved
Copyright © 2018 by Zsolt Rumy

No part of this book may be reproduced or transmitted, downloaded, distributed, reverse engineered, or stored in or introduced into any information storage and retrieval system, in any form or by any means, including photocopying and recording, whether electronic or mechanical, now known or hereinafter invented without permission in writing from the publisher.

Dorrance Publishing Co
585 Alpha Drive
Pittsburgh, PA 15238
Visit our website at *www.dorrancebookstore.com*

ISBN: 978-1-4809-5330-7
eISBN: 978-1-4809-5306-2

ZSOLT RUMY *The will to do, the soul to dare.*
Chi's, Senior Board, W-Club, Swimming '59, '60.

In the senior high school yearbook, the yearbook committee selects a quote for each person that, in their view, defines him or her. The quote next to my picture was, *"The will to do, the soul to dare*."* I don't know who selected this quote, but it turned out to be prophetic as, I believe, I have lived up to this description most of my life.

*By: Sir Walter Scott, Scottish author (1771-1832)

To my wife, Mary. For the last fifty years, she made our good times better and she supported me selflessly through the many disappointing and difficult times while I was building Zoltek.

Contents

Introduction	ix
Prologue	xv
Section 1 - My Family's Life in Hungary	**1**
The War Years	3
Living the "Communist Dream"	15
The 1956 Revolution	39
Escape from Hungary	49
Section 2 - My New Life in America	**63**
The Beginning	65
The Immigrant Life	71
Becoming an American	85
Section 3 - My Corporate Life	**105**
Starting as an Engineer	107
Moving on to Sales	119
End of My Corporate Career	139

Section 4 - My Entrepreneurial Beginning 145
Starting Zoltek as an Industrial Service Company 147
Recognizing the Carbon Fibers Opportunity 167
Initial Challenges of the Carbon fiber Business 183
Going Public - ZOLT, Traded on NASDAQ 197

Section 5 - Beginning of Commercial Carbon Fibers 215
Refocusing Zoltek 217
The Commercial Carbon Fiber Concept 227
The Hungarian Acquisition 235
Building the Carbon Fiber Business 257
Developing the Commercial Carbon Fiber Market 281
Struggle to Survive 293

Section 6 - Building Zoltek's Carbon Fiber Business 303
Breakthrough - The Pivotal Years 305
Breakthrough - Growth Years 317
The Mexican Expansion 333
Another Setback 341
Sidestep – Globalization Attempt 357
Finally, We Made It 365

Section 7 - End of My Carbon Fiber Story 371
Attacked 373
Selling Zoltek 377
After the Sale 383

Epilogue 389
Index 401

Introduction

Allow me to introduce myself.

Unless you and I have met sometime in the past or you were active in the advanced composite business or you were a Zoltek shareholder, it is unlikely that you would know who I am, even if you are a close reader of the *Wall Street Journal*, *Barron's*, *Fortune*, or the *New York Times*. But they have all written stories about me as the founder and CEO of Zoltek Companies, Inc.

Perhaps you have heard of the wondrous properties of carbon fibers. My company did not invent carbon fibers, but we did something equally important: we initiated and drove the commercialization of carbon fibers. That is to say, we developed a low-cost process which made it affordable to use carbon fibers and carbon-fiber composites across a wide range of applications and ordinary everyday products. Our goal was to reduce the price of carbon fibers from the 1988 prevailing price of over $100 per pound to as low as $5 per pound.

My company is, by far, the leading producer of carbon fibers used to build the biggest, most advanced, and cost-efficient wind turbines, giant machines that now produce up to five megawatts of electricity. A wind farm of two hundred machines concentrated in less than a square mile of land or ocean would produce 1,000 megawatts, equaling the output of a modern coal-fired or nuclear power station. The whirling blades of these giant machines now extend to about the length of a football field, and Zoltek's lightweight carbon fibers are the enabling critical reinforcement material that ensures that these super-long blades do not buckle or crack under tremendous structural loads.

Zoltek carbon fibers have also gone into parts for a number of limited-production, high-end cars, including the Chevrolet Corvette Z06, Cadillac, and the Tesla Motors electric roadster, which goes from 0 to 100 mph in 3.7 seconds and can travel more than three hundred miles on a single charge. I believe that carbon fiber will continue to enable performance breakthroughs in the auto industry, and I believe that at some point in the not too distant future, the auto industry will commit to action and begin to consume tremendous quantities of carbon fibers and carbon fiber composites. The automotive industry is destined to become the largest consumer of carbon fibers.

We have proven our commercialization concept, but taking the concept to the finish line will take more resources than Zoltek could put together on its own. After a lot of soul-searching and business considerations, I decided the best option for the future was to sell our company to another company that had the resources to complete the makeover of the carbon fiber revolution that we initiated at Zoltek.

I have called Zoltek "my" company, although in 1992, we became a public company. In 2014, I sold Zoltek Companies Inc. to Toray Industries, Inc. of Japan for $600 million. In purchasing Zoltek, Toray, one of Japan's biggest and most advanced materials companies and by far the world's largest aerospace carbon fiber producer, bought into my concept of the "commercialization" of carbon fiber and carbon fiber composites, bringing an exotic (i.e., rare and highly expensive) space-age material down to earth in terms of its price and availability. The combined global market share of all carbon fibers between our two companies is now close to sixty percent. I look forward to seeing Toray take this market to a whole new level.

As the holder of about twenty percent of Zoltek's stock at the time of the sale, I am not a billionaire, but I am only one decimal point removed from being one, only in America!

To complete this brief introduction, let me offer a short version of my personal history. I was born in 1942 in Budapest, Hungary, smack dab in the middle of World War II. The Russian army "liberated" (i.e. enslaved) Hungary at the end of the war in 1945. My father spent over seven years in communist prisons, first in Russia and later in Hungary. My family, mother, father, older brother, and I, escaped from Hungary at the end of the Hungarian Revolution of 1956.

As an almost fourteen-year-old boy at that time, in a small way, I became a freedom fighter. I witnessed history in the making, and I experienced the incredible thrill that all Hungarians felt in knowing freedom for a few short weeks before the Russians returned in a massive display of force and brutally crushed the revolution.

We spent four months in Austria, trying to decide the direction for our future. My father wanted to live close to Hungary so he could return if the government changed, and he was looking for a job. In the meantime, I enrolled in a Hungarian language school in Innsbruck, Austria. My mother was convinced that America offered the most opportunity for my brother and me, and she worked hard to convince my father. Fortunately, she succeeded, and we came to the Unites States as refugees, arriving at Camp Kilmer, New Jersey on March 30, 1957.

With the help of Catholic Charities, my family moved to Minneapolis, Minnesota, and my mother, father, and brother lived there the rest of their lives. I completed my education at the University of Minnesota as a chemical engineer. After graduation, I accepted a position with Monsanto Company and moved to St. Louis, Missouri, in 1966. I met my wife, Mary Catherine Gallagher, in 1967, and we were married in December 1968. We do not have children, and Mary claims that she is still raising me.

After nine years and too many bad bosses in a variety of corporate jobs, I started my own business in 1975. I borrowed $8,000, cash, by refinancing the mortgage on our home as initial capital, a very expensive loan. After building a successful local industrial service business, I was plunged into carbon fibers in 1988. By 1995, we divested all the other business activities and concentrated exclusively on carbon fibers…and this is when the real fun began.

Over the past 60-plus years, people have often asked me what it was like to live under a communist system. When I told them of the horrors of communism, most people did not believe me, and some even tried to convince me that America is actually a worse place than some communist countries. For many years I tried to stay away from political discussions, thinking that as more and more communist countries failed, Americans would come to better appreciate what they have. As I write this, the popularity of the socialist democratic candidate, Bernie Sanders, is proof that many people still think that a socialist paradise could be right around the corner.

While I have prospered and enjoyed the American way of life, it has been disappointing to me to witness the dramatic loss of personal freedoms that Americans endure. In recent years, it seems to me that we are moving from a society with a strong work ethic and independent thinking to one with a growing dependence on a huge central government. It is scary to see how we are coming closer and closer to a kind of intrusive and oppressive government that my family hoped we had left behind in Hungary. It is my hope that we will be able to reverse this descent into a dictatorial socialist state before we reach a point of no return.

Now at age seventy-five, other than golf, I was looking for a project. Several friends and business associates encouraged me to put my story in a book, thinking that my life experiences would be interesting and the building of my business might be instructive and entertaining, especially for those who share the hopes and dreams, not to mention the disappointments, near-disasters, and frustrations, along with small and large victories, lots of laughs, and fun to go with the tireless work, that comes with being an entrepreneur. Let me say it again, only in America!

Prologue

Smart. Cocky. All of five-six. I thought that I spoke almost perfect English, but I knew that I sounded a little funny to everyone around me, due to my Hungarian accent. Plus, I was not dressed properly for the occasion, not knowing what to expect or what was expected of me. That was me as an incoming freshman at the University of Minnesota, attending the fraternity rush in 1961. A week or two before classes began at the University of Minnesota, a friend of mine from West High School in Minneapolis, John Standal, asked if I would like to go to the university "rush."

I asked him, "What's rush?"

"It's about joining a fraternity," John said.

"What's a fraternity?"

"Not to worry. We'll have some beer, and everything will be cool."

John and I went to a few fraternities, but he already knew which fraternity he wanted to join. He took me to Psi Upsilon, where one of our mutual friends from high school, Arne Svendsen, had already pledged. Psi Upsilon also happened to be the fraternity that attracted some kids from Minnesota well-to-do families. It was a chilly fall day and, not knowing any better, I walked in wearing a sweater, not a coat and tie, like everyone else.

Perhaps the relative I most resembled was my uncle Ede (nickname Édi), my mother's older brother and my father's best friend, a little shrimp of a guy (just five-two, but who am I to talk?) with a booming voice. He was a superb bull-shitter and a lot of fun. In the middle of the communist era, he would go into bars and after a few drinks, make a big speech about how glorious it would be to bring back the Habsburg Empire to replace the communists. Anyone else who pulled a stunt like that would be ratted out and sent to prison. But Uncle Édi got away with it because he was funny and people liked him. Like my uncle, I have always been game for any challenge and have never doubted my ability to get in and out of sticky situations.

This led to an *Animal House* moment. When they opened the door, John and I introduced ourselves, and they ushered John into the living room, along with all the other kids going through rush. Meanwhile, they quickly escorted me to a card room in the back of the fraternity house. With my sweater and Hungarian accent, I must have looked and sounded like a prize mark, a dorky foreigner. They thought that they could have some fun at my expense.

"Do you play cards?" they asked.

"Sure," I said. "What are you playing?"

"Hearts," they answered.

As I had never heard of this game, I asked them to explain, which they did.

"Will you play for money," they asked.

"That would be fine," I said.

I could tell that Hearts was one of those games like bridge where success depended not on chance, but on the skill of figuring out the cards that other players were holding and anticipating their moves.

Over the next two or three hours, I took them for about $20, which in 1961 was pretty good bucks! Then they asked me to come back the following evening. I returned wearing a suit and tie, but I still went only to the card room and beat them again. On the third night, I was still in the card room when the president of the fraternity came in to tell me that they would like me to pledge.

"What about my friend John?" I asked.

He had brought me to Psi Upsilon, and I told the president that it wouldn't be right for me to join and not John. After a short time-out to consult with other officers in the fraternity, the president returned to say "yes," they would also take John.

Through the entire experience over three nights, I never made it into the living room; I spent it in the card room! That was my first college exposure, my first exposure to people whose parents were successful in business, a totally different background than the one that I knew growing up in a European country where being an engineer was highly respected, and most companies were run by engineers.

From childhood, I loved math and science and wanted to be an engineer. In the United States, being an engineer was not such a big deal. I was one of a few engineering students at Psi Upsilon, as most of the members were in liberal arts or business school. The fraternity helped open my eyes to the possibility of becoming not just an engineer, but to finding greater fulfillment in the wider world of business management or entrepreneurship.

Looking back, I can see that I always had a restless entrepreneurial spirit as opposed to a contained and careful corporate mentality. The first thing I learned upon coming to the United States was to take care of myself. Though I could hardly speak a few words of English, within a week of arriving in Minneapolis in 1957, still only fourteen years old, I had a six-square-block paper route. I worked part-time and summers in an assortment of other jobs all through high school and college. Working about twenty hours a week apart from studies, I earned enough money to pay my own way through college.

Nevertheless, upon graduating with a degree in chemical engineering from one of the top three chemical engineering schools in the United States, I did what most graduates, who didn't grow up in some kind of a family business, were doing; I decided to go to work for a giant corporation. I didn't think of starting a company or working for a small company. To tell the truth, I couldn't imagine owning my own company.

Back then, there was no problem finding a job. I had several interviews and multiple job offers from big-name companies. I started at Monsanto (1966 to 1968), went to W. R. Grace (1968 to 1971), spent a couple of years at GE (1971 to 1973), and went back to Monsanto for two more years, quitting in 1975 to go into business for myself.

It took me four good jobs and almost a decade to realize that I just didn't fit the corporate mold.

To succeed in a large company, you don't necessarily have to have a button-down personality, but you do need to project the persona of someone destined for leadership, and you also need to be adept in attracting and cultivating a powerful mentor, someone who will protect you when you inevitably run into that boss from hell sometime during your career, that boss who not only does not have your best interests at heart, but actually wants you to fail.

While I sometimes attracted the attention of potential mentors in top management, I never felt comfortable in capitalizing on those connections and plotting a career. It just wasn't in my nature. I eventually came to realize that I would never rise to a level in a big corporation that would begin to satisfy me.

The final straw that compelled me to make the change happened during my second stint at Monsanto. I had decided to return to Monsanto when it became clear that the department I worked for at GE was going to be divested before I had a chance to move to a more mainstream business unit.

In 1973, I rejoined Monsanto in the Enviro-Chem Division. My department's business was air pollution-control equipment. Unfortunately, this division was destined for abandonment, and it was a place for people who were second-rate and on their way out, not destined to advance in the mainstream corporate hierarchy.

I was in the sales department. I initiated projects with our representatives in the Southeast territory to remove organic mists generated by textile-processing and fast-food restaurants. This was an unusual application, and we were in the initial testing and equipment design phase. I had no support from the rest of the organization and I did the equipment design with fabrication shops in the area.

I was surprised to see a write-up in the Monsanto annual report claiming that this application would be the savior of the Enviro-Chem Division. When I saw this, I went to see the president of the division and told him that the account in the annual report was totally inaccurate and misleading. In reality I was working on this application single-handedly without any support from management. He promised to help fix the situation and asked me to develop a strategic business plan.

After many meetings and discussions, I got approval for the plan. A few days later, the president called me to his office and told me that I was getting a promotion. He had decided to make me the new manager for sales and marketing for this application.

"Great," I said, but I wondered why he stopped short of giving me full responsibility for the entire business.

I was told that a specific engineer would be assigned to do the equipment design. That is when I learned that I would have to accept a certain engineer, a known incompetent, to manage the equipment design.

This was not the first time in my corporate career that I had been set up for failure. But I decided it would be the last.

I went back to my cubicle and called two of my favorite sales-representative companies and asked them if they would recommend me to their principals to become their sales agent for their products in the St. Louis territory. They both offered to help. Within an hour, I had commitments for several product lines.

I went back to see the president again and said, "I decided to resign."

He asked me, "Why now, just after you were promoted to be the sales manager."

I told him, "I was looking to be responsible for the entire business, but what the engineer you assigned to the project could design, I could not sell!"

In 1975, I founded Zoltek Corporation, a manufacturers' representative, engineering, and industrial distributor company. Some thirteen years later, I was becoming restless and impatient with a new status quo in my business life. Rather than being a distributor or agent selling someone else's products and ideas, I wanted us to make some real noise of our own. I began to look at developing a product or for an acquisition that would take Zoltek to a whole new level. That's when carbon fibers loomed into sight as one possibility. I seized the opportunity.

In 1988, I acquired a failing specialty-carbon-fiber company, Stackpole Fibers Company, which was a subsidiary of Stackpole Carbon Company.

Over the years, I have joked that, "It was the perfect acquisition. If Stackpole Fibers had been performing any better, I couldn't have afforded to buy it and if it had been performing any worse, there would have been nothing to buy, just perfect!"

This company produced a special type of carbon fiber, which was well suited for friction products, not for structural reinforcement, which was then (and even more so is today) the primary use for carbon fibers. Shortly after I acquired this company, the aerospace industry and NASA, for environmental reasons, were forced to change from rayon-based to acrylic-based carbon fibers for their rocket nozzle liner application. The only acrylic-based product that had been tested and used for this application was our fiber.

This was a cause for celebration. I could foresee a revenue stream of many millions of dollars stretching out before us for many years to come. However, some weeks later, I was heading for a European vacation and, before boarding the airplane, I called the office one final time. I had a message to call Hercules Chemical Company regarding the rocket nozzle business. I made the call expecting good news. Instead I was told that Hercules had received an $80 million government contract to find a carbon-fiber company to manufacture the product we were already producing. He wanted me to make a case for why my company should be included in this investigation.

I proceeded to write up my case on the plane ride to Paris. The more I wrote, the more upset I became. I realized that the U.S. government was prepared to spend $80 million not to do business with me! Although I submitted my case, I realized I would need to think about other ways to build the business that wouldn't be dependent on the government and a small cabal of government contractors.

When I returned from vacation, I started to study the process of manufacturing structural-type carbon fibers. It became obvious that commercial applications would never develop at then-prevailing prices, and commercial applications would one day dwarf the aerospace business. Ultimately, we developed the process and designed equipment to significantly reduce the cost of manufacturing carbon fibers, with the goal of being able to sell at $5 per pound versus $100 or more.

Our early trouble with the government turned into a game-changing event for Zoltek and the entire carbon fiber industry. While the U.S. government still does not buy our fibers for rocket nozzles, all French rockets utilize our fibers. Further, over the past twenty years, the U.S. government has given Oakridge National Laboratory hundreds of millions of dollars to develop a competitive fiber to what we have been producing since the year 2000. So far, they have not succeeded. The government's return on investment has been ZERO.

Financing a developing and capital-intensive company is a major problem. Obtaining sufficient financing is almost a full-time job. After talking to a number of banks, I met with Southwest Bank of St. Louis. The bank had recently been acquired and was not heavily capitalized. I was looking for a $4 million loan, which was significant for the bank at that time. Although the loan officers recommended approval of the loan, the Chairman had a policy of vetting any new significant potential customer on the golf course.

I was not a good golfer, but tried my best to look like I knew what I was doing. I was teamed with the Chairman, Andrew N. (Drew) Baur, whom I had just met, against his two loan executives: Linn Bealke, Vice Chairman and Bob Witterschein, Executive Vice President.

Drew was a physically imposing, very tall man, matched with a larger-than-life personality. Thanks to his skill and competitive spirit, we were barely ahead through seventeen holes. Things did not go well on the last hole. On the eighteenth green, I had to make a short putt to stay in the game. But I missed! I figured it was all over between the bank and me. But then something funny happened.

Drew stage whispered to Bob, "Zsolt is one of the worst golfers I ever played with, but make the loan."

From this rocky beginning, we became the best of friends. Actually the three of them were the kind of mentors that I had never known during my corporate days. They helped me survive. They trusted me and they had confidence in me and helped me through many difficult periods. My business would not have survived without them. They also introduced me to their friends, many of whom became my friends as well over years.

This brings me to my last short story before I begin my full story. We were raising money for building our continuous-carbon-fiber production facility after we developed our proprietary production process and designed the production equipment. We were looking to raise about $50 million through a secondary stock offering, with Merrill Lynch as our lead banker. We had just completed the prospectus and were ready to go on the roadshow when we received a letter from the Securities and Exchange Commission (SEC) that they were investigating our financial statements. Our share price increased significantly, and it seems that a short-seller claimed that we did not actually buy an acrylic fibers plant in Hungary. Needless to say, it is out of the question to begin an offering when the company is under active investigation by the SEC.

We received a set of questions and prepared the answers. After we submitted our documents, I called our attorney, Tom Litz, to find out the next step in the process. He said that we just had to wait, that there was nothing else we could do. I insisted that we needed to expedite the process and that he should call the SEC enforcement office for a face-to-face meeting to try to resolve the matter. Reluctantly, after telling him if he did not call them, I would, he agreed, and we got a date. Our attorney, CFO, Merrill Lynch's attorney, and their financial person and I went to Washington D.C.

We met for breakfast in the hotel to plan our presentation. There were too many people in the restaurant, so we decided to go to the attorney's office about four blocks away. It was a hot summer day, and we walked. By the time we got to the office, we were all sweating.

I saw this as a problem and I told the group, "Forget my presentation because I will not practice what I am going to say" and I continued, "Next, order a limousine to wait for us at the front door with the air-conditioning on full blast. After that, we needed to find a room with its own air conditioning and set it cold enough to hang meat."

Finally, I said, "The one thing we do not want to do at the SEC meeting is sweat!"

We figured we would get a maximum of thirty minutes to make our case. Our attorney was to go first (five minutes), I would follow and tell the company history (five minutes), and then the CFO would take them through our financial statements (ten minutes), the Merrill Lynch financial person would present the details of the pending offering (five minutes), leaving five minutes for Q&A. I asked them if we could expect to get a positive answer today. I was told it was out of the question, the best we could hope for was positive body language, whatever that meant.

Great plans, but when we were ushered into the meeting room, things changed. The room had no windows, and it was very sparsely furnished. It looked more like an interrogation chamber. Worst of all, the only decorations were framed photographs of about two dozen people who were in prison for securities fraud. I actually thought it was damned funny, but the others did not see the humor.

Finally, three investigators came in with absolutely no expression on their faces. They were all business. After introductions, our attorney started his presentation. He was off his game, clearly intimidated. He repeated himself several times and went way beyond his allotted time. The grim-faced investigators just stared at him.

Then it was my turn. As I started to talk, the investigators maintained the same blank, malevolent expressions. So, I went off script. "We probably would not even be here," I blurted out, "except for the fact that our stock price has gone through the roof."

Then I asked, "Was that something that caught your interest? Did you want to talk about what caused our stock to take off?"

This was something they did not expect, and they opened up. They asked me a lot of questions about carbon fibers, and we talked openly about our company and all about our business potential for the next ninety minutes. They told us to go forward with the offering. If they had any more questions, they would contact us. Otherwise do NOT send them any more information on the offering status. As we said good-bye, the head of the investigation team shook my hand, and she said that she never thought carbon fibers could be this exciting! We successfully completed the offering.

There are many immigrants with stories of success in America and each achieved success in different ways and to different levels. Every one of these stories is unique with lessons of its own. My story is just one of them.

Section 1
My Family's Life in Hungary

The War Years

It was the fall of 1948. I was almost six years old. We were at the Eastern Railroad Station in Budapest where the prisoners of war from Russia were returning home. My mother, brother, and I went to the station every day when the trains were arriving from Russia. Finally, after a dozen or more of these trips, we recognized my father walking off the train. This was my first memory of my father.

When I first saw him, he barely resembled his pictures. It was obvious to me, even as a five-year-old, that he was a broken man, mentally and physically. The only possession he had with him was a picture of my mother, brother, and me that he kept with him all through the three and a half years that he had spent as a prisoner of war in Russia. He had fabricated a beautiful picture frame for this picture out of birch tree bark.

My mother, Ilona Tones, born in 1915, and father, Árpád Rumy, born in 1910, grew up in a small city named Sopron, on Hungary's western border, next to Austria. This was a beautiful ancient city, but, as with most European countries, the capital city is where everything happens. So, eventually, both my parents ended up in Budapest.

Hungary, at that time, was a wealthy country. The Kingdom of Hungary was the most important part of the Austro-Hungarian Empire that became the second largest country in Europe after Russia and the third largest population after Russia and Germany.

The history of Budapest, located on the Duna (Danube) River, dates back to pre-Roman days and was established in its present form in 1873 by combining the hilly and mostly residential villas of Buda and the old city of Òbuda on the west bank with the commercial districts and four- to eight-story apartment houses of Pest on the east bank. In the late 1800s, for the thousand-year anniversary of the establishment of the Principality of Hungary in 895, a major reconstruction of Budapest took place. Most of the magnificent bridges over the Danube River and the beautiful buildings in downtown Pest date back to this time.

Budapest became a vibrant and exciting city, one of the most beautiful cities in the world. Between 1873 and 1914, Budapest was the fastest growing big city in all of Europe, as population more than tripled from 280,000 people to 930,000; today it is over 2 million.

World War I was triggered, but not caused, by the June 28, 1914, assassination in Sarajevo, Bosnia, of Archduke Franz Ferdinand Habsburg, the heir to the throne of the Austro-Hungarian Empire. Hungary was part of the Austro-Hungarian Empire, but it would be inaccurate to assign the real cause or the initiation or a significant part of the war to Hungary. The assassin was Serbian, and Austria blamed the Serbian government and, within a month after receiving Germany's support, Austria declared war on Serbia. Of course, Hungary as being part of the Empire, ended up on the Austrian and German side of the war.

Hungary played a small role in hostilities, but it was singled out for dismemberment after World War I. The Treaty of Trianon, between most of the Allies and the Kingdom of Hungary, was similar to, but possibly even more punitive than, the Treaty of Versailles was for Germany, reduced Hungary's thousand-year traditional territories by about seventy percent, and about three million Hungarians became minorities of the neighboring countries.

The British and French were leading the parade to break up Hungary, based on their notion of "self-determination." They had drawn the new border for Hungary on their own, in spite of recommendations against this treaty by the U.S. President, Woodrow Wilson.

Wilson said, *"The proposal to dismember Hungary is absurd."* Unfortunately, he did not do anything about it.

Hungary's economy was ruined.

Divided Hungary after the Treaty of Trianon

To undo this treaty and regain the lost territory became the primary political direction and goal of the Hungarian people for years to come, including the period leading up to and during the years of World War II. Those were the years of my parents' youth.

In a last attempt to avoid the effects of the treaty, on March 21, 1919, the leaders of the newly formed Hungarian republic resigned in favor of the Russian-backed communist party led by Béla Kun in hopes the Russians would stand up against the Treaty of Trianon. The Kun government immediately adopted the communist model, nationalizing schools, factories, and farmland. When opposition to the government actions started to gain momentum, the communist government transformed the police into a new "Red Guard" in order to intimidate, destroy, and kill all the opposition to communism.

The Russians had no interest in supporting the Hungarian cause. The Hungarian Red Army was formed to resist the takeover of the territories defined by the Treaty. They enjoyed some early success in Czechoslovakia, but the Romanians destroyed the Hungarian Red Army and captured Budapest. The Romanians forced the communists to turn the government back to the Social Democrats, ending Hungary's 133-day exposure to communism. It also ended any hope to derail the imposition of the Treaty of Trianon.

Admiral Horthy, the head of the Austro-Hungarian Navy, consolidated the remaining Hungarian army, ousted the communists, and took control of the government in 1920. He became the regent of Hungary and stayed in power until 1944. To this day, most Hungarians believe that the Allies sold out Hungary after World War I and that the Horthy government was committed to recovering the lost territories and reuniting the Hungarian people under a sensible, if somewhat autocratic, government that opposed extremism on both sides, communist or fascist.

As Admiral Horthy's government consolidated, the communists escaped to Russia or went underground. The Horthy government was determined to keep the communists out of Hungary and put a stop to the communist movement within Hungary. Horthy is viewed differently by different people, but it is undisputed that under his leadership, Hungary's economy recovered, and the country prospered. It became more like the Hungary of old, a cosmopolitan place that attracted visitors from around the world, a place of beauty and serenity where people were free to go about their own business without undo interference from the government.

My grandfather on my father's side died after he returned home from World War I hostilities in the influenza epidemic. My father and his two sisters were brought up by my grandmother. She had limited financial support. When my father finished gymnasium (high school), he decided to go to the University in Debrecen, which is the largest city of the eastern side of Hungary. He enrolled in agricultural engineering. This school also had a military cadet program, which was fitting for a Rumy male (with its long and, I must say, distinguished family history of military service). The ROTC–type program also helped pay for his education during difficult financial times.

My grandfather on my mother's side was an executive in the small local utility company. He also died early, long before I was born. Financially, my mother's family was in better condition and, soon, after my grandfather died, the whole family moved to Budapest. My mother graduated from college in nursing from the Rockefeller Institute's elite Green Cross nursing program, one of a small number of women in her generation in Hungary to earn a university-level education.

After graduation in 1933, my father found a job managing a sugar beet farm for a Hungarian sugar company. This position took him back to western Hungary, to a small village. When my mother graduated in 1936, she took a position as a public health nurse, also in western Hungary. She lived in a town close to where my father was, and this is where they reacquainted and fell in love. They had a nice life, both were in very important positions, but small towns in Hungary were not sophisticated. They visited each other by horseback and by horse and buggy. My mother's family lived in Budapest, and eventually she found a public health nurse position in Budapest and decided to move back to join her family. She was assigned to several schools to oversee their health services. My father was expecting to have to join the military at some point and eventually, when he did, he also moved to Budapest.

Europe was in turmoil. Germany, taken over by Hitler and the Nazis, was making demands on reversing the treaties of World War I. My father's uncle, Rumy Lajos, was ten years younger than my grandfather, but it seems clear that he had a substantial influence over my father's life after my grandfather died. He was a graduate of a prestigious military academy and was commissioned into active service during World War I while he was still at the academy at nineteen years of age. In 1915, he was captured by the Russians and was taken to Russia as a prisoner of war. He escaped from prison and returned to Hungary via China.

He had a distinguished military career, achieving the rank of general, and became a national hero during World War II. For a period between the two wars, he headed up Hungary's military counterintelligence program. When my father entered the military, he was assigned to counterintelligence and essentially worked for his uncle. By 1938, my father was a captain in the counterintelligence section.

Soon after my father moved to Budapest, my parents became engaged. Both my parents had good incomes and flexible work schedules. My parents married on April 21, 1939. My father was twenty-eight years old and my mother twenty-four years old. This was also the year when World War II officially started. It is hard to imagine what they thought their future would be. I am sure they were hoping for a better life than the way things turned out.

However, they still had almost five years of relatively carefree life before it all turned sour. Our family expanded. My brother, Árpád, was born in August 1941, and I was born on my father's thirty-second birthday on December 1, 1942. We were a happy family. My parents lived an affluent lifestyle with a live-in maid and a chauffeur-driven car; they enjoyed an active social life and their children. During the week, they went out for dinners, attended the opera and the theater. On weekends, they socialized with friends and relatives. Life was good.

Based on stories and pictures from that period, it seems they thought that the happiness would never end. Uncle Édi was on a parallel path of building his family, and the two families grew together. In retrospect, it is hard to believe, with the war going on all around Hungary, and some of the domestic turmoil starting to percolate, how normal life could still exist, but it did. All that changed in 1944!

My father's position was important, and his duties were quite interesting. He had an assigned military aide/chauffeur and a BMW. (Later in the war, the BMW car body was manufactured with metal-framed painted cardboard, way before carbon fiber composites!) His initial assignments were to look for any communist activity or plots. There were a number of Hungarian communists who escaped to Russia or disappeared underground and were plotting to return or surface at the right time to interfere with the political system. Later, he had a number of more interesting assignments.

My father and my Uncle Édi, who by then was an attorney and also my father's best friend, had some heated discussions about what Hungary should do if war was to break out. My uncle was a royalist first and staying neutral was his second choice. Any chance of the re-establishment of the Austro-Hungarian monarchy ended with a parliamentary action in 1921, and neutrality was no longer a realistic option as Hitler came to power in 1933.

My father was for an independent Hungary under a democratically elected government, and he was active in the Smallholders Party (National Conservative Party), which was the largest part of the Adm. Horthy government. Considering the political instability after WW I and what happened while the communists were in power, Adm. Horthy's government was a welcome relief. My father was loyal to Adm. Horthy's government.

Once Hitler came to power, there were only two choices for Hungary: become an early ally, but act independently or be occupied by Germany. The thought of relying on British or French support was totally unrealistic. They did not even defend the very countries they had created just ten years before or their long-term allies. The belief was that if Hungary entered an agreement with Germany early, Hungary would be able to remain neutral, maintain its independence, regain part of the lost territories and avoid German takeover. This strategy worked fairly well until 1944.

In September 1938, the Munich Agreement was signed. This agreement divided Czechoslovakia back to pre-World War I borders. Hungary was granted a large part of Slovakia. My father led an advance team to be sure there would not be any opposition or sabotage when the Ceremonial Hungarian Army marched in to officially take over the designated territory. After this assignment, he also administered the takeover of some of the Slovakian government businesses, such as a salt mine.

As the World War II conflict started to build, as part of the counterintelligence, the Hungarian government established a security system to protect the significant companies from communist and fascist sabotage. The concept was to assign a security officer to all major companies who would have no day-to-day involvement with the operations, but would set up the security systems and monitor them. In the event of sabotage or disturbance, the security officer would take control of the company until order was restored. My father was one of these security officers. He had several companies assigned to him.

The Horthy government held the Germans at bay by passing the anti-Jewish laws Hitler demanded, but not enforcing them. Adm. Horthy persuaded Hitler that so many businesses and other institutions were owned and/or operated by Jews that Hungary could not afford to be without them. This arrangement worked for a while. As Hitler invaded other European countries, Horthy's government welcomed people fleeing those countries. The Jews were generally safe in Budapest. However, there was a radical element, the Nyilas (Archer or Arrow Cross) Party, but, for the time being, they were under control.

In 1940 and 1941, Hungary recovered more territory from Yugoslavia, Ukraine, and Romania, in total about half of the territory lost by the Treaty of Trianon. At Germany's command in 1941, Hungary declared war on Russia. Since Hungary was forbidden by the World War I treaties to have a standing army, the Hungarian army was quickly formed from volunteers. They were poorly trained and ill-equipped. Attached to the German army, Hungarian forces had some early success in fighting the Russian army in Ukraine and Southern Russia. However, during the Battle of Stalingrad, the Hungarian 2nd Army suffered huge losses. Some 100,000 men were lost and whatever the Hungarian army was, it was destroyed.

In 1942, Uncle Lajos transferred from counterintelligence to the regular army. He was assigned to lead several fighting units, as the Hungarian army was trying to rebuild itself. The Hungarian army was active only in the southwest part of Russia, trying to prevent the Russian advance toward Hungary. Although the Hungarian Army was ineffective, Uncle Lajos received a number of decorations and promotions for his heroism and for successfully commanding his troops to several victories.

My father maintained his counterintelligence duties until 1944. My mother continued her job as public health nurse. Our family continued to live in Budapest.

In March 1944, Hitler informed Adm. Horthy that he had ordered the German occupation of Hungary. His intention was to remove the government and replace it with a compliant government. The government was taken over by the Nyilas party. This party was exactly like the German Nazi party with its SS Gestapo troops. Adolf Eichmann arrived within days to start the deportation of Jews. The war had finally arrived in Hungary.

Adm. Horthy tried to initiate peace discussions with the Allies to save the country and tried to protect the Jews. While the Allies did execute a treaty with Romania, they did not respond to Hungary's overtures. Adm. Horthy, in defiance of Hitler's demands, ordered a train full of Jews to stop in transit and return to Budapest. In October of 1944, he announced that Hungary would surrender and withdraw from the Axis coalition. At this point, he was arrested and taken to Bavaria by the Germans. (After the war, he was a witness during the Nuremberg trials and lived the rest of his life in Portugal.)

While this entire takeover was taking place, Budapest became a dangerous place. My mother took my brother and me to Sopron, which was much safer. My father stayed on army duty in Budapest. He became part of the Hungarian defense against the Russian invasion as they advanced towards Budapest. Everyone in the military who was left in Budapest participated in its final defense.

The Russian front was not going well for the Hungarian Army. While the German troops were withdrawing, the poorly equipped Hungarian troops were stuck in Russia. There were many casualties, and chaos prevailed among the Hungarian troops as most of the high-ranking officers were evacuated. My father's uncle, General Rumy Lajos, stayed with his men. He refused to return to Budapest when he was to receive a promotion and decoration. He saved many soldiers from certain destruction, but he was captured by the Russians in March 1945. He was initially sentenced to death, but that order was later changed to forced labor. He was finally released and returned to Hungary in 1955.

The defense of Budapest was also crumbling. The Germans saw the beginning of the end and started to pull out as fast as they could. In the process, they blew up all the bridges over the Duna (Danube) River in hopes that it would slow the Russian march toward the west. My father was stationed on the Buda side of the Duna River. During the day time, he was at the battle station, but at night, he and his aide stayed in a nearby apartment owned by my mother's great uncle, who was a retired cavalry officer. The Russian troops broke through one night in mid-February 1945 and started to round up any straggling German and Hungarian soldiers.

My father noticed the Russian soldiers outside the apartment house. He started to dress in a civilian suit as his aide looked on.

At one point, his aide asked my father, "What about me?"

There was only one civilian suit in the wardrobe; the rest were cavalry uniforms. So my father removed the civilian clothes and put on his full uniform and, together with his aide, walked out of the apartment house. Immediately they were captured.

After he was captured, the Russian soldier first removed my father's watch, second, his handgun, and finally, his sword. This is quite humiliating to an officer, as the protocol was that the first thing you did in disarming an officer was to take his sword. My father never wore a watch for the rest of his life.

From this point on, my father was a prisoner of war until that day in 1948 when I first remember him. The outcome of World War I and World War II dramatically affected Hungary during my parents' life. In my early life, I was exposed to the miserable tyranny of the communist system as I experienced how my father was punished for his beliefs.

History is not an exact science, and the history of wars is written by the victors. In the case of World War II, I studied the Soviet Russian and USA versions in school and heard from people who lived through this period and personally experienced these times. There is very little in common among the three versions beyond documented dates and written treaties and agreements.

Soon after the war "officially" ended, with eighty million people losing their lives, the British Empire collapsed, the European countries lost their African colonies, and the world has been in non-stop conflict ever since. Even before the war in Europe was over, the Allies turned over future control of Central and East Europe to Russia, bringing communism to this part of Europe. Hungary was included.

The new world order started to crumble as soon as it started.

Living the "Communist Dream"

As usual in wars, after the fighting stops, the random killing, looting, and crimes against the defeated population begins. Budapest was no different. One more thing happened: the Hungarian communists flooded back into the city like cockroaches from their underground hiding places in Budapest and Moscow. This was a dangerous time to be in Budapest.

In April 1945, a provisional government was formed, which was controlled by the Soviets. Unfortunately for Hungary and other Central and East European countries, even before the war ended, at the Yalta Conference, the Allies agreed to place them under the Soviet sphere of influence. Thereby the Allies conceded the control of these countries to the Soviets, giving birth to the Cold War that lasted over fifty years. Further, the Allies turned their backs when the Russians did not follow the armistice agreement. In time, a reasonable order was slowly returning. The Russian occupying forces moved to western Hungary, about twenty-five miles from Budapest, where they established their permanent base.

We were fairly safe in Sopron, but had not heard from my father. My mother was very concerned and when it looked reasonably safe, we returned to Budapest. She had difficulty finding a place to live, but found an apartment that was used by the German military during the war. The apartment had two big rooms, with one of the rooms used as a stable. Half the apartment was completely destroyed, and we were able to isolate the other half and moved in. A big reason my mother returned to Budapest as early as possible was to find out what happened to my father. Ironically, my father's aide, who did not have civilian clothes to change into, escaped on the way to Russia. He was the source of information about my father's capture and his prisoner of war status.

Another outcome from the war was hyper-inflation. Currency was losing its value so rapidly that any money earned one day would be worth much less or nothing by the next day. People were paid daily and would rush out to buy whatever they could and/or needed the same day the money was received. Many times there was nothing to buy with cash, and people were using any valuables they had to trade for food. The banks were counting their cash all night to get ready for the next day. My mother had a job with the national bank to count money all night and used the morning to shop for food. She was very resourceful and determined that we would have something to eat every day. My mother was wonderful, and she made life seem as normal as possible under the circumstances. This hyper-inflation went on for over a year until the new currency, the forint, was introduced in August 1946.

Elections were held in November 1945. The majority of the votes were cast for the Smallholders Party. This was my parents' party. The socialist and communist parties combined received less than twenty percent of the votes. This is not what the Soviets were looking for, and they did not allow the winning parties to establish a government. This was the last relatively free election for fifty-five years. Future elections had only one candidate, and everyone was required to vote, which is how communists always win elections by over ninety percent.

The siege of Budapest was devastating. The damage in Pest was overwhelming; essentially eighty percent of the buildings were destroyed or severely damaged. In Buda, the Castle Hill was severely damaged. Reconstruction of historic buildings throughout Budapest continues until today. Horrible looking pre-fab apartment buildings started to be built in the early 1950.

Apartment houses were all taken over by the government. Getting an apartment was on a squatter's rights basis. However, communist party members could pull rank and take the choice apartment and/or evict existing residents. All apartment buildings had a caretaker, usually a low-level party member, who would collect rent. They were generally spying for the authorities. Buda still had many private homes/villas, and they were mostly spared the initial confiscation. Their time was yet to come, however.

The communists went into action immediately by nationalizing (confiscating) all types of private and religious properties. All companies and land holdings were the first to go. Private companies were not allowed. Everyone was working for the government, and the economy was centrally controlled. Wages were minimal and basic food prices were low, but there was shortage of everything. Everyone had a job, but spent half their day shopping, trying to find essential items to buy. Service was non-existent. National productivity was minimal.

Eventually the rules for private business ownership loosened up and private companies with a maximum of five employees were allowed to exist. Land was initially distributed to small farmers, but quickly they were taken back and put into large communes. Agricultural productivity also became minimal because no one really cared. Soon, the entire population was poor, which is the socialist approach to equality. Of course, there was the exception. The communist leaders lived like royalty!

When schools went back into operation, my mother returned to her old job as a public health nurse, responsible for a number of schools' health services. My mother's working hours were similar to our school hours, so she enrolled us in preschool and later, when we attended grade school, she did not have to worry about us kids. If she was not yet home when we came back to the apartment, we hung out with classmates outside. In the winter time, we might visit friends and play board games at their apartments. We did not have to worry about crime or traffic in the streets where we would play soccer. All the criminals were working for the government, and there were no private cars, except chauffeur-driven black government cars driving the party members around. If the party member lost his position, he was lucky to save his life and stepped down to the level of the rest of us.

Our apartment complex was on the Buda side; Villányi ut (street), located at the base of the backside of Castle Hill. Our apartment complex consisted of eight three-story buildings with two apartments on each floor. Our apartment, still only half habitable, was on the ground level. In a few months, a couple in another apartment decided to try to escape Hungary. They told my mother of their plans and told her to take over their apartment if they did not return in a few days. They successfully escaped, and we were able to move into their apartment, which was on the second floor in building F.

By Budapest standards, this was a nice, spacious, and bright apartment in one of the best neighborhoods in Buda. The front door to the apartment opened to a rather dark central hallway. On the left side, there was the kitchen, a half bath, a servant's room, a wardrobe room, and a full bathroom. On the right side, there were two large living rooms. One of these rooms had a nice-sized balcony.

My brother and I had our beds set up in the servant's room. Other than the beds, we had a small wardrobe. The large room with the balcony was where we lived during the day. It had a nice big couch, coffee table with side chairs, a book case, and a table with chairs where we could do our homework. The other large room had a dining room table and also a big couch and a cabinet. Hungarian apartments generally did not have separate bed rooms. Instead, the couches had large pullout drawers where the bedding was stored during the day. The other thing we did not have was built-in closets. We had wardrobes. All the rooms had parquet floors except the kitchen and bathrooms, which had tile floors. We were fortunate to get the apartment and the reasonably nice furniture that came with it. Each building had a laundry in the basement. Doing laundry was an all-day affair.

The confiscation of all the country's productive assets brought the economy to a standstill. There was no fresh food in stores and on rare occasions, when some arrived, the news spread fast, and the store was sold out in minutes. We were in school for six days, and we had school lunches, which were our main meal for the day. For breakfast and dinner, my mother did her best to cook something we liked. Sour dough bread was our standard, and it came in a two-kilogram loaf, which was delivered unpackaged in open crates and left on the street in front of the stores. We could buy any quantity, and the store would cut the loaf into desired pieces. We ate the bread with lard spread. Occasionally we were able to put honey or powder sugar on top.

My mother got paid monthly. When she received her pay, we had something special, such as white bread rolls and butter, occasionally some milk or salami. Sunday family dinner, prepared in early afternoon, was the primary meal. My mother did her best to provide something we really liked. Usually pork chops or fried chicken with potatoes or just potatoes of various kinds. Needless to say, with one income and two growing kids, it was difficult for my mother. It was virtually impossible, but she did a wonderful job to make us feel we were special.

I was just starting first grade when my father returned from Russia. It was a happy day. He was able to clean up and wear his own clothes. He began to recover some of his physical and mental strength. For the first time in my memory, the whole family was together, lots of talking, laughing, and crying. Our celebration lasted for several days as my parents reacquainted after so long apart with so much having happened to both of them.

After a few days, my father started to look for a job. He could have been recommissioned into the military if he had been willing to swear his loyalty to the new communist government. Of course, he refused to do so. Ultimately, he received a bookkeeping position with the railroad. The family was now as normal as possible under the circumstances, and with two incomes, we were doing better than before.

As a six-year-old, I could not understand the difficulty my parents had in adjusting to their new situation. For over four years, my mother took care of us by herself, and my father's return seemed to upset the close relationship. I sensed some tension in the family and thought my father felt out of place. One evening, when my father came home from work, he looked unsure of himself.

I ran up to him and jumped in his arms and hugged him, saying, "Hallo, little old man."

My mother yelled from the kitchen to my father. "How can you let him say that to you?"

"He is my son, and he can call me anything he wants," my father responded.

This exchange was totally spontaneous, but it instantly bonded me with my father, and it succeeded to relieve some of the tension in the family.

I liked going to school. I was the youngest in class because I received special permission to start a year early. The regulations were that kids had to reach six years of age before September, but exceptions were made if a kid tested to show that he was ready for school; the cut-off date was extended to December. I qualified for this exception.

School was about two kilometers from home. I could either walk or ride a streetcar. When the streetcar was full and I could avoid the ticket collector, I could get away without paying and ride free from our apartment complex all the way to school. This school was a religious gymnasium (high school) before the war. At this point, it was used for all twelve grades. Both boys and girls were attending the same school, but our classes were separated. Actually, the school for girls started and finished a half hour before the boys' classes. We had about fifty kids in a class. All my friends went to this school, including László (Laci) Korányi, who was my best friend. Laci was the tallest in our class, and I was among the shortest. We remained life-long friends.

In gym class, one of the exercises was throwing a simulated hand grenade, a good practice, just in case we got attacked by the fascists. Outside of school, one of the games we played in the neighborhood was simulating WW I battles. We would split up in pairs, and each pair would dig a shallow bunker. We would find pieces of wood, cardboard and other stuff to cover the bunker. We would then wrap dirt in paper, which served as our grenades. The goal was to throw the grenades at the other guys as they stuck their heads out in the open. Scoring a direct hit was the ultimate goal. Nobody got hurt, but we all got filthy.

We also fabricated our own scooters. We found scrap metal, wood, and ball bearings in the ruins and scrap yards. We had very limited tools that we also found in the scrap yards. Needless to say, these scooters were an accident waiting for a place to happen. They would not last long and generally just disintegrated when you were least prepared. It was not too bad if they failed while pedaling on level ground. But that was not exciting enough. We would take them up on very steep hilly roads and get a thrill riding down as fast as possible. There were no cars, so that danger did not exist. However, we had some spectacular crashes with serious injuries, but the thrill was worth it.

All was going well, maybe life was just too good. In the middle of the night in the spring of 1949, we received the most dreaded knock on the door from AVO agents (AVO, the Government Defense Department, was the Hungarian version of Russia's KGB or Germany's Stasi). They searched the apartment and found nothing, but arrested my father anyway. We did not know what happened to him for weeks until we found out he was in prison at the AVO holding cell where the secret police used torture and other cruel treatment to extract confessions from innocent people.

The Royal Palace was severely damaged during the final battles as the Russians were coming in, and the Germans were escaping Budapest. Prisoners were used to rebuild the castle and for a period, my father was on one of these prisoner labor gangs. His gang worked on removing the rubble. My father was moving rubble in wheelbarrows and dumping it in a chute on the backside of Castle Hill where dump trucks were lined up to remove it. I do not know how, but we found out what he was doing. My brother and I would stand for hours at the bottom of the hill and wait for my father's turn to empty his wheelbarrow. We would wave at him, and he would acknowledge that he saw us. It took many years to rebuild the castle, but the rebuilt Palace is now the Hungarian National Museum, one of the main tourist attractions in Budapest.

Finally, he was charged with crimes against Jews. This was generally an easy case for the government because there was no credible defense possible since so many Jews died during the war. This, however, was not the case for my father. During his assignment as security officer for companies during the war, he was assigned several companies that were owned by Jews. My father protected them during the war years and during that horrible year of 1944 when most deportations took place. Many of these Jews had survived the war, and they showed up at the trial to testify on my father's behalf. So after about a six-month ordeal, he was free to come home. After my father was released, he found a job managing a vegetable farm on the outskirts of Budapest.

At the time, I was seven years old, but I did see how worried and pained my mother was during this entire ordeal. I also saw how helpless we were against the oppressive authorities. It was a confusing time for me. I continued to think of myself as a normal kid, but I started to listen to more adult conversation and tried to understand what was going on around me. Our neighborhood was virtually all professional people, not factory workers. But we did not really know anybody well because no one talked to each other beyond superficial conversation. We did not know who the spies were! People went about their daily lives in a fearful silence.

As kids, we did not know we were poor because we all had grown up in equal poverty and accepted it as a given. However, our parents did know the difference. They had vivid memories of the free society and the prosperous economy of Budapest prior to the war and prior to the imposition of communism on Hungary. They only talked about it quietly and only among their closest friends and relatives.

Everything was reinforcing the communist propaganda. Even as a young kid, I started to see old institutions change. The Boy Scout organization became the Pioneers. We were forced to become Pioneers and wear red scarves and were inundated with the glorification of the communist revolution and socialist system.

It became dangerous to attend church, yes, church! Communist propaganda does not tolerate competition with ideas of any kind, organized or individual. Entire orders of teaching monks and nuns disappeared. Cardinal Mindszenty, the head of the Hungarian Catholic Church and a consummate advocate of free religion, was arrested, tortured, and imprisoned in late 1945. The red star and the hammer and sickle, symbols of communism, along with pictures of Lenin and Stalin, appeared everywhere, on the outside and inside of all buildings. You just could not get away from them.

When I was prepared to enter third grade with a good group of friends, we had changed from crazy child play in the mud and sand to board games and cards. I also liked to do my schoolwork. When I got home from school and was locked out of the apartment, I would start my homework sitting on the steps while other kids were playing outside. We were growing up, perhaps prematurely. My parents did everything possible to give my brother and me a happy childhood. In retrospect, it is hard to believe all they were able to do.

A good friend lived in a beautiful private house next to our apartment complex. One morning I was going over to visit him and, more particularly, his twin sister, with whom I was in love at least as much as an eight-year-old could be. When I got there, I saw a sign on their front door stating that the house had been taken over by the government. This sign was placed on the door during the night and upon entering, I realized my friend's family was not even aware of it. By the end of the day, several families showed up and took over most of the house. There was nothing the family could do about it.

Usually when there was a party, kids went along, but the kids were deposited in a separate room. That is where they stayed until it was time to go home. I never liked this arrangement and usually snuck in to the adult's room to watch and listen. There were other benefits to hanging out with the adults.

The New Year's Eve party in 1950 was at my mother's sister, Aunt Manci's (Margit's), house. She lived in an old part of Budapest called Òbuda. These houses were built in the mid-1800s. They were walled in with small but nice yards. The house was comfortable, but in very bad shape. I started to drink red wine whenever people put their glass down. Next thing I knew, I woke up with a hangover and no one left at the party. I took a street car home in the morning when my cousin went to work. One would think that would cure me, but it did not. Now that I can afford good red wine, that is all I drink.

The year 1951 started with another visit from the AVO in the middle of the night. Again, they searched our apartment and took my father. By this time, along with other institutions, the courts were totally under the communists' control. My father landed in the same AVO headquarters where they were experts at extracting false confessions. We never knew what my father went through, but, finally, after two months, my mother found out where he was. While he was waiting for his trial, he was again put in the forced labor pool clearing the rubble of the Royal Palace.

His trial was a set-up. With a false confession in hand, he was charged with crimes against the communist system; he was convicted and sentenced to three years in prison. He appealed the sentence. To teach him a lesson, the authorities changed his sentence to six years and the confiscation of his personal property.

This meant that a government agent would show up at our apartment and confiscate everything of value, of which we had very little, and remove all the furniture other than three beds, three chairs, and a table. Fortunately, my mother had a friend in the right place, and we were warned twenty-four hours before the agent showed up. We were able to save draperies and some extra furniture by taking them to a neighbor's apartment.

I was just over eight years old and my brother almost ten years old. My father was sent to work in a coal mine in the western part of Hungary, ironically very close to where the Zoltek plant that I acquired many years later is located. My mother would go to visit my father as often as she was allowed. Back then it was an overnight trip. She did not take us kids; she did not want to have us see our father in such a circumstance.

We did do some bad things while she was gone, like starting to smoke. But generally I was serious about things, while my brother pulled some nutty and dangerous stunts, like sitting in a ditch between railroad ties as the streetcars would pass over him. We were fairly independent, and my poor mother felt she was losing control over us. My father's sister unfairly criticized my mother for not paying enough attention to our upbringing. This, of course, made her very angry, and her relationship with my father's side of the family became rather cool at this point.

One time, my mother returned a day early because she was not allowed to see my father. She walked in the apartment where my brother and I were smoking cigarettes. We had our stash of cigarettes still on the table. Needless to say, she was very upset. Fortunately, she always blamed my brother for all bad things. She was mostly correct, and I was safe. She took our cigarettes. To add insult to injury, she smoked them in front of us when she had company. We learned our lesson: not to stop smoking, but to hide our cigarettes.

My mother's great-grandfather, Samuel Hirst, was British; he was born in 1800 in Leeds. He was a graduate of Cambridge in English Language and Literature and came to Vienna with his family to establish an English language private school. He became a political advisor, confidant, and friend of Count Szécsényi István, probably the most prominent Hungarian nobleman of his time. When Szécsényi died in 1860, he returned to England. Before he returned, he sent his son, Theodor, my mother's grandfather, to Budapest to teach English.

Two of my mother's uncles still lived in Budapest and spoke Hungarian with an English accent. They were very nice and liked my mother a lot. They visited us on a regular basis. My mother was quite a gregarious person and knew all the new jokes. I found it interesting that the jokes got better and better as conditions in Hungary got worse and worse. And my mother knew them all. The Hirst uncles looked forward to hearing them, the more risqué, the better from my mother.

To be sure my mother told them all the new jokes, they gave my brother and me money to buy some rolls, butter, and salami to make sandwiches. While we were gone, my mother told them all the dirty jokes. I knew what the program was, and I wanted to hear the jokes myself, but the special treat of the delicacies was worth missing them.

Usually in the summers, we attended camps. It helped my mother to manage us. One year the camp had a ring-worm infestation, and both my brother and I became infected. The standard treatment would have been to shave our heads and coat our hair roots with an iodine solution. Not a pretty picture, but very effective. Nuclear medicine was just coming into use, but no one knew how to use it. Someone at the doctor's office decided that instead of shaving our heads, to nuke our heads until our hair fell out. It was quite a drastic alternative to shaving and did nothing against the ring-worms. As a result of this excessive radiation exposure, we both developed thyroid cancer thirty years later.

Summers were always fun. Instead of camp one summer, I joined my friend Laci's family on a vacation to Lake Balaton. It was a very enjoyable few weeks. While in Budapest, my mother took me to the outdoor opera. I loved the arias, but not the theater in between. All in all, I saw more opera by the time I was thirteen than most people do in their entire lives. We were also able to go to the swimming pool at the Gellért Hotel and Bath. This was a fantastic place built long before the war. It had a large pool with artificial waves, various baths, and sporting pools including high diving boards. This was reasonably close to our apartment and was a lot of fun. Discovering girls helped the fun and excitement.

When I turned ten years old, I started to do things independently. I sometime bicycled to Lake Balaton, about fifty kilometers away, went for a swim, had a lángos lunch, and returned to Budapest.

Lángos is a favorite Hungarian snack, fried potato bread with various toppings. Lángos venders were similar to hot dog vendors in the U.S. and were some of the very few independent businesses allowed by the government. My uncle Édi hated them because they earned more money during the summer than he did as a lawyer all year.

My mother had an unlimited streetcar pass. One beautiful fall Sunday, I decided to take her pass and see all of Budapest that I had not seen before. I started out early morning without telling anyone. It was a great day, and I think that I took every streetcar line and some busses. I arrived back to our apartment at about eight in the evening. There was a commotion at the gate. It turned out to be my mother and some friends, all distraught and worried about me. When I showed up, my mother was upset, but happy to see me. All was forgiven, but clearly I was expected not to do anything like that again.

Winter was a bit different. Budapest can have lots of snow and cold weather. When we had significant snowfall, the snow was removed manually from roads and sidewalks, and many of us lined up to shovel snow for some extra money. For entertainment we had a toboggan, and we would slide down the streets from the local hills. Both of these activities were quite unpleasant. Our clothes were barely okay for short exposure, but after a longer time, we got very cold. We still did both anyway, but at least we received some money for shoveling snow.

Skating was another story. My mother bought us season passes for a skating rink. It took me about an hour to get to the skating rink on several streetcars, none of them heated. Once I got there, I needed to bolt the skates to my shoes. Because the soles were too far worn, they were unable to keep the skates on. So I mostly skated on my backside. After a while, I would just go to the rink and sit by the fire until I got warm and then go back home.

Our apartment was a relatively new design, built a few years before the war, and had a central heating system of sorts. A large built-in wood furnace between the two big rooms heated the entire apartment. It took a lot of wood, which we did not have, to fire up the furnace. We could not afford to buy the quantity of wood it would take to keep the fire going. We only used this furnace once in a great while, like on Christmas.

We had a secondary chimney connection in one of the big rooms where we installed a coal-fired heater. Our coal bin was in the basement, so every morning, my brother or I would bring up enough kindling wood and coal for the day. We would charge the heater in the morning and the first person arriving home would light it. Initially, it gave out so much heat that we had to move as far away as possible in the room, but, as the fire went out and the heater cooled down, we moved closer and closer until we actually had our feet on the heater. We lived in this room all winter.

The only other source of heat was the gas stove in the kitchen. We would turn it on with the door open and heat the kitchen while cooking or washing-up with warm water heated on the stove. Our bathroom was unheated and very cold in the winter. It had a wood-fired water heater that also served as the heater for the room, which we only fired up on rare occasions when we were taking full baths, once a week and on special occasions. In the summer, we just took cold baths.

In the summer of 1952, a truck driver rang our doorbell. He was in a hurry and seemed nervous. He asked us to open our coal bin so he could deliver a load of coal. We had no idea what it was all about, but we certainly welcomed the offer. Later, we found out that my uncompromising and ingenious father had made the arrangements from prison.

The prisoners in the mine were working as helpers while the trained miners were civilians. One of these miners decided to pick on my father. After a number of confrontations, my father picked up a shovel and told the miner that he was in prison because he had killed three people and killing one more person will not make any difference for him. After this incident, the miner refused to go in the mine as long as my father was among the helpers. The prison guards moved my father into the warehouse. Soon he was running the warehouse.

In the communist system, everyone cheats if they can get away with it. In the mine, the guards were stealing blankets, clothes, and supplies for themselves. My father facilitated them by manipulating the inventory reports in exchange for supplying our family with coal. The guards were able to divert a delivery truck to our apartment.

During the time my father was in prison, my mother relied on Uncle Édi for moral support. He continued to contest my father's unreasonable sentence and seek his early release. When someone tried to take our apartment away from us, he was able to put a stop to it. Our families were close, and we saw each other a lot. I liked my uncle, and we continued our relationship to the end of his life. He had a great sense of humor, was forceful, and very likeable. He hated the communist system as much as, or more than, we did, but he had learned to work the system to his advantage. He helped my mother and our whole family a lot.

He remained a royalist. On occasions when he had a little too much to drink in a pub, he would offer a toast to Otto von Habsburg, the last Crown Prince of the Austro-Hungarian Empire. Most people would get hauled away for such a political statement in public. But he got away with it. Much later, during one of my visits back to Budapest, he asked me to mail a letter he had written but was afraid to mail from Hungary, from the U.S. to Otto Habsburg. After this letter, Uncle Édi was invited to Otto's daughter's wedding in Máthás Church (named after Saint Mathias Corvinus, king of Hungary 1456-1490) on Castle Hill in Budapest. That was a very exciting event for him.

Soviet communist propaganda penetrated almost everything we were taught. Even so, we did not buy any of it, and we made great jokes about its stupidity. The essence of the propaganda was that everything was discovered by the Soviets, and all worthy literature was written by the so-called "heroes" of the revolution. In a few cases when they were forced to acknowledge a western inventor, like Alexander Graham Bell, there was a Russian who preceded him by a few days. It was so stupid and transparent that you could only be amused.

On March 5, 1953, Stalin died. This gave us a good reason for celebration. We were listening to the radio the morning when the announcement was made. We literally jumped for joy. We all hoped that changes for the better were coming.

What the communist regime absolutely does not tolerate is any competing ideology or organization. Hungary is over eighty percent Roman Catholic, which was a real problem for the communists. After imprisoning and/or killing most of the monks and imprisoning Cardinal Mindszenty, they targeted the churches. Hungarians, in general, do not attend church every Sunday, but after the communists took over, there was a potential penalty if one was seen going to church.

The most disobedient demonstration was the Easter Parade. There was so much participation that the communists could not control it. The parade started early morning after mass and went all day. People lined up six or eight abreast and the parade took a four-kilometer round trip. When people returned to the starting point, they were replaced by new people. The parade just continued all day with many thousands of participants. It was an impressive sight.

As I entered fifth grade, other exciting things started to happen. A new grade school opened very close to our apartment, and we transferred from the gymnasium building to the new school. We were the first fifth grade class of thirty-six students at this school. The head teacher for our class was a newly graduated teacher. His name was Iván Nobel. We all liked him because he brought youth and enthusiasm to class, and he was a very positive influence on all of us. Also, school started to be more difficult and very interesting, which I really liked. The bad news was that Russian language became a mandatory subject. Most of us refused to learn Russian and to this day, all I can do is count to five in Russian, one for each year I was forced to take it.

The teaching methods and the school system were not yet completely influenced by the communists. We had a good education. Kodály Zoltán, a famous composer and music educator, visited our class to present his studies of Hungarian folk music. He had found pockets of old settlements in Ukraine and at the Ural Mountains in Russia who spoke the ancient Hungarian language. They had folk songs that were identical to the ones in Hungary.

I loved school and did very well, but that did not stop me from having fun and getting into trouble. One day with a friend, we stuffed the chimney with paper and blocked the exhaust. Soon the entire school reeked of smoke that lasted for days. We were caught, of course, and we were severely reprimanded at school and had to take a letter to my mother about my bad behavior. Every student had a small notebook issued by the school, which was a tool for teachers to communicate with the parents. If a kid did something the teacher did not like, the teacher would write a note to the parents. The student then had to have the parents sign, indicating that they had received the message.

I managed to get more than one booklet, so I avoided getting my mother's signature because every time I received a note, I used a fresh book. But once I had a teacher give me two notes within one week. I made a quick decision to use a fresh booklet, assuming the teacher did not remember the previous note. I was wrong, and I got caught with the multiple booklets. Neither my mother nor the teacher bought into my explanation that I just wanted to spare my mother from unnecessary bad news. This became a real fiasco at school and at home. After this episode, I could never get away without my mother signing all teacher complaints.

Needless to say, there was no religious education. Somehow we got connected with an underground boy-scout-like organization run by some university students. It was disguised as a tourist club. We went on retreats along with a priest, and we had a nice camping trip while we learned about our religion.

Good news came in the fall of 1954. My father was released from prison! Soon after he came home, he got a job in his professional field. He became the manager of a significant government sheep farm in western Hungary. This meant that he had to move there, but it was close enough that we could take a train to visit him.

The property was confiscated after the war from private ownership and became part of the government-run farming system. The manager resided in the house the owner used to occupy. It had its own facilities for domestic animals next to the house. My father also had a wonderful small sheep dog named Teddy, more as a companion than a working dog. My father bought several piglets and, eventually, we had a good supply of pork. For the moment, we were living well compared to others.

My father liked this job and did very well. Among other things, he developed a process to make cheese from sheep's milk. He was asked to visit all the other sheep farms to instruct the people on the process.

In the communist system, the sheep were not allowed to get sick! So the first thing that he needed to do was to cheat on the number of births, so there were a certain number of spare sheep off the books. Second, he needed to establish a value chain to dispose of sheep that were hopelessly sick before they actually die. He arranged a deal with the local butcher that any sheep that were delivered alive were officially butchered for meat. The butcher received a few hides for cooperating. Third, he needed to be able to hide the sick sheep from the inspectors. Everyone on the farm and in town liked and respected him. He was able to manipulate the system to do many favors for them all.

I spent the summer of 1955 at the farm. My brother was already there. He finished eighth grade in the country school. During the fifth through eighth grades, students were evaluated to determine if they were destined to academic high school or to a trade school. The academic high school was preparation for the university. Only about ten to fifteen percent of kids went to the university. The law required that children stay in school until the age of fourteen. However, students could not move forward if they did not master the subject matter. So, a number of kids repeated grades, sometimes more than once.

My mother found out that my brother was not going to be allowed to graduate from eighth grade because of his bad grades and behavior. She arranged to transfer him to a country school where my father was living, which was generally easier scholastically. My brother was a difficult kid all his life, and this time was no different. He acted like a big-shot city boy. He worked during the season when the sheep were sheared to harvest the wool. It was a messy and stinking job, but he just loved it. With my father's help, he did manage to graduate from eighth grade, but he did not qualify to enter the scholastic high school, which was just fine with him.

While I was at the farm, I did some work as a helper to the shepherds and farm hands. One day, a runner came to let my father know that an inspection team was on its way. The flock was out grazing, except for about thirty sick sheep. The common sickness was some sort of hoof disease. They had a difficult time walking. I was the only available person to move these sheep over the hill out of sight of the inspectors. It was quite a challenge. Our dog, Teddy, just had puppies a few weeks before. I had two little puppies with me. They were no help. I ran around poking the sheep with a stick to try to keep them moving. The puppies did nothing.

Finally, I got all the sheep over the hill and sat down exhausted. At that moment, the puppies went to work as their instincts took over. They ran circles around the sheep, driving them in a small heap. I had to chase the puppies home to stop them.

That summer, I earned some money and bought a hen with sixteen chicks at the farmers market. I took care of feeding the pigs and keeping track of the chickens. Every day, all the chickens, more than a hundred combining with all the workers' chickens along with ours, were feeding all day in a large yard. I guess today they would be called free range chickens. Over twenty percent of the chickens were lost to the hawks. Teddy would station herself at the edge of the field and watch as the hawks came in for the kill. If the hawk had its sight on one of my chickens, Teddy would chase it away. If any other chicken was the target, Teddy just watched and did nothing as the hawk would take the chicken. We never lost any of my chickens.

When the summer of 1955 was over, it was time to go back to Budapest and to school. This was a very important year because during the eighth grade, the final selection of the students for the scholastic high school was made. The decision was supposed to be made based on the general scholastic achievement of the individual and the results of the final examination in front of a panel of teachers.

The selection process for scholastic high school had a political side. The communist system used this process to change society by not allowing politically unacceptable people to get a university education. Since my mother was working in the school system, she was able to see my record, and she saw that it was marked with a red "X," and I was not going to be allowed to enter a scholastic high school. With her contacts in the school system, she was able to change that, but I needed to do my best to get good grades. Getting accepted into the scholastic high school was not an assurance that I would be allowed to the university, but this was the first step.

Once more, trouble found my father. A mandate from the government came out in the fall of 1955 that non-communists were not to be trusted in an agricultural management position. Of course, my father was included in this purge.

He brought Teddy, a pig, and the chickens (with a few sacks of corn for feed) to Budapest. We butchered the pig right away and kept the chickens at my Aunt Manci's house in Òbuda. We had eggs for a while and once the feed was about to run out, we had fried chicken every Sunday until we ran out of chickens. Once back in Budapest, my father was only allowed to get a manual labor job. After some time, he was able to get a job as an assembly worker in a lock manufacturing company.

At the end of eighth grade, we took a final written and oral examination in math, sciences, and literature. This was a quite stressful examination. It took a full week. For the oral examination, a large number of potential questions were given to the students. At the time of the examination, a student would draw a question and would have fifteen minutes to organize how to present his answer while another student was actually presenting the answer to his question. All went well for me, and I was heading to high school.

After the exams, the entire class went with our head teacher, Iván Nobel, to a restaurant called the Busulo Juhász (Sad Shepherd). We had a nice dinner with wine and played games of bocce ball all evening. Eventually, Iván Nobel was promoted to the Ministry of Education. Much later, he was trying to publish a book, and he asked me to contribute some money, which I did. I met him in Budapest at the Anna Café, my favorite. After forty years, we recognized each other immediately; neither of us had changed a lot and we had a very nice conversation.

During the summer, I got a job as a helper on a construction project. With my pay for the summer's work, I bought a raincoat, a leather briefcase, and a compass set. I felt like an adult.

High school started in early September 1956. We returned to the old school where we started. It was a Catholic high school prior to the communist takeover. The good news was that for the first time, English was offered as an elective language. I signed up. The bad news was that, on the first day, the Russian teacher came into class and talked only in Russian. Very few students understood a word he said, even though we were supposed to have been studying Russian since the fifth grade. The rest of the studies looked to be very challenging and exciting. But before I really got into the routine of the new challenges, life changed abruptly and completely.

On October 22, 1956, our undercover religious retreat group, also known as the University Tourist Club, had a meeting scheduled at the

Technical University of Budapest. As we walked in to the main lobby, we were shocked by what we heard. There was a large crowd that filled the entire lobby, and more and more people kept coming in. There was a lot of shouting as a group of students were reading a list of demands they developed. The students were trying to present their demands to a government representative, who was less than receptive. A short version of the demands was as follows:

- Immediate removal of the Soviet occupying forces.
- Free and secret election of the officers of the Communist party.
- A new government to be constituted under the leadership of Nagy Imre (an earlier president, from 1953 to 1955, who was considered to be a reformist communist and much more reasonable than the current president).
- Public inquiry into the criminal activities of the current government.
- New free (secret) general elections for the entire country.
- Revision of the Hungarian-Soviet political and economic relationship.
- A complete reorganization of the Hungarian economic system.
- All foreign trade agreements to be made public including the exploitation of the Hungarian uranium deposits by Russia.
- Adjustment of wages and salaries according to economic contribution.
- Reorganization of the agricultural production system.
- Review of all political and commercial trials and repatriation of prisoners.
- Complete freedom of opinion and expression.
- Immediate removal of the statue of Stalin.
- Replacement of all non-Hungarian emblems and symbols.

- Technical University of Budapest students to declare solidarity with workers.
- Technical University students to organize a Youth Parliament.

The meeting went on for many hours without any success in achieving an agreement for discussion with the government officials.

The next best thing was to try to get the radio station to read these demands on air. That was also unsuccessful. The group came to a final decision: mimeograph thousands of copies of their demands and post them throughout Budapest during the night. Also, plans were made to demonstrate in front of the radio station the next afternoon to continue pressing for these demands to be read openly on air.

I was so excited, and I would not leave the university until the meeting broke up late at night. I sent my brother home to get my father. I wanted him to come and see what was happening. My father did not believe it was possible and did not come. I knew this was the beginning of a very important change and started to imagine what that might be.

The 1956 Revolution

I could not sleep all night after I got home from the events at the University. I could hardly wait to see what would happen in the morning. It was Tuesday, October 23, 1956, the official beginning of the Revolution.

The demands were posted everywhere. People were reading them in shock. It is hard to find words to describe the change in people. Usually people were walking around like zombies, looking down to avoid eye contact with anyone. On that day, it all changed. People looked happy, smiled, and discussed these demands openly with strangers. People expressed their hopes and openly speculated about what changes these demands might bring. It was like the weight of the world was lifted off the Hungarian people.

Almost the entire city's daily routine changed. Everyone just wanted to see what would happen next. Several spontaneous demonstrations started all over Budapest. A large group of students were joined by workers coming off the morning shift, and they started to march toward Parliament. By the time the demonstrators arrived in front of the Parliament building, they numbered over one hundred thousand. For the first time, Nagy Imre appeared to address the crowd and accepted their demand to become president and change the political system of Hungary.

The planned gathering at the radio station turned into a huge demonstration. Later, it was revealed that large contingents of AVO agents were sent to the station, and they were ready for the planned demonstration. The demonstrators tried to break through the doors, threw bricks through windows, but were unable to enter. Finally, the AVO fought back with bayonets and clubs. The violence escalated when the leaders of the demonstrators were allowed to enter the station and were immediately shot. My cousin, Aunt Manci's twenty-year-old son, Laci, was one of the unarmed demonstrators, and he was killed at the very beginning. He was a very nice and happy young man, and his death was senseless and a huge loss. He was buried in a temporary grave on a tennis court close to our apartment. Aunt Manci never got over her loss.

What happened next is not completely clear. I read several accounts later, and they do not differ a lot, so I will tell the version I remember. The Hungarian army, which was similar to the U.S. National Guard, was called in to control the demonstration. As they arrived, the officer of the troops was standing in the tank turret overlooking the situation. All of a sudden, the AVO inside the station started shooting. It's not clear if it was by accident or by deliberate act, but the officer in the tank was shot. As most troops usually do, the army returned fire in the direction the shot came from.

More shooting broke out. The army shot at the AVO and the AVO continued shooting at the unarmed demonstrators. The situation quickly went out of control as the soldiers and the local police protected the demonstrators from the AVO inside the fortified radio station. The local police opened their gun storage and distributed whatever firearms they had to the demonstrators. Soon after, workers from Csepel, an island in the Duna River where the communists built what they considered the model industrial complex, arrived with trucks of guns and ammunition. They distributed them to the civilians, and the spontaneous shootout started. The Revolution had officially begun. The battle at the radio station lasted for several days.

Soviet troops had been stationed about forty kilometers (twenty-five miles) from Budapest since World War II. They were called in overnight. Wednesday morning, the Soviet tanks arrived on the streets of Budapest. They were not prepared for what they saw. Using tanks for close combat with untrained and unarmed demonstrators was not what they expected.

I ventured out every day, either by myself or with my father, to see what was happening. My brother was always looking for trouble, so this was just the perfect opportunity for him. None of my friends were as venturesome. My first exposure to the action was on Wednesday, not far from my school. There was a large square with shops and a streetcar terminal where some of the Soviet tanks arrived.

Since there was no obvious enemy in sight, the tanks were moving slowly and aimlessly in the confined area around the streets. We had no weapons, but as most of the revolution was random spontaneous reaction to the situations, we quickly figured out how to stop the tanks without weapons. If we could get close enough, the guns that were controlled from inside the tank became ineffective. In close quarters, we would take railroad ties or logs and shove them between the wheels and the track, making the tank immobile. When we succeeded, most of the tanks just stopped and were towed away. But some started to fire wildly and did a lot of damage to buildings, and a number of people were killed in the process.

To fight back when the tank started to shoot, we would throw a Molotov cocktail at the back of the tank. A Molotov cocktail is a bottle of gasoline with a wick that is lit. As the bottle broke, the burning gasoline spread over the tank's armor and, due to surface tension, the burning gasoline would actually flow upward under the armor and light the fuel tank. At that point, the soldiers inside had two options, escape the tank or burn to death. Once they exited the tank, the people attacked them either by hand-to-hand combat or with guns, if they had them. After a few tanks were destroyed, the tanks stopped coming into the square. Fortunately, nothing happened to me, and I left the area. However, the tanks came again later, and a battle started in the evening and lasted most of the night. Much damage was done to the surrounding buildings, and a number of Hungarians and Russians were killed.

For the first time in my life, I saw dead people. They were lying all over the pavement. It was hard to process what I saw and connect it to actions I had actually taken that might have contributed. Over the next few days, I was exposed to so much death and destruction that it became commonplace. It was hard to comprehend what the final outcome we should have expected. The people had been oppressed for so long that they were not really thinking; they were just reacting. I certainly shared this feeling, and we all hoped for a better future.

There was no public transportation of any kind, so I needed to walk everywhere. The Pest side was much more active than the Buda side, so I walked over the river to see what was happening. All the confrontations I saw were spontaneous. They would last for a short time, no more than a few hours. Once the fighting was over, the Soviet tanks would be removed, and the dead bodies of the Hungarians would be taken away by ambulance while the Soviet soldiers would be removed by personnel carriers. At the time, it all seemed so routine. However, I had nightmares for many years until the memory finally faded away.

I went to Hero's Square where a huge statue of Stalin had been toppled earlier in the day. I found a side street where a large part of the statue was being broken up by a lot of people with sledge hammers. I waited for my turn and was able to break off two pieces. An American reporter asked me for one of them. I traded a piece for a pack of L&M cigarettes. It was my first business transaction, I think.

There were two or three more organized and much larger confrontations. I did not see them, but we all knew about them. The largest was at the Kilian Barracks where the regular Hungarian Army, along with a number of young people, students, and workers, stood up against the best the Soviet army was able to dish out. This confrontation lasted the longest time, essentially nonstop for the entire revolution. The other one or two large confrontations were mostly Hungarian young people fighting with small arms against the organized Soviet Army with its tanks and heavy weapons.

On Thursday, my father and I went to visit our relatives to see how they were doing. On the way, we saw Soviet tanks with Hungarian people riding on them with the Hungarian flag. Within one day, the occupying Soviet troops understood that the revolution was an act of ordinary Hungarian people. A number of them had married Hungarian women, and their families were just like the freedom fighters. Many of them just did not have the stomach to shoot at the young Hungarians.

Later that afternoon, we were near the Parliament Square when we heard shots being fired. We rushed to see what was happening. The Parliament Square was filled with unarmed demonstrators. The square was surrounded with government buildings and there were AVO agents on the rooftops of these buildings. When the square was packed with people, the AVO agents started to shoot randomly. The Soviet tanks aligned in such a way as to protect the people and help them escape. In all, several hundred unarmed people were killed or wounded. This incident really energized people to seek out and punish the AVO.

Almost immediately, whenever an AVO agent was identified, he was beaten to death by the people. Some were hung on trees by their feet and beaten with anything people were able to find until they were dead and even longer. This was pure hatred. I saw at least fifteen to twenty such incidents. It was hard to understand the cruelty people can administer on others, but clearly in the case of the AVO, it seemed to be justified.

Friday was much quieter. Although the organized action was still going heavy, the spontaneous confrontations with the Soviet Army were infrequent. However, the search for AVO agents escalated. Many more were killed that day. There was evidence that the Soviet occupational troops were moving out. Friday evening was like the last stand. Some of the troops did as much damage as they could on their way out.

On the way home that afternoon, my father and I ran into a group that had trapped an AVO agent in a basement. They asked us to help, gave us guns, and informed us of the situation. We were blindly shooting into the basement, and our shots were returned. After about a half hour, no more shots were returned from the basement. We were thanked for our help, and we moved on, but I kept one of the guns.

Saturday, October 27 was quiet. There were almost no gun shots to be heard. The Soviet troops were gone or on their way out. Nagy Imre was now in control of the government, and he announced his Cabinet officers. Ceasefire negotiations were in progress. We all thought the Revolution was a success. The only negative was that the AVO was still active, and the retribution against them continued.

During the next few days, political parties started to organize in hopes of stabilizing the government and preparing for elections, hopefully to be held soon. My father was involved with the reactivation of the Smallholders Party. Political prisoners, including Cardinal Mindszenty, were released. There was still a certain level of uneasiness as people looked at the damage that was caused. The dead were buried in makeshift cemeteries, and the hospitals were full with the wounded.

I still walked all over the city every day to see what was happening and trying to make sense of everything. I was not yet fourteen years old, but I was trying to project how our family's lives would change in the future. I could not help but feel optimistic and full of hope. The violence had not stopped completely, and the new government had not completely taken control. There was a park in the area of the AVO headquarters. We could hear noises coming from below the ground. Upon inspection of the decorative planters, it was obvious they were ventilation ducts. We could not find the entrance to where the people were inside. This really bothered me and certainly gave me the feeling the bad guys were still in control.

Sunday, November 4, we woke to increasing intensity of the sound of gunfire. The Russians were back! Deep down, we all knew it was over.

Mostly, two major confrontations were going on: at the Kilian Barracks, which was organized and still holding out, and a second at Csepel, the industrial district, which was the pride of the communist regime representing the glorification of the worker. The Soviet troops were all over Budapest. There were few spontaneous confrontations, but when they occurred, the response from the Soviets was brutal and extreme, nothing like at the beginning.

The constant presence of Soviet soldiers in the neighborhoods was intimidating. During the day, we were able to talk to them as they walked around in our neighborhood. We were harmless looking young kids and we knew some Russian, enough to have a simple conversation. They were clearly different from the occupying forces who withdrew only a few days earlier. Obviously, they had not been told and had no idea where they were.

On the same day, the Soviet tanks rolled into Budapest, the formation of a new government supported by the Russians and headed by Kádár János was announced. Nagy Imre and several of his government's officers fled to the Yugoslav Embassy. Maléter Pál, the Defense Minister, was in Russia to negotiate a ceasefire, disappeared, and never heard from again.

As a desperate final hope, the Hungarian radio station constantly repeated the plea to the U.S. and Western Europe for help until the radio station was taken over by the Russian army or the secret police.

We heard gunshots and the radio station went silent. ==Help never came. Quite to the contrary, President Eisenhower announced that no help would come.==

About the same time, Cardinal Mindszenty entered the U.S. Embassy and asked for political asylum. (With the help of the U.S., he defied the communist government's demand for his extradition. He lived there until 1971.)

Hungary continued under the Soviet military administration as the conflict came to an end, and a certain normalcy was restored. It would take another 30 years-plus for the entire communist system to be rejected globally.

As the conflict was winding down, more and more people started leaving Hungary and emigrate toward the West. One afternoon I noticed the reflection of binocular lenses in Building A of our apartment complex, which was recently renovated and was occupied by active military officers. Clearly, someone was watching our apartment. We had been talking about leaving Hungary, but my father was reluctant to leave the country his family had defended for centuries. Now it became clear that our lives would be like before, if not worse, if we stayed. By this time, there was no hope for future improvement; there was no reason to stay.

My brother got impatient and joined some of his friends leaving for Austria. I wanted to be sure my parents would decide to escape, and I was willing to wait for them to make their decision.

On November 22, my father visited our close relatives, including Uncle Édi, to inform them of his decision to leave Hungary and asked if any of them wanted to join us. No one did.

On the same day, I buried my gun in my friend's yard. I have considered almost every time I visited Hungary since then to dig it up and bring it home for a reminder. I lost contact with my friend, but much later, I found out he had a rough time after the revolution and he still lived in the same house. I hoped the gun was not discovered and was not the reason for his problems. If it was still there, I might cause more problems for him, so I decided not to try to retrieve it.

On November 23, we left our apartment for the last time. We took nothing with us; we had nothing of value to take, and we did not want to look like we were going for a long time.

I did not say goodbye to my friends in fear of possibly being discovered by the authorities.

There were over two hundred thousand refugees who left Hungary after the revolution, approximately two percent of the population. It was a difficult decision to leave the country where generations of our family had lived and died. Hungary, in particular, had a troubled and proud history, and my father's family was an integral part of that history.

Escape from Hungary

We took a train to Sopron where my father's mother and sister lived. I think the entire train was filled with people trying to escape. The train engineer knew this and decided to stop a few kilometers before the railroad station. The news spread rapidly. The police were there to check identification papers as the passengers were arriving at the station. We got off the train and walked the rest of the way.

One of my grandmother's neighbors was a border guard. He was willing to show some people the area which was least guarded. There used to be a fence at the border and a 10- to 20-meter strip that had been cleared of all vegetation and mined. Fortunately, a treaty had recently been signed that required the fence and mines to be removed just a few months before. We had to trust the border guard and hope for the best. He asked to take all the cash we had, which was very little, since it had no real value in the event we escaped or if we were captured. Sunday, November 24th, after dark, we left for Austria.

It was a cold evening, and we needed to walk about ten kilometers. At one point, our guide stopped, pointed us in a direction, and told us to walk until we ran into someone who would hopefully be an Austrian border guard. We followed his instructions and found the border area within an hour. After another half hour or so of walking around, hoping not to return to Hungarian territory, we did run into an Austrian border guard who was looking for Hungarian refugees.

The boarder guard walked with us to a nearby town that had a restaurant open all night to welcome the refugees. They gave us warm food and took care of us for the rest of the night. By morning, there were about seventy-five refugees collected by the border guards in this area. After we had breakfast, special busses arrived and transported us to the prime collection camp for the refugees in Eisenstaedt.

Eisenstaedt camp was the barracks and/or stables of an old Eszterházy castle that had been reactivated to deal with the Hungarian refugees. The International Red Cross kept track of everyone who arrived at this camp. We were able to find out that my brother was in Belgium and how we could contact him. After a few days, we left for another camp which was more equipped to handle a limited number of refugees for longer periods. At that camp, I found information about the Hungarian language school in Innsbruck. Later, I applied to this school.

My mother believed going to America provided the best opportunity for my brother and me. My father wanted to stay in Austria to be close to Hungary, so he could return if the political situation improved. It is hard to comprehend his attitude after the punishing years he spent as a Russian prisoner of war and as a political prisoner in Hungary after World War II. However, when I considered the Rumy family history, it was easy to see his point that his suffering was based on his loyalty to Hungary and to his family heritage.

The Rumy family was one of Hungary's historical noble families. Current day Hungary's history dates back to the Magyar tribes from west of the Ural Mountains who occupied the virtually abandoned Pannonian Basin in the eighth century. The Christian Kingdom of Hungary was established in the year 1000.

Our family's history spans almost a thousand years, essentially from the beginning of the written history of Hungary, dating back to the eleventh century. The patriarch of the Rumy family, Doroszlò, of noble rank (meaning a free man, exempt from taxes, and committed for military service), lived in Vas (Iron) County, which is one of Hungary's western-most counties. He made significant contributions in defending Hungary's western territory during the Mongolian war in the twelfth century. For his services, Doroszlò was granted an estate by King Andrew III in 1274. Part of the granted estate was the town of Rum, which is the origin of our family name. (In the Hungarian language, an "i" ending of a noun means "from." In the case of a family's name, when the "i" ending is replaced with "y," it indicates the family's noble rank.)

The twelfth century Mongolian wars were devastating for Hungary; almost fifty percent of the population was killed. To repopulate some of the lands, Hungary invited people from neighboring countries to occupy the devastated territories. Also, to improve Hungary's defenses, a fortification project started. This is the period when our family rose to prominence.

For continued services to the Hungarian kings during the following three centuries, the Rumy family was granted significant additional land holdings. All such granted property was exempted from the royal family control and taxes. At one time, our family owned a number of towns, with large land holdings attached, in the western region of Hungary. The Rumy family was also granted the toll rights for the Rába River that had to be crossed on the way from Budapest to Vienna. The location of the bridge was a town that our family named Rábadoroszlò. At that point, our family changed its name to rumi ès (and) rábadoroszloi Rumy. Clearly the family was prosperous and highly influential.

During this period, the Rumys fought wars, protected members of the royal families, and they were counts and vice-counts in Vas County, representing the royal family's interest. The last king the Rumy family served directly was King Sigismund, the last king with Hungarian royal family ties, whose reign ended in 1437. A member of the Rumy family was the wine taster for the king, which was an important position; the king's wine taster was one of the most trusted allies, given that the most popular way to kill your adversary was to put poison in his wine or food (liking good wine must be in my genes). After King Sigismund died, there was no clear royal family succession and contest for the royal throne followed. There were Hungarian nobles and foreign royal families with distant connections to Hungary claiming the throne.

János Hunyadi, from a noble family in Transylvania, gained prominence by successfully leading battles against the Ottoman Empire and capturing Belgrade. His son, Matthias Corvinus, became the first Hungarian king (1458-1490) with no relations to the Árpád Dynasty. He became one of the most loved and respected Hungarian kings. After his death, the country fell into disarray and infighting among the wealthy nobles weakened the government and the defenses of the country, resulting in the successful Turkish invasion of Hungary. Buda was captured in 1541 and Hungary became divided into three parts, Royal Hungary in the west, Ottoman Hungary in the center, and Transylvania in the east. The Rumy family was located in the region of Royal Hungary.

The politics became complicated. The Austrian royal family, the Habsburgs, gained control over Royal Hungary, which also included present day Slovakia. The claim to rule Hungary originated from a Habsburg marriage to the daughter of King Sigismund. They were exploiting the region and were in conflict with the Hungarian nobles. In defiance of the Austrian rulers, many of the Hungarian nobles changed religion from Roman Catholic to Calvinist. The Rumys did the same. However, some wealthy and powerful noble families of Hungary supported the Habsburg takeover. The property grants from the king came with tax exemptions, which was a great opportunity to grow wealth and provided significant temptation to support the Habsburg takeover.

After one-hundred-thirty-five years under the Ottoman Empire rule, in 1686, with the help of several European countries, the Turks were defeated, ending their control over central Hungary. The Habsburgs were able to consolidate their control over both Royal Hungary and Ottoman Hungary. The eastern part of Hungary became the Principality of Transylvania, but the Habsburgs continued to battle for its control. Finally in 1718, the entire Kingdom of Hungary was restored, but under Habsburg control.

Centuries of wars wiped out large numbers of the Hungarian population. The Austrian government settled large numbers of Slavs and Slovaks in the southern and German Swabs in the northern part of Hungary.

All these political changes resulted in additional land grants to the loyal noble families, but the Rumy family was opposed to the Habsburg takeover in favor of independent Hungary. Further, by consolidating multiple family properties under the leadership of the oldest or strongest male family member, created a class of hugely wealthy and influential magnate families. The Rumy family did not follow this practice and over time their property was divided and, in some cases, absorbed through marriages into wealthier families.

The most prominent Hungarian noble family, the House of Eszterházy, was the prime example. They were a small noble family in northwestern Hungary that gained its original wealth by marriage in 1539. While most nobles were trying to break away from Austria's dominance and the Roman Catholic religion, the Eszterházys became close allies with both. After the Habsburgs gained total control of Hungary, the House of Eszterházy accumulated property from the redistribution of property taken from the dissident nobles, redistribution of land taken back from the Turks and through strategic marriages. The House of Eszterházy became, by far, the largest landholder in the Austro-Hungarian Empire.

Dániel Eszterházy (1586-1654) was a contrarian member of the family and favored Hungary's independence. He established a new branch of the Eszterházy family and became a baron in 1613. In 1623, he married rumi és rábadoroszloi Rumy Judit (1606-1663), and the part of the Rumy family property that she controlled became part of the new branch of the House of Eszterházy. After this branch made peace with the rest of the Eszterházy family, their oldest son, János (1625-1692), became a count in 1683.

The Rumy family mansion is still in existence just outside of the town of Rum. It is now a home for children with learning disabilities. The little church in town was maintained by the Rumy and Eszterházy families for generations.

The Habsburg attitude toward Hungary was inconsistent, mostly oppressive and exploiting dictatorship. Without question, much of the wealth of Austria came from Hungary. The Habsburgs initiated a number of changes to the social structure, favoring a few Hungarian magnates. As the Habsburg control over Hungary strengthened, the Rumy family's prominence continued to decline.

It is not clear how the family property was diluted. There were indications that some of the granted properties were taken back after the Habsburgs took full control of Hungary. Also, the family suffered many casualties in their military service and probably caused the families to sell part of their property. By the eighteenth century, there were no major property holdings left in the Rumy family. There are indications that the Rumy family supported the 1848 revolution against the Habsburg control over Hungary and contributed whatever wealth was left to this losing cause.

The most prominent member of the family at the time of the 1848 revolution was Rumy György Károly, a very well-known scholar, scientist, and author. After a number of teaching positions, he moved to Vienna in 1824. While he was there, he converted back to the Roman

Catholic religion. In 1828, he was invited to teach and establish a library in Esztergom, the home of the primary Hungarian Cathedral. He was a member of twenty-five international scientific associations and academies. In Hungary, he was elected a member of the Association of Natural Sciences. He was the grandfather of my grandfather.

Uncle Lajos, my father's uncle, was born in Esztergom and lived there much of his life. When he returned from Russian prison in 1955, he returned to Esztergom and lived there until he died at the age of eighty-seven. Ironically and unintentionally, some one-hundred-fifty years after Esztergom became my modern family's home base, I established Zoltek's Hungarian plant about ten kilometers from there.

As far as we know, at the time we escaped from Hungary, my father's uncle, my father, my brother, and I were the last male descendants of our branch and probably to the entire historic House of Rumy.

After the 1848 revolution, the Habsburg rulers became more benevolent, and Hungary began to prosper after Emperor Franz Joseph came to power in 1849. In 1867, the imperial and royal Dual Empire was established. Under this arrangement, Austria and Hungary coexisted as equal partners in the Austro-Hungarian Empire.

Hungary began to change and universally adopt the Hungarian customs, culture, and language for its entire territory. At the same time, Hungary started to modernize. The building of new industries throughout the country was the primary indication of significant changes as Hungary became one of the wealthiest countries in the world. The economy grew faster than most European economies. Budapest was rebuilding into an international city.

Although the Rumy family lost its wealth, our family was respected in Hungarian society and continued in military and public service during the Habsburg reign. Our family members continued to hold high-level positions in the military. The family represented the region in the Diet and also had a few Calvinist religious leaders. However, with the family losing much of its wealth, openly opposing the Austrian Habsburg dominance and in defiance maintained their protestant religion, its prominence declined.

World War I changed everything for the Kingdom of Hungary. The ultimate settlement of the war was the Treaty of Trianon, which dismembered Hungary. Also, communism was brought upon the world, in Europe in particular, by the Bolshevik Revolution of 1917 in Russia. Ultimately, after World War II with the Allies' help as agreed at the Yalta Conference in February 1945, all of Central and Eastern Europe was handed over to the Soviets. The communist system was imposed on the countries taken over by them, including Hungary.

Consistent with the Rumy family history, my father's loyalty was for an independent Hungary. From the age of twenty-six to the time we escaped at age of forty-five, he sacrificed his youth for this cause and was still hopeful that he could contribute if the political system changed.

All this history and the Rumy family's and his own commitment for an independent Hungary weighed heavily on my father. He felt that he had betrayed his family legacy by leaving Hungary and wanted to be ready to return if the opportunity presented itself. I think that he eventually realized that once he left Hungary, any possibility of a significant role he may have played in any renewal of the country was unrealistic. At that point, he started to look for the best opportunity for the family, particularly for my brother and me.

I understood this dilemma my father struggled with, and I had no reason or was in no position to try to influence or expedite his decision. However, living in refugee camps was depressing. So, while my parents dealt with their decision and continued to move from camp to camp, I wanted to move on. I applied to the Hungarian language high school in Innsbruck, and I was accepted. On January 7, 1957, I left my parents and headed to Innsbruck. This was my first time being truly on my own; I looked forward to this new experience and just loved it.

The school arranged for me to live in a summer camp site halfway up the mountain where the Olympic Village was later built for the 1964 Winter Olympics. Our building, which would normally be closed during the winter, was used as a temporary dormitory for young Hungarian refugees. All the other guys were eighteen years and older, and they all had jobs. I was younger and the only one going to school, and I was assigned a private room which was normally used by the counselor. We needed to take a funicular from the city to reach this level on the mountain. This was a beautiful setting. It was like a resort.

I was a short and skinny kid, and immediately people tried to help me get on my feet. The Austrian people were very nice to me and the charitable organizations, primarily the Catholic Relief Services and the International Red Cross, were funding much of the support given to the Hungarian refugees. I received $5 per week in vouchers for extra food. I could use these vouchers just like cash in any food store. I also received a $100 voucher for clothing. I was able to buy brand new clothes to add to the used clothing I received in the refugee camps. I also received a small amount of cash that was provided to all refugees.

It was amazing what the U.S. dollar was able to purchase at that time. I felt rich! After arranging all my documents and buying the streetcar pass, I was ready to see what Innsbruck had to offer. Quickly, I got into my routine of going to school in the morning and sightseeing in the afternoon. I had to get back to the house for dinner. After dinner, I studied, but a number of times the older boys took me with them to the pub. These outings were a lot of fun. The boys were trying to meet girls, mostly unsuccessfully. Invariably, it did not turn out well. The girls were not alone, and their boyfriends did not appreciate the Hungarian guys taking over. I had to watch for and be sure to disappear before the fights eventually started, and the local police showed up to break it up.

I spent more time with two of the younger kids, István (Pista) and Imre. I think they were a little jealous of me because all the attention and special support I was getting. I used the food vouchers to buy chocolates and delicacies that I had been unable to get or had never seen in Hungary. I shared some of the goodies with them, which they appreciated.

We tried skiing. The huge ski slopes were above where we lived. We had to take a cable car to reach these ski slopes. We were beginning skiers, and these slopes were much more demanding than our skills. We spent more of our time sliding on our behinds than skiing. We had great laughs and fun anyway, but decided not to repeat the experience.

I also started to spend time with the caretaker's daughter, Anneliese. She was a couple years older than I, but we enjoyed being together. We went tobogganing, went to the movies, and started to spend a lot of time together. Being together with Anneliese helped me to learn German very fast. She was very nice to me. I noticed that her father was getting a little concerned about us, but he seemed to like me, and he was looking out for me. Other than being the caretaker for the facility, he was the chief operator of the funicular, so I saw him often.

At the end of January, my father was still thinking about staying in Austria and asked me to talk with the headmaster at school to see if he could assist my father in securing a job. The headmaster promised to make some contacts. Two weeks later, he informed me that the agriculture system was being revamped and that land reform was going on, making it impossible to get a job in that field. My father had the same kind of bad luck on other fronts. I think this started him to worry, and he finally started to listen to my mother about going to America. In the meantime, my brother managed to return from Belgium and join my parents at the refugee camp.

I was having the greatest time of my life when, on March 8th, I received a telegram from my parents. They had registered to go to the

USA, and, they had already arrived at the screening camp in Salzburg. I needed to get there as soon as possible because the entire family had to be screened at the same time. I really hated the idea of leaving Innsbruck! I had new friends, lived independently, and I had enjoyed everything about it. But going to America also sounded intriguing and not joining my parents was not an option.

The following morning, I informed the school of my needed departure and said my goodbyes. I picked up the remaining vouchers and aid that I had been programmed to receive in March and went on a shopping spree. I spent all the remaining clothing allowances. I was able to dress quite well for the circumstances and had a suitcase-full of extra clothing. I spent about five week's worth of food vouchers. I bought all kinds of delicacies: chocolates, bread, butter, salami, and two bottles of Jamaican rum.

That evening I said goodbye to Anneliese and her father after dinner, and Anneliese helped me pack my two new suitcases, one full of clothing and the other full of food. Later, I said my goodbyes to the guys. After that, Pista, Imre, and I went to my room and drank one of the bottles of rum.

Early the next morning, I said my final goodbyes and headed for the railroad station. Imre accompanied me and helped me carry the two suitcases. I boarded the train I had coordinated with my parents. When I arrived in Salzburg, I could not find anyone waiting for me. I proceeded to find out how to get to the refugee camp. I took the bus that let me off about a kilometer from the gate. I carried the two suitcases with frequent rest stops.

It turned out that, because they had no money for the bus, my father and brother walked to the station to meet me. By the time they arrived, I was already gone. After a while, they assumed I was not on the train and walked back to the camp. They could not believe their eyes as they saw me all settled in when they finally arrived at the camp.

I had already registered with the camp administration, and it was time to celebrate. We enjoyed the food I brought and drank the second bottle of rum.

We had our medical examination the next day. It all went well. It was followed by an interview. The interviewers were more careful by this time because several people before us had either exaggerated their stories or were communists fleeing the revolution, resulting in a number of bad actors and communists being among the initial group of refugees. The investigators questioned my father's story. Since we did not bring any documentation, we had no way to confirm his past. We had a problem. Uncle Édi was one of the few people in Hungary who had a phone. So my parents called him to see if he could forward my father's documents. There was nothing we could do but wait.

In the meantime, we signed up to go to Canada in the event we could not go to the USA. While we were waiting, we went sightseeing in Salzburg. We also looked at the daily roster to see if we could find people we knew. We found some and, in particular, Domokos Jobbágy (nickname Domi), who was a civilian detective who had worked with my father before the war. He was sentenced to death after the war, but his sentence was later commuted to life in prison. He escaped during the revolution. He was already scheduled to leave for the USA in a few days.

Ten days after we called Uncle Édi, on March 25th, our documents arrived. We later found out how he did it. His former secretary was working for the Swedish embassy. She was able to put a pre-addressed letter in the diplomatic pouch that was sent weekly to Vienna. Once it arrived in Vienna, someone mailed the letter. The next day, after the documents arrived, my father returned for his second interview. Immediately after my father showed his documents, we were given approval to go to the United States of America. We were scheduled to depart on the next plane, which was the last evacuation plane carrying the Hungarian refugees.

On March 29th, at 1:15 PM, we left Salzburg. We landed at Ireland's brand new Shannon airport. From there, we flew to Newfoundland and on to New York.

On March 30th, 1957 at 1:45 am, we arrived in America. We went through immigration and physical examinations and took busses to Camp Kilmer, New Jersey. After that, we settled down to start making plans for where we might be able to establish our new life.

The following day, the CIA interviewed my father. At that time, the world was at the height of the Cold War, and the CIA was looking for any information about my father's prison experiences and what my father might know about the current political situation.

Section 2
My New Life in America

The Beginning

Camp Kilmer, New Jersey was a dormant military installation which was activated to handle the incoming Hungarian refugees. It had been open for at least four months by the time we arrived. It looked like some families had been there for a long time, and they were pretty well settled in. The accommodations were simple, but the barracks were clean and well maintained. They were set up like dormitories. Families who had been there for some time sectioned off their beds with blankets hanging from the ceiling. This gave them a certain amount of privacy that, for some of them, was probably as much as they were accustomed to in Hungary.

Very quickly it became clear why, compared to the circumstances we all came from, it was like going to heaven without having to die. The camp was operated as a military camp with soldiers doing all the work. The food was regular army cuisine, which was better than I had ever experienced. Every day we had afternoon and evening movies, USO entertainment, and a recreation hall with pool tables and pinball machines. We also had access to the army PX for shopping with coupons that were allocated to each person. Why would anyone leave?

With all these freeloaders, I had to figure out what skill I could develop in order to get myself to the front of the service line. My few hours of English classes in Hungary and the German language I learned in Innsbruck came in handy. I did not know much English, but it was easy to figure out what was going on with just a few words of comprehension. Every afternoon, a few soldiers came between movies to serve refreshments. They had to move a table and coolers out from a small storage room. Each day they asked for help. It was not hard to figure out what they wanted, and I would call on people to help. After a couple days of this, everyone thought that I knew English, and I was considered the interpreter for both sides. I was rewarded by getting in the front of the line. After about two weeks, the fun became routine, and we were all getting anxious to move on.

My parents reviewed opportunities posted each day. Also, the army wanted to close the camp as soon as possible, so there was some urgency. We were not familiar with the U.S., and it was difficult to sort out what would work or not. My mother's education and skill set were quite marketable in any city. My father's education should have also been marketable, but not quite as easily, particularly in a city environment.

We also looked for people we knew to discuss the available options. We did find Domi again. He had been in Camp Kilmer and was scheduled to leave in a few days. He introduced us to Miklos Fözö, who was also leaving at the same time and to the same place. Domi gave us his destination before he departed, which we wrote down and promised to contact him when we settled down. They both left on April 10th.

As an option, the authorities promoted to contact relatives to see if they could sponsor us. My parents found a distant relative, a lady in her late eighties who lived in New York. She came to visit us. She was very nice, but also very poor, and sponsoring us was out of the question.

Things started to look discouraging, but on April 24th, we were told that Catholic Charities of St. Paul, Minnesota, was willing to sponsor five families. We were encouraged to sign up since Minnesota is quite agricultural, and there might be opportunities for my father. We had no idea where St. Paul was, but it seemed like the best option we had. On April 27th, we departed for St. Paul. We took an overnight train through Chicago. The sheer size of the country was imposing in an unexplainable, but positive way. The morning we entered Minnesota, we heard dogs barking and saw all the small towns and prosperous farms; things were looking up.

I found a very interesting reflection of this period in my life. I had started a diary with daily entries when we arrived in Austria, which is why I am able to recall exact dates and times during the period that followed. However, the last entry in my diary was the day we departed Camp Kilmer for St. Paul.

We were very impressed with St. Paul. Downtown looked very European, and we truly felt at home. Within a few days, we were offered a situation that seemed like a reasonable start. We moved to Minneapolis to a nursing home where my mother did the cooking and took care of the old people. For that service, we were provided an apartment in the attic and meals for all of us. Back in those days, nursing homes were small and usually located in large homes where the owners resided as well as their patients. It was not the best situation, but it was a start. My father found a nighttime janitor job at the local TV station. It was a disappointing job, but it gave us cash, and my father had time to look for a better job during the day.

As we started to venture out, we found life in the U.S. to be amazing. Probably the biggest surprise was the number of cars. Budapest had outlawed horse-drawn wagons just a year before we escaped, but there were still very few automobiles. There were trucks to move materials, but they were noisy and smoked like a chimney. There were very few cars and essentially all the passenger cars were carrying government officials. A few East German Trabants and Russian Ladas started to appear, but it took years to get one delivered after the buyer paid for the car in full and in advance. The difference was amazing. Not only were the trucks much larger, cleaner, and so numerous, but there were so many cars, not only in numbers, but in styles and colors.

Equally amazing was the sight of all the private homes and green spaces in the city. Budapest was very compact; in Pest, low-rise apartment houses were built closely together with shops on the street level and in Buda, there were more private homes, but they had very little space between them. Minneapolis/St. Paul was smaller in population than Budapest, but significantly larger in geography, with roads and highways to support the automobile culture and with less emphasis on public transportation. Even so, we were able to get around town on busses without much difficulty.

Going to a grocery store was an unbelievable experience. Self-service supermarkets were unknown in Hungary. We were used to going to empty stores with limited product choices, and everything came in bulk and was dispensed manually into paper bags or into containers that we took with us to the store. The quantity, quality, and packaging of the food was amazing.

The department stores were just as strikingly different. We just could not believe the quantity and quality of the clothing available. The prices were also unbelievably low, and the standard of living was overwhelming to us.

Minneapolis was very nice, and the numerous single family homes had a lot of green space. It was different from Budapest where most people lived in big apartment buildings. When I walked around in Buda Hills, which had many old villas, all built in the 1800s, I dreamed of one day owning one myself. I immediately thought Minneapolis offered that possibility.

The most striking difference, however, was the people. It was clear that people were upbeat, prosperous, and generally happy. Clearly there were no restrictions in movement, and no one was watching us. The signs of freedom were everywhere. You could not help but feel empowered to do what you wanted and be able to accomplish whatever you were able or willing to work for. The openness of the people and the fact that they were so genuinely accepting and helpful were very pleasant surprises. We were all looking forward to becoming an integral part of the American way of life.

At the same time, my parents sought out the Hungarian community. There were around seventy-five Hungarian families in the Twin Cities. The range went from workers, managers, and engineers to college professors. The only common denominator was that they were Hungarians. My father became the main organizer for the group. I was required to attend some of the activities, which I considered harassment. I used to ask my father if he had known these people in Budapest, would they be his circle of friends; the answer was no. I finally concluded that maintaining contact with the community gave people, my parents included, acceptance they may not immediately have felt in an American social setting. It also gave them an opportunity to compare experiences, which helped them to adjust to their new lives.

This was not uncommon among all immigrant groups, but none of them believed that maintaining their ethnic community was a substitute for immersing themselves in the American way of life. They also knew that they could not make a good living and be a productive part of society without learning the English language. Generally, the ethnic contact was maintained, but it became less and less important.

Unfortunately, I was dragged into some of these activities. The Hungarian group decided to participate in the international festival in St. Paul. It was a nice event. Several ethnic groups participated in the entertainment and served their national foods. The Hungarians decided to do a dance number with a professional dancer couple and several amateur couples who danced at the beginning and at the end of the number. In the middle of the musical number, the professional dancers performed while we were to get down on one knee and the girl sit on the raised knee. When I got down on my knee, my pants split in half. My white underwear was hanging out of my black pants. There was nothing that I could do but finish the dance. That was the last time that I let my father talk me into participating in such Hungarian activities.

I did keep in touch with several of my old friends from Hungary for a while, but as I got more involved with my American life, these contacts started to be less and less frequent. My friend Laci was the only one who I maintained contact with throughout our lives. He became a doctor and specialized in diabetes and genetics research. With my help, he came to St. Louis, completing a significant part of his research at Washington University over a number of years.

I have to admit, for several years after arriving in the U.S., I wondered what would have happened to me if we had stayed in Hungary. The thought was not how good things would have been, but how bad it might have gotten. All my curiosity was cured when I returned to Hungary for a short visit in 1969.

The Immigrant Life

Once we settled down in Minneapolis, it was clear to me that I needed to get my life on track. By the end of the first week in May, I enrolled in Jefferson Junior High. The school assigned me to two hours of math and three hours of English. Three hours a day of English helped me learn the language much faster, but unfortunately, the math was a total waste. They were teaching beginning algebra, but I had already started calculus as a ninth grader in Hungary.

I immediately looked for a job and by mid-May, I got my first job, a paper route. I delivered the *Minneapolis Star and Tribune* evening and Sunday papers in a six-square-block area, about one-hundred-twenty-five papers per day. The neighborhood consisted of two streets of two- and three-story apartment buildings and nine streets of single-family homes.

It was like a small business. I was responsible for delivering the papers to the front of the apartment doors and to the front door of the houses. Other than delivering papers, I was also doing the weekly collections and trying to find new subscribers. Bundles of papers were delivered to a street corner, marked with my route number, at 3:00 PM on week days and 5:30 AM on Sundays. After delivering the papers in the afternoon, I would return in the evenings and Saturdays to collect payments and solicit new subscribers. I submitted cash payments to my manager on a weekly basis for the papers and kept what I had left.

After successful Saturday collections, I would go to the local drug store soda fountain for a banana split. Unfortunately, there were some deadbeats who would not pay, but I was not authorized to stop delivery. At Christmas, I decided to give each of my customers a Christmas card, hoping that the deadbeats would pay up and the good customers would give something extra. One of my good customers wrote to the local paper, which was my first appearance in the press:

"Mrs. Newell Griffith of Pleasant Avenue has been a subscriber of our gazette for 25 years. Each year she has remembered her carrier salesman. This year, for the first time, she says, her carrier salesman remembered her with a card. The Christmas greeting came from Zsolt Rumy, a Jefferson High student and a Hungarian refugee who has been in this country six months."

The idea worked with the good customers, and I received tips from most of them, but not so much with the deadbeats. This idea of sending Christmas cards to customers became a standard procedure for paperboys in Minneapolis.

When the new school year started, I went back to Jefferson Junior High. It did not even occur to me that there was no tenth grade. We did not have anything like a junior high school in Hungary; when we completed eighth grade, we progressed to "gymnasium," which was ninth to twelfth grade. It took me a week or two to finally conclude that I was still in ninth grade. To me it was like "kindergarten" or worse. I went to the principal's office to explain that I was supposed to be in tenth grade. She was not at all sympathetic; obviously she thought highly of the ninth-grade education the school had to offer.

When I explained that I had already taken chemistry, physics, and calculus in Hungary and the classes in junior high were a waste, I did not think that she believed me. Between my poor English and unfamiliarity with the system, I was unable to change her mind, even with tears rolling down my face from the frustration of trying.

So, I ended up staying in the "kindergarten" for a full year. This is where I met and became friends with John Standal and Arne Svenson. We have been friends and in contact with each other ever since.

We all took a number of aptitude and intelligence tests. The teachers knew that my language skills were not adequate to take these tests, but they made me take them anyway. I am not sure of the results, but I took many tests later that would negate these early test results. One thing continued to follow me all the way to college. Filling out the personal information on the first test I took, one question was: what is your sex, with M and F as choices. I understood the question, but I did not know if I was M or F. I took a chance on F which resulted in numerous invitations to join girls organizations, including several sororities when I entered the University of Minnesota.

My school situation was disappointing, but our family settling into the American way was more exciting. After a few months at the nursing home, we were all ready to move on. My mother had to work way too hard, and our living conditions were strange. The owners of the nursing home, our family, and the residents were all living together.

My mother found a position at Deaconess Lutheran Hospital as a practical nurse. The hospital accepted my mother's diploma from the prestigious Rockefeller Green Cross Nursing College and promised that as soon as her English language skills improved, she would be promoted to a professional nursing position. We had to move from the nursing home by the time my mother started her new position. By the end of 1957, my mother's degree was confirmed, and she received her nursing license. She was immediately promoted to a professional nursing position. She was highly respected for her knowledge and her strength of character. Eventually, she was asked to be the head nurse.

My parents' combined incomes provided us with enough to begin our own household. We moved into a South Minneapolis apartment in October 1957. As we set up our household, it was amazing how easy it was to purchase what we needed. Prices were low and credit was easy. We found this amazing.

What was even more amazing was shopping for groceries. Before coming to America, we had no idea about supermarkets. The idea that we could buy everything from one store instead of shopping all day in specialty stores, which were chronically short on merchandise, was unbelievable.

We found that pork and chicken, which are what we were used to, were almost given away. We just about panicked when we could not find lard. I happened to notice two half-pound packages on top of a display cooler. We bought both. When we took them home and found they were white in color and tasteless, we panicked again. I suggested heating it until it started to smell more like the lard we were used to. It worked—my first successful chemistry experiment. We soon, however, switched to butter, which we loved but could rarely afford in Hungary.

Shortly after we moved, my brother started to have severe headaches. It got so bad that he had to be taken to the hospital by ambulance in the middle of the night. It turned out to be a brain aneurism. Today, this would not be as a major life-threatening medical crisis as it was back then. It was our luck that we were in Minneapolis. The University of Minnesota Hospital was one of the very few places in the world where they operated on the brain. He recovered very quickly. Although for a while, there were some after effects including occasional seizures. The doctors told my mother to let him say what was on his mind to remove any strain on his brain. As a result, she paid a lot of attention to him. They became very close and, unfortunately, my mother made more excuses for him rather than helping him as the years went on. As my brother and I had very little in common from our early childhood, my relationship with my mother drifted apart. At the same time, my father and I got even closer.

Our next adventure in the American experience was to get a driver's license and to buy a car. We decided that my father and I would be the first to get licenses. He also used this opportunity to learn English. He translated the entire driver training book and learned every word. I just read the book once, and we were ready to go. My role was to be with my father while he was taking the test. My father was so concerned about his accent that he was reluctant to talk, so I was translating for him for the eye test. We took the test; he got a hundred on his test, and I skated by with just over eighty.

Once we had our permits, we needed to buy the family car and learn to drive. We bought a lime green '55 Oldsmobile. We learned how to drive together. My father had a car in the 1940s, but he also had a driver, so his experience was just enough to practice driving and to teach me. In early spring of 1958, my father took the driver's test. Again, we went together, and I was translating for my father during the driving test. He did okay. I received my learner's permit, and I was allowed to drive with my father until I could take the driving test when I turned sixteen. After I received my license, my mother and brother also learned to drive in the same car. Before we were all done learning to drive, we had so many fender benders that, it seemed, the roof of the car was the only part that was still original.

My contribution to the systematic destruction of the family car came about a year after we bought it. Once I turned sixteen, I could drive by myself, but there was no reason for me to use the car until one beautiful summer Saturday afternoon. My father took a nap, and I worked on my mother to let me take a drive. I finally wore her down, and she let me take the car. I headed toward the beach on Lake Calhoun. On the way there, I saw a very good looking girl walking toward the lake. I just had to take a better look at her and at the same time, show off my driving. Unfortunately, a parked car suddenly appeared out of nowhere, and I hit it before I ever saw it. The girl was truly very nice looking and was well worth a closer look, but I failed to impress her with my driving.

When we felt like we were settled, once again, we made connections with other Hungarian families. We finally looked at the address where Domi indicated he was going. By pure coincidence, he and Miklos Főző both ended up in St. Paul. By the time we connected with Domi, he was working as a caretaker for a well-to-do family living in a beautiful mansion at Lake Minnetonka. My parents and Domi became good friends and frequently met socially.

Miklos was employed at a fruit and vegetable stand in the St. Paul farmer's market. In Hungary, he owned a food store before the war, and he was anxious to get back into the business. He convinced my father that he could duplicate the success of the St. Paul market stand in Minneapolis. Within a few months, they agreed to become partners in what became the Forum Fruit and Vegetable Market.

I quit my paper route and became totally involved in the negotiations and in the opening of the store. I actually came up with the name. It was very easy to make all the arrangements to start a store. We had a lot of support from future vendors. Used refrigerators and walk-in coolers were supplied without initial payment by future suppliers. We built the counters ourselves, and we were able to buy inventory on credit from the wholesalers. We did, however, make a major mistake. We found an ideal store, but we had no idea about the importance of the location. The store was on the corner of a busy street and a one-way street going downtown. We quickly realized that nobody buys fruits and vegetables on the way to work. We were open for business in September 1958, about eighteen months after we landed in the United States of America.

While we were putting together the store, I needed a job to have some spending money. I went to work in a downtown Greek restaurant as a bus boy at eighty-five cents per hour. It was a part-time job during lunch and dinner. It was an okay job, but I was always looking for a better opportunity. I noticed that dish-washing was a much harder job and that the restaurant had a new worker almost daily. I assumed, which one should never do without verifying the assumptions, that the pay would be significantly higher. So, I asked the owner if I could trade for this job. He was happy to accommodate. I worked very hard for a week, when I received my paycheck, which I expected to be considerably larger. As it turned out, I received seventy-five cents per hour. After the shock wore off, the only honorable thing I could do was to quit.

In September, I started tenth grade at West High School. High school proved to be just as backward scholastically as junior high school. The only new subjects were English language, literature, and American history. Beyond those subjects, I was not exposed to anything I had not already learned in Budapest.

About half of the Jefferson Junior High kids, including John Standal and Arne Svendsen, also went to West High along with kids from other schools. I was the only foreign regular student. In addition, there were two foreign exchange students. I was no longer on a special schedule like I was in the junior high school, so I always felt this was the time of the true beginning of my American life.

I started to meet kids on an equal basis. As normal in high school, there were several cliques. In our school, there were three, and I was part of all three of them. I did go out for swimming and made the team. I did receive a letter, not as significant as football, but a letter nevertheless, which qualified me in the jock group. My grades were very good, and I was invited to join the Chis, which I called the smart clique. Arne was also a Chi, but John joined the Dekes, which I called the fun clique. They were the most fun. I liked the Dekes the most, so I was mostly hanging around with them.

Since I was almost a year older than my classmates, I was the first to drive. On Saturday evenings, I would pick up three or four friends, and we would look for things to do. This was a strange experience for me because I thought we should have plans if we had wheels. In those years, kids really did not have a lot of options. This was so unusual for me because kids in Hungary had minimum age restrictions and could go anywhere for entertainment, but we had no means to do anything. At this time, I had money and a car, but had no place to go. So, we would drive around or go to drive-in restaurants and sit in the car until we were chased out. If we did not spend money, we would be ordered to leave.

After about an hour or so, I would say, "If we have no place to go, I am taking all of you home." The parents were happy to see us kids being home within two hours, but my friends always complained, but we repeated the same schedule the following week.

Our store did quite well for a short time, but as the novelty wore off, things slowed down. My father depended on Miklos's expertise, but within a short time, it became clear that Miklos did not really know how to run the business.

As business got worse, more and more tension developed between the partners. The two of them would count the cash every evening after the store closed. One evening there was $10 extra in the cash register. My father remembered that he made change, but forgot to take the $10 out of the register. Miklos insisted that whatever money is in the register is company money. That was the final straw for my father. He ended the partnership right on the spot. He gave Miklos the choice to buy out my father's interest or be bought out. Unfortunately, Miklos was smart enough to take the second option. We never saw Miklos again.

After my father was by himself, I spent the rest of the summer working at the store. Since I was not getting paid at my father's store,

I needed a source of income. I took a part-time job at McDonald's. I worked the weekends and some evenings. Initially I was earning seventy-five cents per hour. Later I was promoted to assistant manager with $1.25 per hour pay. I bought my first car from my savings; a '53 Ford for $125. The car and my expanded social life also brought on additional financial needs, so I needed to work as many hours as possible. I always needed spending money and continued working there for three years, most of the time as a second job.

Very fortunately for our store, the Super Value stores, the largest grocery chain in Minneapolis, went on strike. Our business immediately increased by a factor of ten. The strike lasted for several weeks, and we did quite well. When the strike was over, within weeks our business started to decline. In about three months, we were back to the same level as before the strike. The final clue that we would not return anywhere near to the business level we enjoyed during the strike came when one of our regular good customers was making a left turn off the busy street in front of our store and was hit. She never returned to our store.

My father worked very hard. He started out at 5:30 in the morning at the wholesalers' where he handpicked the products. The wholesalers were very helpful and wanted my father to succeed. They gave him the best merchandise at a competitive price. Since my brother did not help, I took over from my father every day after school at about 3:30 in the afternoon so he could go home and rest. He would come back to close the store at 7:00 in the evening, and we would go home together.

In July 1959, we bought a house. Getting a mortgage on a $14,500 house was quite difficult at the time, but even more so for an immigrant family with no credit history. We asked an older well-to-do Hungarian couple to guarantee the loan, but my mother was still required to get a doctor's letter assuring the bank that she was unable to have more children, meaning that she would not stop working. The house was in South Minneapolis in a very nice neighborhood. So, in just over two years, we were living like true Americans: a car, a house, and a business.

In eleventh grade, I decided to go out for football. The practice started right after classes. When I was given the uniform, I was totally speechless. I had no idea what I was to do with all of the gear. Even more shocking was to see the ball; it was not round. I needed help and time to get dressed. By the time I was all dressed, I was totally intrigued. I was anxious to find out what this was all about, clearly not soccer, which is what I was expecting. I did okay during practice, and I was one of the fastest on the team with all the gear on. However, by the time I got to the store, it was almost closing time. My father was very tired and clearly upset. I thought that it was best for all of us that I quit football the next day.

It had become painfully clear that the business would not support the family and that my father needed to do something different. Just at the right time, some people came forward who were interested in buying the store. My father did not waste any time and, seizing the opportunity, he sold it.

There were no obvious opportunities in the agricultural business, so he took a training course in mechanical drafting. Once he completed the course, he was able to find a position in a small manufacturing company producing well screens in St. Paul. He worked there for the rest of his life. He was well liked and respected in the company. He continued to be very self-conscious about speaking English in public, but he became proficient in the written language to a level that the company had him proofread for correct grammar and spelling of all publication and technical books before they were printed.

After sophomore year, I found a summer job in a commercial bakery as a general helper wherever help was needed. I did a good job, so I was rewarded by being asked to fill in for regular operators when they took their vacations. This was a great opportunity because I received the same pay as the operator I replaced, which was more than triple that of the helper's wages. My first assignment was as an oven operator for the angel food cake line on the night shift. The only instruction I received was the storage place for the raw cakes, which needed to be placed in front of a moving arm that dragged the pans into the oven. There was enough room to stack ten pans in front of this arm. I tried to load all ten pans per cycle to be sure I got all of the cakes baked. Halfway through the shift, I realized I would shortly run out of pans. I had finished loading all the pans in the oven with three more hours left in the shift. I was quite proud of myself until I went to the other end of the oven. To my surprise, heaps of unpackaged cakes were stacked all over. The packaging ladies were in a panic. I immediately took charge and organized everyone, and I went to work helping with the packaging. We successfully completed the packaging before the shift ended. The next day, I paced the baking to make life easier on the other end of the oven. Lesson learned about teamwork.

Entering into twelfth grade after a financially successful summer, I upgraded my car to a '55 Ford convertible. My options in social life improved. I started to date more, and there were parties to go to. These parties were quite interesting. Usually if a kid's parents were out of town for a weekend, they would invite a few friends. As the word got out, a huge number of uninvited kids would show up. There was drinking and noise and generally ending up with the police being called by the neighbors.

It was quite an interesting new experience for me, a totally different life style from Budapest. We did a lot of partying, probably too much. We did drink beer, and the parties got a little wild sometimes. We knew drugs were around, but to my knowledge, none of our group was involved with the use of drugs, with a few exceptions with marijuana. I was fairly careful with my drinking since I had been used to it at home. However, the car added an extra dimension that worried my father. Many times when I rolled in at 2:00 AM or later, I could see a lit cigarette in the dark living room and knew my father was waiting up for me. He did not discipline me, and he did not have to. His concern worked on me more effectively than an argument would have.

Senior year was very interesting. It started with the election for class president. Several kids asked me to run, and I went along. My campaign manager was a very popular girl. She and her friends worked hard, but we were unsuccessful. However, I was elected to the senior class council and felt that I was fully accepted by the rest of the kids.

There was one more very important event that year. It seems that the good life in America had caused me to start growing again. In my senior year, my height shot up from five-foot-two inches all the way up to five-foot-six inches!

We saw the end of our high school days coming and started to make plans for the future. I had decided back in Hungary that I wanted to be a chemical engineer. I liked math and sciences, but I had no interest in being a research scientist of any kind. In Europe, engineers were the ones running businesses and, in my opinion, chemical engineers had the best potential.

I was not aware of all the possible universities that I could have chosen, so I concentrated on the University of Minnesota. I took the entrance exam and scored very well and was accepted. Some people suggested looking at other universities, such as Stanford or MIT. I, of course, could not afford them, and it was suggested that I look into scholarships. I went to the counselor's office to inquire. She clearly knew my grades were excellent, and my entrance exam score for the University of Minnesota engineering was the highest in the school, but she still suggested that I should get a job instead of going to college. Obviously I was not going to get any financial support, so I accepted my fate. As it turned out, University of Minnesota was one of the top three chemical engineering schools in the U.S., so I ended up with a great education at an affordable cost.

In the senior high school yearbook, the yearbook committee selects a quote for each person that, in their view, defines him or her. The quote next to my picture was, *"The will to do, the soul to dare."* I don't know who selected this quote, but it turned out to be prophetic, as I believe I have lived up to this description my whole life.

During the school year, the bakery had gone out of business, so I needed to find a new company to work for during the summer. My father recommended me for a summer job in the shop at the company he worked. I was hired.

The company manufactured screens for water wells and oil wells. The owner was a Dartmouth graduate and he usually hired four or five Dartmouth students. I was the only outsider. We became good summer friends with the Dartmouth students and did get together with them over the summer and during holidays. They were more mature and grown up than my high school friends. I enjoyed their company, but ultimately lost track of them once I started my college years. I continued to work for the well screen company in the shop for a few summers and later in the laboratory during summers and part-time during the school year. I ended up working there throughout my college years.

Becoming an American

After being accepted as a candidate for U.S. citizenship, usually signified by getting a "green card," it takes five years of residency to actually become a citizen. At the time we came to America, each country had an annual quota for immigrants. After the revolution, the number of refugees coming to the U.S. far exceeded the Hungarian quota. We received a "white card" to designate us as permanent residents until the annual quota caught up to us. It took over two years to get our green card, but our residency time counted as part of the five-year mandatory waiting period. So, we all became U.S. citizens on June 16, 1962.

It was a memorable day. There were about a hundred new citizens that day in Minneapolis from a variety of countries. It was a special day for all of us, and there were a number of people to assist in making the celebration special. We had politician speakers, government officials, a few musicians, citizen volunteers, and marine flag bearers to assist with the swearing-in ceremony. To round out the celebration, the organizers looked for a couple of new citizens to make a short speech. They selected a good-looking blond German girl and me.

When we walked up onto the stage, everyone's eyes were on the German girl, and I felt like they had just forgotten about me. After the official program was complete, we both got our chance to speak. The

German girl went first. She told the audience that America should be happy that people like her were willing to come to America and become a U.S. citizen. My message was different. I thanked everyone and especially the American government for welcoming us after we had to leave our homeland; I committed that we would try our best to become valued citizens. Needless to say, I became the hero, and everyone wanted to say hello to me, and no one paid any more attention to the German girl. Welcome to America!

I was just finishing my first year at University of Minnesota in the chemical engineering curriculum; it truly felt great to be an American. The Psi Upsilon fraternity members were mostly made up of kids from well-to-do families, and joining it gave me a very important experience and helped me to understand the American way of life. Acceptance did not come automatically. Not knowing what fraternities were all about and not knowing about the rush program resulted in a memorable experience. I was not properly dressed and, coupled with my accent, I was separated from the mainstream candidates and tested. Fortunately, the testing was playing cards, for money, no less, and I was not intimidated. I always thought this was a fun experience, but when the *Animal House* movie came out many years later, it became even funnier to me in retrospect. The entire idea of a fraternity was completely new for me. It added some cost to the school, but it also added a new and valuable experience. And a whole new set of friends.

I followed my earlier decision to become a chemical engineer, and I was even more excited because I realized it was the most exciting technology and the newest engineering curriculum, making it more interesting and challenging than other engineering disciplines. My score on the entrance exam to the university was high enough to receive the highest degree of confidence that I was going to finish.

Although I had a fairly good command of the English language, I had only been in America for five years, and American life continued to offer a number of surprises. Most of these surprises were positive, but occasionally they presented some contradictions to my understanding and expectations, which caught me off guard and resulted in some embarrassing situations. However, on the surface, I did my best to exhibit a strong self-confidence.

My father and I had a serious, but very short conversation about how to finance the cost of my university education. He gave me two choices. The first choice: my parents would pay for one hundred percent of my expenses if I would concentrate on school and give up the car, fraternity, and social life. The second choice: if I wouldn't give up all of those activities and managed to pay for them, then I should be able to pay for school myself. He barely got the question out before I gave him my answer. I would be happy to pay my way.

This was the right thing to do anyway because my parents were paying for my brother to get a college education, and they would have been stressed having to pay for both of us. My brother always wanted to be an electrician, but my father wanted him to go to the university. He was never a good student, but he managed to finish the university in eight years with an electrical engineering degree. I don't believe that he appreciated the sacrifice my parents made to put him through school.

My freshman year was full of activities and new experiences. At the end of the year, I became a U.S. citizen, which was an emotional experience, and I really believed that the memories of the horrible life under communism were behind me. However, I was very surprised to find out that several of my new friends in the fraternity, who were from well-to-do families and were born and raised in the U.S., actually believed that socialism was desirable over the American way of life. I had a number of heated discussions about how miserable life was under a communist/socialist system, but they would not believe me. I stayed away from political discussions for a long time.

I encountered a similar experience in class. I was taking a social science course which was taught by a turban-wearing Indian communist. We were required to turn in a book report on a specific book. I went to the book store and thumbed through the pages of the book for a few minutes. It was virtually the *Communist Manifesto*, and I decided that I did not need to read the book to write a report. I received an "A" on my report. I just could not help myself and went up to the professor after class to tell him I did not read the book; I did not need to because I had escaped from the system he was promoting. He was not happy with me.

For the first time in five years, I was taking courses that were new. Unfortunately, I got out of the habit of studying, and all my exciting new experiences over the prior four years diminished my interest in school. At the same time, the fraternity was quite interesting and a lot of fun. We played cards for hours, and there were many social functions. To fund school and my social life, I needed to work during the school year to supplement my summer earnings. I worked a few hours in the afternoons at the well screen company's laboratory.

On weekends, I still worked at McDonald's. Occasionally, I was asked to help out on Friday evenings as well. It was getting to be too much. Although I was a part-time assistant manager, the son-in-law of the owner became a permanent assistant manager for afternoons and evenings. One Friday evening when I arrived, I asked to be released as soon as possible because I had plans for the evening. When the evening rush was over, he told me that he would not let me off because I always ask to be released in the evenings. He proceeded to release everyone else, including kids who wanted to work additional hours. He indicated that he had the authority as the full-time assistant manager, and I assumed that, in his mind, I represented some sort of competition for his position. I had already thought that it was about time to quit McDonald's, and this confirmed it. My pay at $1.25 per hour was much lower than my pay at the well screen company, and it was too little for all the time it took away from my other activities.

The early McDonald's stores were just a small building with the grill, the French fry cooker, milk-shake machine, and the soda machines in the front room. The office and food preparation and inventory were in the back room. More inventory was stored in the basement. Customers would walk up to one of two serving windows to place their order and receive the food. Coincidentally, as I was thinking about my situation, a basketball game was over at the high school just across the street. Within minutes, there were about a hundred kids in front of the service window screaming for food and drinks. I was in the front room and the son-in-law just sat in the back. It seemed to be the perfect time to quit, which is what I did. I went to the back room and took off my apron and handed it to him, saying, "I quit" and walked out as he was trying to gain his composure; not my proudest moment, but I still think that it was funny to see the shock on his face. A few days later, I went back to pick up my final paycheck, and the manager asked me to return. I told him that it really was time for me to move on.

I was introduced to golf by my frat brothers. One of them gave me his grandfather's old set of clubs. The university had a beautiful golf course, and we played for free. I could have taken a golf class or lessons also for free, which was included in the activity fee we paid in addition to the tuition, but I did not realize that at the time. I learned on my own, and it showed. Golf turned out to be large part of my later business and social life, and I always regretted that I did not take advantage of these opportunities to learn the game.

Although I felt I was well on my way toward becoming a true American, I still liked Hungarian cooking. My father and his friend, Domi, decided to make Hungarian sausage one Saturday, and I assisted them. It was quite a process. The ingredients were simple: ground pork and beef, plenty of paprika, onions, and garlic. It didn't get much better. We cooked some of it to taste, and the rest was to be smoked.

The evening after the all-day sausage making, we had a fraternity party. We took a tour bus to the club where the party was held. I was stinking from garlic and could not hide. Needless to say, I was reminded of it all evening and was subject of many jokes. It was embarrassing, but the sausage was well worth the trouble.

My trouble was nothing compared to what Domi ran into. Domi fabricated a smoker and set it up in the old barn at the estate where he lived. Unfortunately, the estate owner's "his and her" new Cadillacs were also parked in the barn. Every morning Domi would bring the car up to the front of the house for the owner. The morning after the smoker was activated, the smoked grease and garlic smell in the cars was overwhelming. They attempted to clean the cars, but it was not possible. Ultimately, they decided to sell both cars.

I finished freshman year with grades far lower than I had been used to in my entire school career. I blamed everything but my lack of interest and commitment to studying. My wakeup call came the first quarter of my sophomore year. My grades were so bad that under normal circumstances I could not have registered for the next quarter. Fortunately, my high score in the entrance exams qualified me to pre-register for the second quarter, but I was not allowed to register for the third quarter without approval from the head of the Chemical Engineering Department, Dr. Amundson.

This was my first meeting with him. He was a wonderful and brilliant person, the head of both the Chemical Engineering and Mathematics Departments. If he got excited, he would stutter.

When he looked at my record, he asked me with a very serious stutter, "What are you doing still attending classes?"

I said, "No one told me not to attend," as I gave him my second quarter grades, which were all As except one B.

He said, with a distinctly less stutter, "Nothing I can do about it now" and signed the approval form.

Fortunately, later we had a number of meetings that were more pleasant. Several years later, after I graduated and moved to St. Louis, the annual meeting for the American Institute of Chemical Engineers was held in St. Louis. Dr. Amundson was there. I overheard him talk to other professors about the difficulty of finding graduate students with the Vietnam war going on. It was my time to have some fun.

I interrupted their conversation. I said, "Dr. Amundson, I would be willing to come back."

I had him stuttering as much as he did when I first met him, but this time, he thought I was funny, as he said, "We are not that desperate yet!"

During my sophomore year, I started to think I might want to change to a business degree. It seemed most of my frat brothers were in that program, and it was considerably easier and shorter than the chemical engineering program, which, at the time, was five years. I approached my father with the idea. He was not happy about it. His first objection was that when the U.S. eventually became a socialist country, there would be no jobs for business graduates. I never knew if he was just paranoid or if he actually saw the changes that were coming. The second reason he gave me was more compelling. He reasoned that if I wanted to have a business degree, I could always get it after graduating from engineering. The second argument was convincing because I had to admit to myself that to quit engineering was a way to admit failure, which I was never willing to do! I continued with chemical engineering.

Very soon, school, fraternity, and work started to collide. Once I decided to stay with the engineering program, I also decided that I had to concentrate on my studies. I significantly reduced my social schedule.

By the end of my junior year, I was back in the good graces of the engineering school. I had cut back on social activities, but not completely. For the first two years, our courses were actually in the Chemistry

Department and starting with our junior year, we officially transferred to the Chemical Engineering Department. By this time, we only had about thirty students in our class, down from over one hundred and fifty starting two years earlier. So things were much more personal.

My fall quarter results were okay, but I expected better. In an important lab course, I had a perfect report, but I received a "C" grade. When I complained to the teaching assistant, he told me that I got higher grades in my other courses, which did not seem to have any relationship to my grade in his lab. After some more conversation, I realized that all the professors reviewed each student and decided which grade would be awarded to the student in each of the classes he took during the quarter, not necessarily according to the student's actual performance in any particular class.

I concluded that I needed to demonstrate more interest in my classes and spend more face time in the department. So I substituted the usual afternoon card games for the library, although sometimes I was actually looking at *Playboy* magazines. Once, I actually overheard two professors talking in the hall, remarking that I was spending time in the library. I also joined the student chapter of the American Institute of Chemical Engineers and soon became its social chairman. As I became more immersed in school and continued working in the afternoons, I dropped out of the fraternity. My grades significantly improved.

After the fall quarter of my fourth year, the chemical engineering curriculum requirement was changed from five years to four years. By this time, I was doing well in school and after coordinating the old and new course requirements, I could finish one quarter early. With that possibility, I started to interview for jobs.

Engineers were in high demand, and top chemical companies were coming to campus to recruit. I tried for a sales position, but all possibilities came with a one-year or two-year training program. I wanted to get started in a real job as fast as I could. So, to avoid training programs, I considered an engineering position as a starting job. Although I had had a job from the time I was thirteen years old, I looked at this job hunt more seriously, figuring that I was choosing a lifetime career path.

With the end in sight for school, I needed time to study and at the same time, keep an open schedule for interview trips. Therefore, I had to stop working in the afternoons. But I still needed to earn some money. One evening, I substituted as a bartender for a private party. The host expected two of my friends, and he was very upset when I showed up by myself.

It was a party at a 3M executive's home. The bar was set up in the kitchen, and no one was leaving the conversation in the living room for drinks in the kitchen. I decided to walk into the living room and take people's empty glasses out of their hands and replace them with fresh drinks. The party became a roaring success, and I was in high demand for future parties. For a while, I was the first person people called to plan a date for their party. This job was a lot of fun and quite lucrative. I still remember how disappointed that lady who called me just before I moved to St. Louis was to find out that I would not be available for her party.

The entire job interview process was very interesting and challenging. It also had some lighter moments. My parents were hoping I would not have to move away from Minneapolis, but the only real opportunity I found there would have been with 3M. My interview schedule was apparently cancelled because I did not respond to the request for my flight information. When I showed up at the appointed time at 3M, I reminded them that there was no flight scheduled between Minneapolis and St. Paul. They quickly organized an interview, but it was with an uninspiring business unit. The person with whom I interviewed was embarrassed and promised to get me a better opportunity if I wanted to come back. I did not see the reason because there were so many more opportunities to investigate.

My Union Carbide interview was in Chicago. My parents asked me to try to make contact with the family of my father's cousin, Tibor Rácz. The evening before the interview, I tried to contact him to introduce myself and to say hello. He was not home, but returned my call the next morning at the hotel. I told him I was on an interview trip and would try to meet on another trip to Chicago. He was the Chief Accounting Officer at Harris Bank and was not about to take directions from me. He decided to come to Union Carbide, where he asked to see me in the middle of my interview. It was embarrassing, and I am sure that it left a strange impression.

The dress code at Union Carbide was quite formal, and I was severely criticized for not wearing a hat, although I was dressed in a three-piece suit and a camel hair overcoat. After the interview, I did buy a hat, which I never wore. I did not get a job offer from Union Carbide, but we did establish a relationship with the Rácz family.

The real fun interview trip was my Goodyear interview in Akron, Ohio. A classmate, who graduated a quarter earlier than I, had taken a sales position with Goodrich Chemical in Cleveland. I arranged for a Friday interview and stayed with him for the weekend to compare notes and have some fun.

My friend had a date and arranged a blind date for me on Saturday evening. We decided that just the two of us would go to a Hungarian restaurant, called the Gypsy Cellar, for dinner and pick up our dates after dinner. The two of us had a great dinner and as we were leaving the restaurant, the entertainment was just starting. We asked the hostess to save our table, and we would come back with our dates.

As we walked in with the girls, the violin-playing band leader jumped from the table-height stage to our table and performed a Hungarian dance called csárdás. Dishes and silverware were flying all over. When the number finished, he jumped back onto the stage and while the waitress cleaned up the table, he proudly announced that the two young American gentlemen had come for dinner earlier and liked the place enough to bring their girlfriends back. Needless to say, being exposed to our dates as two cheapskates, the evening did not go well.

By the end of 1965, I had several job offers. All of them were for training programs in sales except one, which was from the Monsanto Company in St. Louis. The job was a process engineer position in their W. G. Krummrich plant. With the promise to be considered for a sales position after gaining experience in the plant, it seemed better than one- or two-year sales training. So Monsanto was my choice. My first impression of St. Louis during my interview trip was positive. I thought that St. Louis had a very European look and would be a nice place to live, and I became friendly to the idea of starting out as an engineer.

My offer of $700 per month was more than my parents' combined earnings. I was embarrassed to show them my offer, but they were happy for me. I had no idea how I could spend it all. I got a quick start by purchasing a new '65 Mustang for about $3000 before I had formally accepted the job offer. In order to get the financing approved, I had to show the car dealer my offer letter.

Back then, the starting salaries were close to the same at all the major companies. Engineers were in high demand, and each year the starting salary increased by about ten percent. Since I received my offer in 1965, but expected to start in 1966, I was hoping to negotiate for the higher salary. The next day after I bought my car, I called my prospective boss with intentions to negotiate. Before I could say a word, he told me how happy he was to learn that I would be coming to work for Monsanto. That ended any chance I might have had to negotiate. During the conversation, I realized that the car dealer had called him to confirm that my job offer was for real, a negotiation lesson I never forgot.

My father—as cadet at
University of Debrecen—1932

As entering in military—1938

My Mother—Rockefeller Green Cross, Nursing college, Budapest—1936

Early career as a public health nurse in a rural district.

Transportation in the rural life

My parents reacquaint during their first professional jobs in rural district

My mother—1937

Great Uncle
Gen. Rumy Lajos—1941

Uncle Ede & Aunt Irén—1937

My mother and I—1943

Mother, brother (right), and I (left)—1944

Budapest Zoo—my mother and I in back, my brother in front and our maid—1944

My father and mother—1939

Sixth grade class, 1953—I am second from right in the front row.
My best friends—Laci (the tallest in the back row) and Pista (third from left in front row)
My favorite teacher Nobel Ivan

A very serious ten year old

Standing front of my school
Pictures taken in 2014

Standing in front of our apartment
(2nd floor)

First apartment with our own phone and television

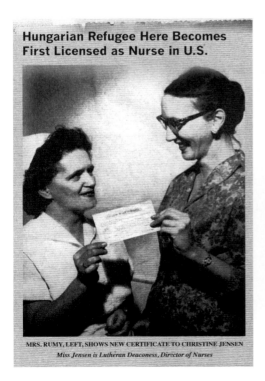 

Family house and first car, a '55 Olds
Minneapolis 1958

Forum Fruit and Vegetable Market—Minneapolis 1958

Parents in front of new house

First Christmas at new house

Vacation with friend, Domi

West High School days

My first car—'53 Ford

Family in 1960

The Last Hungarian Dance

College graduation

On my own again—in my apartment, St. Louis

Mary's first trip to Minneapolis

Section 3
My Corporate Career

Starting as an Engineer

On April 1, 1966, I started my professional corporate career with Monsanto Company at the W. G. Krummrich plant in Monsanto, Illinois. It was a complex chemical plant. In the corporate structure, the plant was assigned to the Organic Chemicals Division, but the Inorganic Chemicals and Agricultural Chemicals Divisions also had operations at the plant. I was a technical service engineer in the Inorganic Chemicals Division, assigned to the ACL facility. ACL stood for "available chlorine," and its chemical name is chlorinated cyanuric acid. This facility was considered extremely important and highly visible to the division management because the product was sold at over one dollar per pound, while most of the Monsanto industrial chemical products were sold for a few dollars per ton.

The first day I was introduced to the ACL facility and the people running it. I have to say, I was quite excited and anxious to get started. A maintenance superintendent asked me what kind of engineering degree I had. When I proudly told him that I was a chemical engineer, he summed up my education as he said, "Oh, you are plumber with a diploma."

As if that was not enough, he added, "The only thing plumbers have to know is that shit does not flow uphill."

This brought me down to reality.

I took over all the projects from my predecessor, who had just been promoted to production supervisor of the ACL operation. My first day was a Friday, and I spent the entire weekend reviewing the project files. There were too many projects for one person to handle efficiently and expeditiously. Clearly, they had not been handled well for years. I began to complete the current and significant projects as fast as possible and cancel the ones that were dying of old age. I started to like engineering.

ACL is a powder that at a certain low moisture level will decompose; at room temperature, the decomposition products condense into a liquid, which behaves just like nitroglycerine. Potential explosion was a constant danger. The plant was designed for a single product, but over the years, additional versions were added, and the original plant design needed to be modified.

 Most of these design changes were handled at the plant level and for almost two years, I was responsible for process and equipment changes, as well as for managing the project installations. After preparing the project approval documents for my first significant project, my supervisor and I met with Elmer Boehm, the superintendent who was the head of our division at the plant. He was feared and respected by most people because he was smart and demanding. He questioned me on every detail of the process, the project design, and the project cost. I answered all of his questions for at least a half hour. When he had almost run out of questions, he asked me what kind of gasket I planned to use. I had no idea and told him so. We were done.

I went back to my desk, kind of upset about the finish, when my supervisor came to tell me that I had done great. Elmer's way of testing people was to find out if they knew what they were talking about and if they were able to admit it when they did not know something. I passed his test, and he never questioned me again. This turned out to be a valuable lesson, and I effectively used this management technique in the later years of my career.

I had a number of successful projects, which was unusual at this facility. The plant was a difficult place to work because it was controlled by the Organic Chemicals Division, which produced products that were generally based on hydrocarbon technology with more complex chemical reactions, and the units owned by the Inorganic Chemical Division, where I worked, were producing more corrosive industrial chemicals based on easier chemistry. These production units were treated as bastard children. The maintenance people made it almost impossible to complete any work without frequent confrontations and intimidation. So I needed to figure out how to deal with this.

I was good at developing the projects, but drafting was not my strong suit, and I used hand sketches and schematic diagrams. I hated electric system-drawings even more, and I never included one in my project package. One day I was called to come down to the electric control center. When I arrived, I saw the electrician looking at my schematic in front of a control unit. He asked me to show him what he needed to do. Of course, I had no idea what to do, so I told him that if he could not figure out such a simple system, I would need to call the foreman and ask for a better qualified electrician. He immediately figured out what to do. Neither he nor any other electrician ever challenged me again.

In order to make the maintenance group's performance look better, their management wanted to push any maintenance costs onto operations and projects. The quickest way to do this was to charge maintenance work to open projects. All this was done with our division management's direction, and proper documentation was maintained. However, the project costs were beyond what would be considered reasonable over-runs, which brought scrutiny from upper management.

By this time Elmer had been promoted and unfortunately, the new plant management did not support the engineers. I was the biggest violator of the rules pertaining to cost overruns. The managers pretended they never knew anything about the maintenance charges assigned to projects, which they themselves directed. Instead of coming clean and developing a better procedure to deal with maintenance, they started a phony program to train engineers to do a better job of estimating project costs. To add insult to injury, they gave an award to one of the engineers who, after spending over $500,000, realized he had made a major mistake and that his design was wrong and the project could not be fixed. Management decided to cancel the remaining part of the project and scrap the $500,000 worth of new equipment. So the project was closed with a lower cost than estimated, never mind the waste of time and money spent without any benefit. This engineer also got promoted!

Adding to all this dysfunctionality was a strong union. Working with the operators could also be confrontational. As an engineer, I was constantly being tested and challenged by the operators. Once a project was completed, the production supervisor negotiated with the union for what level and how much time was required for operator training. All training was done on overtime. I was overseeing the training for each of my projects. This was always a challenge.

For a period when the plant was running poorly, a supervisor was assigned for each shift. I was assigned to be one of the shift supervisors. It was quite a combative experience. Three incidents were defining of my experience with operators and unions.

On one of my shifts, we had an incident requiring an operator to clean a piece of equipment before maintenance could start repairs. It was a very ugly job, but it was the operator's responsibility. The operator refused to do the work. I gave him a direct order, which he could not refuse, but he could request a grievance, which he did.

The next day I was called into the grievance hearing with no support from the permanent production management. I stated my case, which was that the unions always demanded eight hours pay for eight hours of work, and that is all I had asked. I actually learned this in communist Hungary. No one listens in a grievance process, but everyone shouts. I waited until the shouting stopped, and I repeated my statement. This went on for a number of times, but the union representative could not come up with an opposing argument and after a bunch of screaming, the grievance was over. The operator was disciplined.

While I was on the shift supervisor assignment, one of my projects was activated, and an operator from an earlier shift stayed over for four hours of training. Once a shift started, the minimum pay for an operator was four hours. About fifteen minutes into the shift, the equipment broke down, and the operator being trained was demanding to go home and claim his four hours of pay for fifteen minutes of work. However, I ordered him to assist the regular operator to clean the equipment to get it ready for maintenance.

The operator was really upset and tried to figure ways to get out of doing the work. After several unsuccessful tries, he called for a Health and Safety Grievance, which was the only way to stop a direct order. In such a case, the union representative, the HR manager, and production superintendent all had to inspect the job to be sure it was safe to do. To comply, I either had to rescind the order or have all the required people called in to make the decision. I had all of them called in at 2:00 AM. Within minutes after they had all arrived, the operator was cleaning the equipment.

Ultimately, he was fired, the first in over ten years at this plant. I was never quite sure what the management thought of my actions, but the union committee man caught me in the hall and pulled me into a closet to tell me that what I had done in these two incidents had led to a major troublemaker's being fired, and this was the best thing that management had done in years to build operator cooperation and morale.

One morning as I arrived at the plant after being off for two days, I saw a hose spewing chlorinated recycle material on the ground instead of into the recycle storage tank. I called this to the operator's attention. He happened to be one of our best and before he went to correct the problem, he responded by telling me that it had been that way for three days, but no one noticed or cared.

After he returned to the control room, I asked him why, if he knew there was a problem for three days, he hadn't corrected it. His response was that management apparently did not care, and I was the first one to notice or say anything. As for his lack of initiative, he said that there was no recognition or reward for good performance and that only union seniority counted. This perfectly demonstrated to me that weak management principles combined with a strong union is a formula for disaster.

After two years of this kind of experience and after several negative changes in the management, I thought that it was time to try to move into sales. I reminded my manager that I was promised that after some engineering experience, I would be given an opportunity to move on to sales. He refused to consider it; he said that I was needed at the plant.

But unexpectedly the opportunity I was looking for came to me. One day an engineer from central engineering, Dick DeSchutter, showed up at my office. He was sent to "assist" me in a significant and difficult project. With typical headquarters arrogance, he asked me what the problem was and said that he would take over the project. With all the humility I could muster, I told him that if I knew what the problem was, I would already have solved it. He assured me that within a week or ten days, he would return with the solution. When he returned in two weeks, he was humbler. He did not have the solution and suggested that we should "work together." By then, I had the problem defined, and I was well on my way to designing the solution.

At that point, we became friends and got together socially. Over the following few weeks, we realized that we both were looking to get into sales. After I told him that my management was not willing to support me, he promised to help me. In these kinds of situations, the first step was to see if the sales people would be likely to offer me a position by getting an unofficial screening interview. Dick helped me to arrange this interview, which I passed.

Next, the sales organization would place an advertisement in the newspaper for the sales position, to which I would respond. In this way, I was just an unsolicited applicant, and I was officially invited for a full interview. I was accepted for the position, and I was hoping to be in the same training class as Dick. But the plant refused to release me. Dick went on to the sales position and over time, we lost track of each other. He achieved a fantastic career with Monsanto and later with DuPont companies, while I went on to make my own way.

The managers at the plant tried to put a positive spin on torpedoing my career move, but I decided to look for a new position with a different company. I did continue completing my projects, and I did tell management that I had no interest in spending my career at this plant as I certainly did not get my degree to work in the confinement of the ACL plant. I started sending out my resume by responding to job advertisements and taken a number of interview trips to see a number of companies.

During this time, I was asked to complete a project in a different operation. The challenge was to significantly increase the production output and quality. The project had been going on for some time, and a significant amount of money had been allocated for this project.

Within fifteen minutes after I set foot for the first time in this plant's control room, I had recognized the problem, and I realized how easy the solution to the problem would be. Back then, control instruments worked electro-mechanically and control charts with colored pens indicated the process conditions. Usually there should be a distinct and fairly straight line indicating that the process was under control. This instrument had a chart completely covered in green ink with the pen jumping from one side of the chart to the other; obviously this part of the process was out of control.

After discussing the process with the foremen, the solution was obvious. The plant consisted of three continuous reactors in series, with a purification absorption column following the reactor series. The out of control chart represented the feed rate to the purification column. Right in the middle of the control panel was an instrument that indicated the feed rate to the absorption column. The production rate was controlled by the feed rate to the first reactor, and the purification column was jumping back-and-forth to recycle. The process should have been controlled by the feed rate to the purification column. This change would cost no more than $10,000.

After I went back to the office, I reviewed the process documentation and confirmed that the design capacity of all the equipment was sufficient to meet the desired production rate increase. When I told my manager my idea, at first he did not believe me. Once I explained the concept, he saw an opportunity to look good. My manager placed me on the night shift to complete the totally unnecessary and useless sampling program the previous engineer had set up. By the time I came off the night shift, others had claimed credit for my engineering solution. If I had any reservations about leaving Monsanto, they disappeared at that point. Soon after this incident, I followed up with companies I had interviewed with earlier. Within a few weeks, I received several job offers. I accepted a sales position in Chicago with W. R. Grace & Co.

In many ways, the Monsanto job and the work atmosphere at the plant was very unpleasant. I never could understand how so many people worked in this environment for so many years or for their entire careers. On a positive note, I am proud of what I accomplished professionally and valued my experience, which was priceless, but I would never do it again.

On the personal side, I enjoyed living in St. Louis and made a number of friends in and out of Monsanto. Of course, the most important outcome was meeting my wife, Mary. There were a number of young engineers hired by Monsanto in a three-year period, and we were all looking to enjoy our new lives. The secretaries were local girls and way before the aid of computers, they were keeping track of all the single engineers in the company.

In the fall of 1967, the secretaries planned a big picnic. They made sure plenty of their friends were there. One of the girls was Mary. Other than being very attractive and very nice, she was petite. For that reason, her high school friends, who were Monsanto secretaries, selected her to meet me. She was working that day and arrived late, just before I had to go to work myself. We barely had a chance to talk, but it seemed that we were destined to meet again.

A few engineers rented a house, and it became a perpetual party house. Shortly after Mary and I met, there was a large party at their house. Mary's friends were there and kept asking me when we were getting married. I insisted I was not even sure if we would meet again. But they knew what they were doing. Mary and I met again in a few weeks at the next party the engineers arranged. We spent the entire evening together and really enjoyed each other. After that day, we went everywhere together. She worked at a radio station as traffic manager. Her office was downtown, just across the river from the Monsanto plant. Occasionally, we would meet for lunch and many times we met after work. She took the bus to work, and I could pick her up and take her home after we had dinner together or met with friends.

By August of the following year, Mary and I got engaged. I bought an engagement ring and took it with me when we went for dinner at Trader Vic's restaurant. After we finished dinner, I worked up enough nerve to give her the box with the diamond ring in it and said, "I bought a fortune cookie for you."

As I said it, a waiter walked by and hearing the word fortune cookie, he rushed to get us some. He arrived with the cookies just as Mary was opening the box, causing some confusion. Finally, after we were able to shake off the waiter, I had my chance to ask her to marry me. Happily, she accepted.

After we were engaged, I was invited several times for Sunday dinners with the Gallaghers. It was quite an experience for me; I was not used to so many people at the dinner table. There were twelve people around the table, including Mary's aunt and her uncle and me. I was seated where Mary's oldest brother usually sat, which resulted in some hidden conflict. Mary's mother, also named Mary, was not a gourmet cook, but how could you be when cooking for so many people every day? I really enjoyed the experience and learned to like green beans, which were part of dinner almost every time.

We also visited my parents in Minneapolis, and they just loved Mary. We also met their Hungarian friends, and everyone thought Mary was the greatest. So did my friends who we met during several visits to Minneapolis.

We planned our wedding for December 7, 1968.

When we got married, Mary was twenty years old, the oldest of seven kids. She had three sisters and three brothers, and all of them were still living at home. Mary was ready to move out, and it seemed like the family was ready for her to move as well. During the rehearsal dinner, my mother and Mary's father, Marty, were having the typical new in-law conversation.

"We are so happy to have Mary join our family," my mother said.

Marty responded by saying, "We are not looking at it as losing our daughter…"

My mother smiled in anticipation that he would say something, like they are happy for gaining a son.

But he finished the sentence by saying, "…we are looking forward to gaining a closet."

My mother was never sure if he was just joking, or he was really serious.

Mary's uncle, her mother's brother, Father Joe O'Brien, was a priest. He was very close to the Gallagher family, and I am sure Mary was his favorite. He married us at St. Ferdinand's Parish, and we had the reception at the school gym. This was long before destination weddings!

Mary's two friends, Vicky and Judy, who introduced us, were included in the wedding party, and Mary's sister Patty was the maid of honor. Two of my friends, John Standal and Mike Duffy, came from Minneapolis to be part of the wedding and Denis Fitzgerald, a friend I met at Monsanto, was my best man.

All of Mary's brothers and sisters were included. Mary's favorite thirteen-year-old little sister, Joan, decided to dress as an adult. She was very cute, wore a nice dress, and for the first time, she wore nylon stockings.

My brother was still in school, and he claimed he was just too busy studying to come to St. Louis for the wedding. My mother convinced him that he needed to attend the wedding, even though he refused to be my best man. He finally did come, of course, at my parents' expense, just in time for the wedding ceremony. One of my friends picked him up at the airport. He was wearing an ascot and carrying three text books to be sure he could study while he was in St. Louis, as if he just did not have time to waste. My friend made him take his ascot off and wear a tie. He acted like he was the center of attention at the reception party and left his books behind when he returned home the next day. I guess they were not that important.

The next morning, we went on our honeymoon to Aspen, Colorado. Our wedding day was the coldest day in St. Louis in years and as we boarded the airplane, we wondered why we were not going south.

Going to Colorado seemed to be a great idea when we planned it in August with over 100°F temperature in St. Louis. Mary tried skiing and did not take to it, so we enjoyed snowmobiling and the winter scenery. We built fires in the fireplace at our rented condominium and burned most of the firewood that was stacked for the entire season.

After we returned from our honeymoon, we visited Minneapolis for Christmas, and my parents had a reception for their Hungarian group and my friends.

During the time I worked for W. R. Grace & Co. in Chicago, Fr. Joe visited us a number of times. He and I became good friends over the years, even though he knew I was a fallen-away Catholic. Among other things, he reintroduced me to golf. When we moved back to St. Louis two years later, I joined Norwood Hills Country Club, where he had been a member for over thirty years. I was hanging around him and his priest friends so much that people thought I was also a priest.

Many years later, I was playing golf at St. Louis Country Club where Joe, one of the waiters from Norwood Hills, was working in the refreshment shack.

As he saw me, he greeted me, "Hello, Father. How are you?"

Of course, I answered, "Just fine, my son."

My friends were shocked and thought it was hilarious that anyone would believe I was a priest. I continued the charade for two more seasons until he was promoted to waiter in the dining room. One evening he saw me with Mary, and the gig was up; he looked shocked, and I was too slow to save the day. I should have introduced Mary as Sister Mary.

Moving to Sales

On November 1, 1968, I started as a sales representative for the Dewey & Almy Division of W. R. Grace & Co. I worked in the Midwest territory out of the Chicago office. We were selling latex chemicals, which were resins suspended in water. The primary customer targets were the paint and adhesive producers and the paper coating industry.

I had been attracted to technical sales since my fraternity days. Many of the guys in the fraternity were starting in sales, and I figured they knew what they were doing. Once I was actually working for a chemical company, I convinced myself that a sales career was the right career approach. I found engineering interesting, and I enjoyed the problem solving, but I also found it very confining. I was certain that, in all career paths, if one could get to a high level, then things would become equally challenging and interesting, but I was convinced that getting there was more direct from sales and marketing.

On my way driving from St. Louis to Chicago to report for work, I managed to make some introductory calls on potential customers to get an idea of what sales was about. By the time I arrived in Chicago, I realized that to become a successful salesman, I had a lot to learn. On the surface, sales seemed to be an easy job. Meeting customers and discussing our products was the easy part and just the beginning.

After I officially started my job, I spent some time in the Chicago office and Boston headquarters on initial sales and product training. Before I got immersed in my new career, I returned to St. Louis for our wedding and ten-day honeymoon in Colorado.

When we returned from our honeymoon, we went to Chicago to find a place to live. By the end of December, we found a brand new condominium close to Oakbrook. We did not have enough money to pay the necessary down payment, and neither of us felt we could ask our parents for help. I ended up borrowing from Beneficial Finance to cover the down payment. This was an expensive, last-resort type financing. When we paid back the loan on time, and it seems not too many people did, we became a preferred customer for life.

We moved in after the holidays. Our neighbors were Jim and Diane Betts, who had also just moved in. With my new job, I had to travel a lot, and Jim did the same. Mary and Diane were left by themselves while Jim and I were gone. Their friendship helped Mary deal with being in a new city by herself while I was traveling. We all spent most of the weekends together, and we became best friends and have been ever since.

After we settled in our new condominium, Mary found a job in a retail store until she found a more reasonable job as a secretary.

My first assignment was to prepare a budget for 1969. Since I was not yet familiar with the territory or the customer potentials, I received a lot of help from my sales manager, Alfonzo Baraccani, and the prior salesmen in the territory. The process was very interesting. It was generally accepted that a ten-percent sales increase was a reasonable goal. So the idea was to spread the ten percent among the most likely customers that were expected to grow. My territory was geographically huge, which included southern Illinois (half of Chicago and south), Indiana, Kentucky, Missouri, Kansas, Iowa, and Nebraska. Organizing coverage of this much territory was a real challenge.

My initial sales calls were quite an adventure. One of my largest customers was Union Carbide in Chicago. During the first week after settling in Chicago and starting to take control over my territory, I took the purchasing manager out for lunch. He started to down one martini after another. Being a rookie salesman, I thought I needed to keep up. I could not drink gin, so I drank manhattans. I quit after three, but my guest had five martinis before lunch and one for dessert. I dropped him off at about two in the afternoon. It would have been smart to call it a day, but I felt that I needed to make more calls. I drove all the way to Gary, Indiana to the Montgomery Ward paint factory. I saw the technical director, who had a typical small office. After pleasantries, I started to get into my pitch. I thought I was doing great, and he had a pleasant smile on his face. When it was time to go, I had to choose between two doors to exit his office. Unfortunately, I picked the closet. In an instant, I realized that it was a grin, not a pleasant smile. The smell of bourbon filled the small office, and he knew as soon as I opened my mouth. Fortunately, he understood exactly what had happened and eventually, he became a good customer. This was my first day in sales.

My boss was Alfonzo Baraccani. Al was a fantastic salesman, and he was by far the best boss I ever had. He had worked for W. R. Grace for over twenty years, mostly in the Midwest territory. He knew almost all of my customers. He was also a very good family man. He had a daughter in a home for mentally impaired children in Wisconsin and visited her monthly. He asked me several times to drive him, which gave us an opportunity to talk uninterrupted for three hours.

I liked Al a lot, and I think he liked me. Our conversations were very productive, and we had a lot of laughs about crazy sales situations. One important personal direction he gave me, that I have practiced all my life and have recommended to everyone who has worked for me, was to call home every evening when traveling. This would keep you involved with your family and avoids a flood of issues when you finally arrive home. I learned a lot from Al.

Al always supported taking time with the family. I quickly challenged him by taking two weeks off right away for the wedding and again, in the summer of 1969. My father had his fortieth high school reunion in Budapest. He really wanted the whole family to go. I took two weeks off work. It was not exactly what we wanted to spend a lot of money on at the time, but it was important for my father, and Mary went along.

This was Mary's first visit outside of the U.S., which was bad enough, but going into a communist country was a bit stressful. We rented a car in Munich and drove to Budapest. The rental car was an NSU, which was a sporty small car. There were very few cars in Budapest and every time we parked, a crowd gathered to admire it.

Mary and I stayed in a hotel on Margit Island in the Duna (Danube) River. The hotel was a beautiful place, and it was quite modern and luxurious when it was built in the 1930s. Nothing had been done to it other than minimum maintenance since. Even the bath towels dated back to the beginning, they were worn, torn, and full of holes.

On the second day, when we got back to the room to get ready to go to dinner, we were going to take a shower, and I noticed that the towels were still wet from the morning, and the bed was not changed. I took Mary to the balcony and told her not to say anything, just to follow my lead. I walked back inside and sat at the edge of the bed and made my speech.

"We are paying $17 per night, which is more than what a worker earns in a week, and they have not even cleaned the room properly. I am so upset, I need a drink." We slammed the door as we left the room. We came back in 20 minutes, and the room was totally made over, with clean dry towels, and the bedding changed. Obviously the communists were listening.

The next morning, we had breakfast on the patio. A sudden summer storm appeared, and we watched two waiters argue over what to do with the awnings. One argued for keeping it down to protect the guests, the other argued for protecting state property and rolling it up to be sure it would not be damaged. Protecting state property was the winning argument, and they rolled up the awnings, and we had to run for cover.

We were followed the entire time we were in Budapest. Not much changed in Hungary under the communist system after the revolution; it was still a police state.

Mary meeting all my family, none of them speaking a word of English, was a sight to see. They all got along, and everyone just loved Mary. My brother was also on the trip and again, my parents paid for it. He acted the part of the rich American relative. Every time we were out for dinner and drinks with our cousins, he ordered and then handed me the check. In America he had no social life, and my father was concerned about it. During the reunion parties, my father found out that one of his classmates had a daughter who was unattached. My father made sure to meet the family and arranged for my brother to meet her.

While it was a learning experience for Mary, being back in Hungary for the first time in thirteen years and seeing a few of the old friends in person, it was a little emotional for me. My best friend Laci had become a doctor. We had communicated by letters, but it was great to see him again. His wife, Beatrix (Bea), was pregnant with their second daughter. Mary liked them both. We spent lots of time with them. We went to Lake Balaton for a day before we left for Sopron and on to Austria. We dropped off Laci and Bea at the train station and watched them board a slow, smoky train. As the train started to move, Mary started to cry as she was thinking of them having to go back to live in the miserable circumstances that existed in Hungary at the time. They would later come to live in St. Louis for about five years.

Before leaving Hungary, we visited my aunt, my father's sister. She never moved from Sopron. Her husband and son were out, and she really wanted us to meet them. So we stayed until they got home. When we finally left them, it was much later in the evening than what we had planned. I was driving fast. It was dark, and we could see the lighted border station about a kilometer away. All of a sudden, a red traffic light appeared out of nowhere. As I came to a screeching halt, the barrel of an AK-47 emerged on Mary's side of the car. I thought that she was going to lose it right there. After checking our passport (back then we could get a family passport), the guard let us proceed to the border. There, they virtually dismantled the car looking for something. After a delay, we were free to exit. We ended up decompressing in Vienna for a couple days and then visited Innsbruck.

We stayed in a hotel in the Olympic Village, near to where I had stayed while in school many years earlier. The first evening in Innsbruck, we found a pizzeria, and Mary was quite anxious to go there for dinner. When it came time to order, I took charge with my minimal German. All Mary wanted was a simple cheese pizza, but I let the waitress talk me into all the toppings that she had recommended. When the pizza arrived, it looked like a mountain of sausages and strange vegetables with canned peas for garnish. Mary took one look at it, and tears started to roll down her face.

Finally, she was going to have a familiar meal, and I had ruined it for her. It took me some time to console her, and I realized the trip to Hungary was much more stressful for her than she had shown on the surface. Fortunately, she came to like visits to Hungary, and we have visited many times over the years.

Two years later, a full fifteen years after the Hungarian Revolution, as a closure to history, Cardinal Mindszenty was actually forced to leave Hungary. The cardinal had lived in the U.S. Embassy in Budapest since the revolution and continued to be a problem for the

Hungarian communist government. They had tried, unsuccessfully, for years to negotiate to force the U.S. Government to expel him. When negotiations between the U.S. and Russia started to make progress, they prevailed on the Pope to call him back to Rome. So, in 1971, he left Hungary. Coincidentally, the Cardinal Mindszenty Foundation was established in St. Louis by very strong Catholic conservatives and in 1974, just two months before he died, Cardinal Mindszenty visited St. Louis. He celebrated a mass at the Hungarian-sponsored St. Mary of Victories Catholic Church. I was an usher and after mass, I had the opportunity to personally meet him.

After my brother returned to Minneapolis, much drama of letter writing to Kinga, the girl he met in Hungary, followed. If response to his letter was not immediate, he panicked. Finally, he invited her to Minneapolis, at my parents' expense. While she was in Minneapolis, he married her in front of the Justice of Peace. Further drama followed when she needed to go back to Hungary for a period before she could qualify for a permanent residency visa and begin the five-year citizenship eligibility. My brother was worried because he was not sure if in fact she would return.

I was happy to be back in the USA and felt a little guilty for taking time off while I was not yet confident about my sales performance. During my first year at W. R. Grace, I traveled the entire territory on regular intervals. I traveled three out of four weeks. When my travels took me to St. Louis, I tried to visit Mary's family. I would have dinner with Mary's parents, and sometimes Fr. Joe would also join us. Mary's mother would inform me, in great detail, about all of Mary's friends and happenings in the neighborhood. While in Chicago, I did mostly paperwork and spent time in the office.

I started to realize that working hard and traveling so much did not necessarily translate into success. All of the travel and calling on so many customers brought acceptable results, but I was not satisfied. I got along well with existing customers and did develop a few new accounts. But I only barely achieved the ten percent increase in revenue that was expected of me. It was a very uneventful year. I realized I was missing something, and it was necessary to analyze my entire territory and to concentrate on identifying new opportunities. I needed to develop a process to understand the customer's needs and develop a way we could satisfy them.

My second year was a whole different story. In preparing the 1970 budget, I looked at the potential of my territory in total, not by customer. It became clear that the old eighty/twenty concept worked, eighty percent of the potential business was with twenty percent of the customers. For example, we never did business with Sherwin-Williams, by far the largest paint company at that time. A single paint line would require more product than my entire existing territory.

Developing a large customer takes a lot of effort and time. However, I was too busy calling on much smaller customers that were spread out over a huge territory. The eighty percent potential was almost exclusively in the Chicago area. I prepared a conservative sales budget showing the new customers, but projected less sales than I believed was their full potential or what I thought I could generate. Even so, my budget showed about thirty percent growth. I changed my travel schedule and stayed in Chicago three weeks and covered the rest of the territory in one week. I resumed my MBA evening program at Loyola University of Chicago that I had started at St. Louis University.

Covering my large territory one week per month had its challenges. For example, one week I started out from Chicago and met a customer for lunch in the Omaha airport. Later, I flew to Kansas City for dinner with a customer and spent the next day calling on other customers. That evening, I attended a big Paint Society Christmas party, which was quite wild, and most of my customers in the area were attending. The following morning, I flew to Des

Moines for a lunch meeting. After this meeting, I was supposed to head home to Chicago.

The flight to Des Moines was delayed, and I was too late for my lunch date. My customer had a meeting, but we decided to meet after. Later when we met, I spent too much time and missed my Chicago flight. This was before cell phones and by the time I called Mary, she was already on her way to pick me up. I called my customer to have cocktails while I was waiting for my next flight. He invited me for dinner at his home, and I accepted. Of course, I missed the second flight while Mary was on her way for the second time. Finally, I waited for the third flight without leaving the gate. Mary did come to pick me up, fortunately without the divorce papers, but she never picked me up at the Chicago airport again. It is hard to believe, but back then, there were actually that many flights between Des Moines and Chicago.

W. R. Grace participated in a huge packaging show in the spring and decided to combine all divisions serving the packaging industry in one booth. To ensure everyone would work together during the show, we all met at dinner the evening before the show opened. I arrived quite late, as usual, after the cocktail party, and everyone was already sitting at the dinner table. I walked up to the bar for a drink, and another person joined me. We struck up a conversation and when I found out that he was from corporate headquarters, I invited him to our hospitality room at the Hilton. He accepted the invitation.

When he arrived at the hospitality suite, we continued where we left off. We had cocktails and a friendly discussion, but the rest of the people stayed away like we had the plague. Finally, when I had an opportunity, I asked them what was wrong. They asked me if I knew who this guy was, which I did not. They informed me that he was the right-hand man to Peter Grace, the company's president and CEO, and further, that he was on the wagon. Both were news to me, since by that time, we had had a number of drinks. He wanted to meet Mary and take us to dinner the next evening, and we actually went out every evening during the show. Mary was a wonderful partner in winning people over. She was good looking, smart, and enjoyed going out.

He organized a publicity film about the show, and I was featured as the youngest W. R. Grace salesman at the show. He also introduced me to Peter Grace's son when he came to visit the show. One warm and muggy spring evening when we were leaving the show, he asked me to turn on the air conditioning. When I told him my company car had no air conditioning because we were north of the Mason-Dixon Line, he told me all about the corporate car policy, which was quite different from our division's, they were air-conditioned Buicks. The next afternoon, he told me that he had made arrangements for our division to get corporate air-conditioned Buicks.

On Friday, we said goodbye, and he told me to call him if I needed some help. I did not think much about his offer because I knew I would never take him up on it; right or wrong, it was not in my personality.

Soon after the show, our division split, and our business became the Polymers and Chemicals Division. Nothing really changed, except a whole new layer of management was added. Al continued to be the sales manager, but he became the highest-level person for our division in Chicago, and we became a tenant in the building. Al was given an office suite in the front of the building. This was an old factory, and the entire building was a wreck. As the office was cleaned up for occupancy, a cheap curtain was installed to cover a damaged glass block window. It was still an unattractive mess of an office.

About a month after the show, when I called in to the office, Al was excited and had good news. "Hey Zsolt, you will not believe, but I was informed that we will upgrade our company cars, including air conditioning," he said.

"I knew this for over a month," I told him, busting his bubble. And I told him the story about the company cars and took credit for making it happen.

He thought that it was really funny and called the VP of Sales and Marketing to tell him my story. The VP did not think it was funny at all because he considered it as interference from the corporate office, and we were the instigators.

A national sales manager was named in addition to the VP of Sales and Marketing. The two of them came to Chicago to meet with Al. When they entered Al's new office, they noticed the curtain. The new national sales manager said, "Al, your office is nice, but your position does not entitle you to have curtains."

Al thought they were joking and still laughing while he pulled back the curtain and said, "These are cheap curtains, and they are here for covering the broken glass block window."

They did not care. The national sales manager said, "They still have to be removed."

Finally, the VP said, "Al, you do not seem to understand. Either the curtains go, or you must go."

In total disbelief, Al chose to leave the company after twenty-five years of service! He was not about to work for these two impossible, arrogant people. I missed him, but I certainly understood his position. Unfortunately, he was replaced by a clone of the other two.

I continued my efforts to increase sales, and things were starting to go my way. I obtained qualification for a paint line at Sherwin-Williams, and we were preparing to initiate railway tank-car shipments, which were rare. Tank trucks were the common mode of shipping because the sizes of our customer orders were much less. Even though I was showing success in achieving my sales objectives, the new sales manager started to give me a hard time for not traveling as much as I had previously.

While my territory was doing well, the rest of the company was not doing so well. The sales team was challenged by management to find a single customer who would take a very large volume of a single product at a significant discount. This would improve the incremental cost of all the products, boost revenue, and make the division profitable. I immediately had a customer in mind, a huge adhesive company headquartered in Chicago. If I could pull this off, my sales would be off the charts. It took me about a month to convince the customer and complete the necessary testing to approve our product. They selected the right product that would be profitable, even with the significant discount. I reached an agreement with the customer, and it was approved by our management.

    The national sales manager insisted on coming to Chicago to close the deal. I assumed he was trying to take the credit for the deal. My new manager and I met him at a cheap motel next to O'Hare Airport for breakfast and to discuss our pending meeting. It turned out that the cheap motel did not have a restaurant. I suggested breakfast at a hotel close to our customer's office. After breakfast, he looked around and saw people at only one other table. He complained that we could not talk there because we might be overheard. So I suggested that we could go to my condominium a mile or so from the hotel, which we did. Even there he was asking about my neighbors before he was willing to start talking. There was nothing he said, that anyone, including me, would care about, but it quickly became clear that he was going to try to extract a higher price from this customer than what was our verbal agreement.

    Finally, at 11:00 AM, we were in the customer's office. After introductions, I turned the meeting over to my managers. Just as I thought, the national sales manager started off by telling my customer that he came out to negotiate a great deal. The customer said that he thought we already had a deal negotiated and that we were meeting just to seal it. When we did not confirm the preliminary agreement, the customer ended the meeting. We were out by 11:07 AM.

    Both of my managers were speechless. I dropped the two of them off at the Sheraton without saying a word and called my customer to apologize. I knew that my manager would try to get a second chance, so I asked the customer if there was any circumstance in which he would be willing to meet them again. He firmly told me, "No!"

As expected, my manager did call me to ask me to see if they could get back to the customer to try again. I told them it was not in the cards. They were very upset, but I did not care. It was clear to me that I had no interest in working with these people any longer, but I wanted to stay until I could successfully complete my sales plans.

Several weeks later, the national sales manager came back to Chicago. He scheduled individual meetings with each of the salesmen in the afternoon and for a group dinner in the evening. Everyone started to buzz about the meetings and try to figure out what it was all about. I told everyone that I thought there would be some kind of reorganization and that the person with the first appointment would get fired and that the one with the last appointment would get promoted. When the appointment schedule came out, I was the last appointment.

I could not figure how that was possible, given how I felt about the management team. I was at a customer meeting in the morning. When I called the office, my secretary was in a panic. She had been looking for me all morning to let me know that the schedule had changed, and I was now the first appointment. I was fired.

I took pride in being able to figure out how it would go down, and I was not surprised with the outcome. The only regret I had was that I should have quit after what happened to Al. That way, I could have searched for a job on my own schedule.

Mary still had the secretary job, and I was trying to earn some extra money while I was looking for a new job. I started to prepare tax returns. It was an unprofitable enterprise since most of the people calling me in response to my ad in a local paper were old with minimal incomes, not required to file a tax return. I did not have the heart to charge them for this advice like other tax preparers and quickly stopped my tax advice business.

The job market was still good at the time, and finding a new position was faster than I expected. In about three months, I decided to join General Electric's Insulating Materials Department and started in April 1971. The product line was less than inspiring, but I thought that GE was a good company. We were selling several products in electric insulation applications, from underground high-voltage cable termination and splice kits, to mica electric motor insulation, to wire enamel and transformer paint. Our customers were distributers and original equipment manufacturers (OEMs). Between all the products and different sales outlets, things were more complicated than the size of the business would normally dictate.

I was hired for the Chicago territory, but before I could get started, the St. Louis territory manager was promoted, and his territory opened up. The management went to the second choice for the Chicago position, but he did not want to move. So I was asked if I would be willing to move to St. Louis.

Of course, this was viewed by Mary and her family as a divine intervention, and we were on our way back to St. Louis.

When we moved back to St. Louis, we bought a house in the western suburbs. Mary's father looked at the house and thought it was a good deal, so, I made an offer contingent on Mary's approval. Once more, I needed to borrow money from Beneficial Finance to make the down payment. Mary never liked the house and always claimed I independently chose the house.

We went to the Lake of the Ozarks for a long weekend and looked at vacation houses. On the way back to St. Louis, Mary told me she would no longer complain about the St. Louis house if we bought a small vacation home that we both liked. I did buy that vacation home, but she just could not get herself to accept our place in St. Louis. It took me over five years to realize that she would never like living there. We finally sold the house and moved closer in town.

Once we settled in St. Louis, Mary went back to school at the University of Missouri, St. Louis to complete her art history studies. I also tried to return to St. Louis University to complete my MBA program. However, I had the same reception as I did at Loyola of Chicago. They would not accept each other's credits, but St. Louis University had another surprise; they would not accept their own credits either because by the time I could finish, they would expire; it was hard to imagine what part of accounting principles would change over three years. I made an ugly scene, questioning Jesuit charity, and left. I decided it was not worth pursuing.

Many years later when I had the means to donate to the school, I was seated at a cigar dinner next to Fr. Biondi, the president of St. Louis University. It appears that one of my old friends, who was on the University Board, told Fr. Biondi, who was known not to miss an opportunity to solicit contributions, that I had some past affiliation with the University.

"Did you attend St. Louis University?" he asked me to break the ice.

"Yes, but it did not end well," I said and after he urged me, I told him my story.

"So," he said "you want an MBA? Given your experience, you should have one."

In 2013, I received an honorary MBA, a little too late to help my career. I did make a nice donation, but I still regret I did not ask for a PhD.

Headquartered in St. Louis, my territory was southern Illinois, Missouri, Kansas, Nebraska, and Iowa. My sales manager was located in Ft. Wayne, Indiana, and his prime responsibility was to handle the wire enamel business of the internal GE motor division. The technology was easy, but the sales strategy was quite challenging.

Sales to OEMs were similar to the sales process at W. R. Grace. But the distributor sales were very different. Many times, the distributors were handling competitive products along with ours, and we needed to convince them to prefer selling our products over our competitor's. We also needed to create demand. To do this, we needed to make calls on electric utilities and contractors in the field and demonstrate our products to their mechanics. We had a van which was fitted with samples of all our products. The van was rotated among the sales team and from time to time, when it was my turn to have it, I drove the van to construction jobsites to demonstrate the products. It was like a carnival.

The culture at GE was much different from that of Monsanto or W. R. Grace. There was no pressure to conform to a standard dress code or behavior; only performance counted. This process permeated from individual performance, to division, and to the total corporation. My compensation was directly tied to my sales performance. In addition to direct compensation, there were many long-term benefits, including a stock purchase plan. Many of the wives referred to the company as "Generous Electric."

The accepted guideline was that if the performance was outside plus or minus ten percent of the budget, the business was out of the management's control. This produced some interesting unintended consequences. In 1972, our group was doing exceptionally well. Even after pushing as many sales as reasonably possible to the following year, our profits were still more than ten percent over budget.

We had an emergency sales meeting just before the end of the year with the goal to spend around $200,000. We went to Marco Island, Florida, for four days. We played golf, had great dinners, and enjoyed the local entertainment. All turned out well; we were successful in spending the designated money or more.

Jack Welch took over the Chemical Division in the fall of 1972. Our department belonged to this division. He and his management team assessed what was each of the product department's business to see how it would fit in GE's long-term plans and also evaluated the management team. We had a sales meeting in the Bahamas in the spring of 1973. Three of his close associates, including his key Personnel Manager, as they were called then, attended the meeting.

The personnel manager made a presentation that stuck with me for a very long time. His presentation described what it would take to get ahead in the company. He had a drawing of three circles; the first represented individual skills, the second represented the company's needs, and the third represented luck. These circles could be the same or different sizes, representing each person's situation. Where all three circles intersected, there was a small sliver that represented a person's chances for getting ahead. It was hard for me to see how I could improve the size of that sliver based on my department's rank in the company and my position within the organization.

In retrospect, based on Jack Welch's history, his three key people were probably looking for higher potential people to move to other groups before the Insulating Materials Department was divested because it clearly did not fit the GE Chemical Division image.

GE had supported the idea of spouses joining at the end of the meeting and staying for a few extra days after the meeting ended. Mary came to the meeting, and we had a very enjoyable dinner with two of the key guys. Jack's associates had to leave the morning of the last day of the meeting because there was a serious accident in the Lexan plant in Evansville, Indiana. One of the guys we had dinner with told me to contact him after we get back to St. Louis. Once again, I did not follow up.

I had reasonable success in developing new business and had learned how to deal with distributors, gaining more confidence in my sales and strategic abilities. So much so that I started to represent my regional manager at the monthly management meetings at our headquarters in

Schenectady. By any measure, GE was a good place to work, and it looked like I had an opportunity for advancing in our non-strategic department. I was more relaxed than I had ever been in my prior jobs. Life was good, but the job was not very exciting. The likelihood of being divested looked more real as time moved on. As I turned thirty years old, I was also getting restless, believing that I was running out of time to move into a significant role at GE or any other company.

My old friends at Monsanto were encouraging me to return because a number of our old gang had been promoted into significant management positions. I started to look at ways to return to Monsanto. In the late 1960s, the chemical industry was concerned about the cyclicality of their business, and all the major chemical companies started to migrate into non-traditional businesses. Monsanto's answer was to start a New Enterprises Group. Initially, some existing business units like Astroturf and sulfuric acid plant technology provided the core businesses. Later, additional new businesses were added.

Prior to the formation of this new business strategy, Monsanto was selling its sulfuric acid technology that was constructed by Leonard Construction of Chicago. In addition to selling the technology, Monsanto continued to sell the catalyst and replacement specialty equipment, including the mist eliminators to operating plants. As part of the new strategy, Monsanto expanded its equipment offerings and acquired Leonard Construction in order to maximize revenues and profits. This group of products became part of the Enviro-Chem unit. It seemed like a new opportunity for growth and a possible fresh start for me. When an opportunity came up in this division, I decided to make the move.

When I told Mary about my decision, she was not happy. My main argument was that a chemical engineer had no real opportunity in an electric company. Several years after I left GE, Jack Welch was named CEO and Chairman. For many years, Mary reminded me that he was a chemical engineer and obviously there had been opportunities at GE. I do not regret leaving GE, but it was the best company I had worked for. As I expected, shortly after I left GE, my department was sold, so the party would probably have come to an end anyway.

As I was training my replacement, we were in Iowa when I got a call from my mother in the middle of the night; my father had died. He had been having some health problems for a few months, but none of them seemed to be life threatening. But one day, after he got home from work, he decided to check his garden. While working in the garden, he felt tired and went in the house to lie down. Apparently he had heart failure and died. He died one month after he made the final payment on the family house, which was a major goal for him. He was not yet sixty-three years old.

His death was a shock and a very sad time for me. He and I had gotten much closer as I became an adult. I used to meet him for long lunches when I was in Minneapolis to have some quality time together. We had a number of intimate conversations about his life in prison. He had told me some amazing stories of his experience in the Russian prison camp, where the prisoners were doing all the farm labor for a commune. My father, who was the senior officer and had the agricultural background, had the role to negotiate how much work the prisoners had to do. There were interesting and revealing stories of the Russian system and life in Russia at that time. But we never got to talk much about what happened in the Hungarian prison, where I am sure he was tortured. It was difficult for him to talk about it, and I did not push him, thinking we would have a lot of time to talk.

America provided our family the opportunity to live in freedom and in comfort. But all the upheavals and persecution through my father's life had done their damage. Being close to him for most of my life, I realized that he had considered his life unfulfilled and had thought he had not provided his family with the legacy and prosperity that he had always wanted. I still miss him, and I know my ultimate success would have helped him overcome the disappointments in his own life.

Fr. Joe knew I could use a lot of moral support, and he came to Minneapolis to celebrate the funeral mass and the burial. We were able to spend some time together, and his counsel was very thoughtful and helped me deal with my father's early passing. His support also helped my mother through the funeral.

My father's death was very difficult for my mother. With the house mortgage paid off, she was doing okay financially, and she continued to live in our family house alone. My brother lived six blocks away and spent time with my mother almost every day. She was able to retire when she turned sixty years old with Social Security and my father's and her own pension.

A few months after my father died, one of their Hungarian friends had a big party. My mother was invited, but my brother was not. When my mother called to let them know, they told her that it was not an oversight. This rejection of my brother was devastating for my mother. She never socialized with the Hungarian friends again. This unfortunate incident defined the rest of her life and for the next thirty years, she lived to defend my brother.

End of My Corporate Career

My job at Monsanto Enviro-Chem was to sell Brinks mist eliminators, a unique pollution control device, through manufacturer-representatives. Brink mist eliminator removed very fine mist from air. The primary application for this product was the removal of sulfuric acid mist from sulfuric acid manufacturing plants. There were a few other developed applications in the chemical industry, and potential new applications were virtually nonexistent. Our group was very small, offering mostly application engineering and sales support to our manufacturer-representative group around the world. Fabrication of the product was done outside Monsanto.

The entire chemical industry's move into new enterprises turned out to be a huge failure. Monsanto was no exception. One by one, the New Enterprises Group was dismantled. Even successful products that were included in this division became dispensable. Enviro-Chem, which essentially consisted of the sulfuric acid technology, was the one last remaining business. My idea of crossing over to the mainstream of Monsanto was fading rapidly. Moving on to another job was also looking like a problem. At the age of thirty-three, it would be my fifth job in nine years and explaining this to a potential new employer would be difficult. I felt I had to work hard and hope my performance would earn a promotion into mainstream Monsanto.

My objective was to look for new applications to expand the business. Our representatives in the Southeast region reported to me. They were a bunch of successful young guys, and I got along well with them. Almost the entire U.S. textile industry was in their territory. Many of these textile plants were covered with a constant blue smoke. Formation of this very fine smoke was chemically different than sulfuric acid fumes, but the consistency and formation of the small-particle mist was the same.

We started to look at how we could apply the Brinks mist eliminator to this problem. The technical solution was not difficult, but the textile customers were not staffed to design their projects and were looking to purchase a complete system that they could just put on the roof and connect to the utilities. Offering a system through Monsanto was not an option. We did not have qualified engineers to design and fabricate a reasonably cost-effective system.

We decided to work with local metal fabricators in the Southeast area. I designed the system, and the fabricators developed the detailed drawings and built the systems. Monsanto would sell the mist eliminators to the fabricators and pay commissions to our representatives. Our representatives would sell the completed systems at a profit to the ultimate customers. It was a good business for Monsanto and a great business for the representatives. However, it was not very challenging, but I enjoyed dealing with the sales representatives.

Our management was not paying attention to the business. One particular episode stands out. A technical service manager sent out a memo to the upper management of our group, describing a customer problem that questioned the basic design of the sulfuric acid application. This memo caused serious concern, and for days there were high-level meetings.

The management's decision was to give the person who recognized the problem the responsibility to fix it. However, if you really understood the situation and the application, you could not miss that the problem was non-existent. In about a month, without doing anything, the same person sent out another memo, claiming the problem was fixed. He was congratulated and rewarded with a pay increase and a promotion. He eventually went high enough by creating other issues and "solving" the problems, to get promoted out of Enviro-Chem. I have to admit, I was jealous of him. However, he was promoted once too often. He finally ran into a boss who knew his business, and he was fired, but he did have a good run for a while.

With our success in the textile application behind us, we started to look at Hardee's fast food restaurants that were using open-fire cooking versus grilling. The blue haze produced by open-fire cooking was not dissimilar to the textile application. The possibility of tens of thousands of fast food restaurants using our mist eliminators was exciting. We got as far as obtaining EPA approval, but ultimately, we could not make the economics work.

When I saw the Monsanto annual report, I noticed that the part about Enviro-Chem claimed that these applications would turn Enviro-Chem's fortunes around. I informed the head of the division that this statement was incorrect and that I was the only person in the organization working on this application without management's support. In retrospect I realize why my comment would have alarmed the management. Shareholders could cause serious problems if they thought Monsanto might have misrepresented its financial outlook.

My comment resulted in the head of Enviro-Chem joining me in visiting some of our customers and fabricators to try to understand this business. It seemed to me that he was more interested in covering his behind than in developing a plan to support building this business. He drank way more than he could handle when we met our representatives and customers for dinner.

After a lot of meetings and planning to make this application look bigger than its potential really was, management decided to put me in charge of sales and marketing of products for the organic mist applications. Management also decided to design and build complete systems. As I described this episode in the prologue, there was no possibility for success the way management organized this business effort. When I received this promotion, which was a clear set-up for failure and for me to become the scape-goat, I realized I had to move on.

This episode confirmed for me that I was not mentally prepared or suited for the corporate life. I still thought that if I could reach a certain level in the organization, the quality of the people would improve. I realized my personality and attitude could not tolerate the stupidity and incompetence experienced at the lower levels of management long enough to get promoted above it.

Working with the manufacturer-representatives gave me confidence that I could do well financially on my own and that I would not have to put up with the corporate politics. The representative organizations I worked with the most promised to help me obtain product lines to represent.

My friends in Minneapolis had started a distributor business a few years earlier, and I had signed them up to be the Monsanto representatives. I did all the sales for them, but the commissions helped them succeed in their other business and when I visited customers, it gave me a chance to visit my mother. They asked me to partner with them in starting a branch in St. Louis, based on their business model. This gave me a second option to start my own business as a distributor.

The decision to make the move was easy for me, but convincing Mary was a bit more difficult. I am sure that by this time she was wondering if I could hold a job for more than two years. When I told Mary of my decision, she was disappointed. We were doing okay financially, and Mary was finishing her degree in art history. The future looked good. Suddenly, facing the uncertainty and the possibility of failure was, again, a reasonable concern. I fully appreciated her concern, but, as I indicated before, we made a good team and very quickly, Mary accepted the reality that I would continue to move forward on my own. She did all she could to support me getting started.

Fr. Joe was enthusiastic about my decision because he was always trying to come up with ways for the family to get into business. He had come up with all kinds of ideas that required a lot of work by everyone in the family, but with marginal likelihood for financial success. I used to enjoy making fun of his ideas, but he continued with his suggestions. He lost his energy for thinking of new ideas as my business was getting successful, but what finally cured him once and for all was when he responded to a twenty-five dollar get-rich-quick advertising scam. He sent his money in and received a prayer card; he was beaten by his own game.

Section 4
My Entrepreneurial Beginning

Starting an Industrial Service Company

At the end of 1975, I started my business with great enthusiasm and energy. I quickly received verbal commitments to represent several companies in the St. Louis territory, and I started the manufacturer-representative business as soon as I left Monsanto. I was not interested in starting a St. Louis distribution branch for my Minneapolis friends, headed by Mike Duffy, but I agreed to start it after the manufacturer-representative business got going. To simplify things, I took their company name, Power Dynamics, Inc.

I firmed up the representative agreements with as many principals as I could, collected product literature, and made introductory sales calls. Mary was still finishing her university degree, but she worked with me part-time while in school. After she graduated from the university, she continued at the company for over three years.

Very quickly I found a significant waste-heat boiler project at Monsanto. The boiler price was about $2 million, and I would earn an $85,000 commission if I was able to get the contract. I spent a lot of time on this project and after several months, it came down to our price versus a competitor's. Our product was preferred, but our price was higher than our competitor's. I had a good estimate of where we needed to be on price, but the boiler company refused to review their cost estimate and would not consider lowering their price.

The boiler company was a small company, and they were bidding on three similar-size projects and realistically, they could only handle one. That is why they decided to hold their prices, figuring they would succeed with at least one of the three projects. Of course, this misguided attitude resulted in their losing all three. In doing damage control, the company re-estimated their cost and found they could have reduced their price to well within the price level that I had recommended. Unfortunately, they informed me of their decision the day after Monsanto issued their purchase order to our competitor. The potential eighty-five-thousand-dollar commission evaporated. After a disappointing year of working on the manufacturer-representative business, it was time to review my business strategy, and building the distribution business started to look more interesting.

The distribution business seemed more attractive than the commission-based sales because, in theory, we would have more control over our business by actually buying and reselling products. However, the distribution business needed more employees and more money. It also incurred significant business expenses, hence, taking on more risk.

After I decided to start this phase of the business, I spent the first few weeks setting up an office and a small warehouse with Mary's help. As a matter of fact, Mary hired our first employee, Roger Seers, to take care of our warehouse. He was a simple young man, just out of the army. He turned out to be the most loyal and reliable employee who ever worked for us and, later, for the successor company until he died forty years later. Mary was a great judge of people, and I should have listened to her over the years when she did not approve of my choices and they turned out to be disappointing.

This part of the business also requires capital to fund inventory and receivables. Mary and I did not have significant savings, partly because

I was so confident that I would continue to increase my income, so we felt we still had time to begin saving. Asking for support from our families was out of the question.

There were a number of options available in seeking to finance a business. Some were better than others, but the initial business plan limited and, in some cases, defined the available options. My initial approach was defined by the business plan for a regional industrial service company. This kind of business did not have an appeal to outside investors because the upside potential was usually not very attractive. My only option was bank financing.

I got off to a bad start. I developed a business plan, but I had no credit history or contacts. Although I had lived in St. Louis for some time, I did not know people who could help me. I started with the bank where I had my checking account. Not only did they refuse to give me a loan, but the day after they turned me down, they rented the building that I had selected for my business for their own use because it was an attractive building with a very competitive rent. The only asset we had as collateral was our home. I went to the bank that held our mortgage. Instead of giving us a second mortgage, they insisted on refinancing the original loan, freeing up $8,000 in new money. The overall cost for this loan was prohibitive, but they knew I had no other option. They were terribly greedy and happily, soon after writing my loan, they went out of business.

After several financing rounds, I realized that the best outcome for the bank was for the loan to be repaid with interest; there was little upside opportunity, and there was no room for a mistake. So they needed to feel confident about the borrower's integrity and ability to repay the loan. To make or not to make the loan was a judgement call, which does not follow standard rules. It took me a while to understand that rejection by one bank is not the final answer. Other banks may look at a business and an individual borrower in a completely different manner, and/or their lending criteria may be totally different. The objective was to find the right banker.

The initial products available for us to handle were the same as those that the Minneapolis business represented: gaskets, mechanical packing, and seals. The product lines they were handling were second tier, and their manufacturers were unknown in the St. Louis market. Our potential customer base was committed to an existing supply chain of higher quality and better known product lines. The only approach available to us was to supply whatever we could find that our potential customers wanted to buy. This was an unacceptable business plan. We needed to find new products and services that we could grow our business around.

Many of the products contained asbestos, which was starting to be identified as a health hazard. There was a lot of opposition to these findings by both the producers and customers, and the industry was slow to change. I recognized an opportunity to concentrate on non-asbestos products and believed this was the way for us to enter the market. In addition, we were looking for other service opportunities. After a year or so of trying to build our business in St. Louis, our business was very different from my friend's in Minneapolis. We were unable to reconcile our differences, so we decided to break up our business relationship. Unfortunately, this negatively affected our personal relationship, but our businesses prospered in a completely different way.

Part of our agreement was that we were to change our name. I contacted a friend in the advertising business, Tom Frasier, to ask him to come up with a name. My criteria were to make it short, make it sound like an international technical company, and not use my name. After a short time, he came back with ZOLTEK. It sounded good, but I really did not want to use my name, even my given name, so I rejected it.

Finally, we were running out of time and had to make a decision. He promised to get back to work on it. A few days later, Mary and I were having dinner and saw Tom in the bar. I invited him for a drink at our table and, when the waitress came over, he wrote ZOLTEK on a napkin and asked her what she thought that was. She said quite enthusiastically that to her it sounded like a large international technology company. Of course, Tom set her up to say those things, but I thought it was so funny that I decided to go with it. The name turned out to be a good one for our business, but it has forever caused people to misspell my name (Zolt versus Zsolt).

On the manufacturer-representative side of our business, we recognized a lucrative service opportunity to also manage the installation of the equipment we sold. We sold a major heat recovery system to a breakfast cereal producer in their Canadian plant. They did not have an in-house project group that could handle the installation. They requested that we handle the construction, which we gladly did. After this project, we routinely offered engineering and construction services. This capability helped us increase our revenue and income. Almost as important, the progress payment schedules also helped us finance the rest of our business.

The eight-thousand-dollar loan and our savings would have been good enough to support the manufacturer-representative business. However, when we added the distribution business, we needed more money. Soon after starting the business, I met some other business people and some bankers, so I was able to find a lender who would likely look positively at my request. He did, and he approved a twenty-five-thousand-dollar loan. I knew this would not last long, but I also knew I needed to start with a modest request. A few months later, I was able to increase the loan to $50,000. Unfortunately, our friendly banker left the bank and moved out of town, so I was left unsupported at the bank. Soon after, the new president reviewed our loan and could not understand our business. He immediately called the loan and forced us to find another bank.

The asbestos replacement strategy turned out to be the right one for several reasons. The asbestos health issue became much more clear and intense, and every responsible customer realized the change must come soon, and we were there to help.

By the end of our fourth year, we were optimistic that we had found our way to success, and the risk of failure steadily diminished. Mary had completed her studies at the university and received her degree in art history. We never meant to build a mom-and-pop style business, so Mary transitioned into her own career, first in real estate and later in travel. Regrettably, Mary never pursued a career in art, but her love of art rubbed off on me. Over the years, we have acquired art during our travels throughout the world and enjoyed them at our home and business.

With Mary not working at Zoltek, we were able to do some traveling together, usually when business took me somewhere we could enjoy. Mary would accompany me and take side trips before or after my business concluded. We took many nice trips and had good times. Too often when we took a trip, Mary had a real estate deal in the final stages. To ensure the transaction would go smoothly, she generously shared her commission with other agents.

Since we both enjoyed travel, she decided to change her career to become a travel agent. At that time, there were travel benefits for agents, which was a good deal for us. She was very good at her job and eventually we bought a travel agency, but unfortunately, at the wrong time, just before deregulation. Soon after, the airlines stopped paying commissions to travel agents, and the travel benefits quickly disappeared. She did well, but it was too difficult to make it into a profitable business. So, at the right time when the lease for the office and the airline computer came up for renewal, she decided to close the agency.

Mary was a beautiful young woman, and she started to turn gray early. I thought it looked great, but she was concerned about it. One evening when she was particularly feeling down, we went out for dinner.

I asked Mary if she recognized the couple a few tables down from us who kept looking at us. She did not. I asked several more times, and she could not identify them and after a while, I looked at her as if I realized who they were.

I told her, "I finally figured out what they are saying. They are saying that it is nice for that young man to take his mother out for dinner."

That helped Mary to snap out of her downer.

Zoltek's business continued to grow, and we doubled the size of our facility every three years from 1977 to 1986.

The asbestos replacement products generally had much higher performance capabilities than the asbestos-based products, but they were higher priced. Although the initial cost was higher, the lifetime costs would prove to be quite competitive.

The best example was Union Carbide's flexible graphite called Grafoil. It would last for a lifetime if one understood how to apply it. Six of the major mechanical packing producers were the Union Carbide's master distributors. I believed in the product so much that I campaigned to make Zoltek a master distributor. I went to Union Carbide in Cleveland and met the general manager and the product manager. I convinced them that we would do a great job for them. After they visited our facility for inspection and further discussions, they agreed to sign us up.

When we went for our initial business meeting and training session at Union Carbide, the general manager put a press release in front of me to approve. The press release was announcing our distributor agreement. In every business, established companies hate a newcomer. I knew that it would upset the other master distributors, so I was not sure if I should ask him not to make the announcement. Of course, that was not a good option, so I let it go.

Two weeks later, the Union Carbide sales manager, Des Baker, whom I had not met before, called me. He wanted to come to St. Louis to meet. When he came in, I introduced him to all of our sales team, but he seemed anxious to get away for a private talk between the two of us. He and I went out for lunch. He seemed edgy and after downing three beers, he finally asked the question he had come all the way to St. Louis to ask.

"Well, Zsolt, what do you think our other distributors think of you?"

I told him, "They think I am an asshole."

He was quite visibly relieved and said, "I am so glad you know it, and I did not have to tell you."

Des was relieved, and we had a good laugh. We have been friends ever since.

Grafoil was a relatively high-priced product, and it was difficult to install in the field. To facilitate its use, we were pre-fabricating the seal rings, so that it became very easy to use and quite cost effective. We also started surveying the equipment in the plants of prospective customers, both to determine the size of rings required and then propose a full package to replace the high pressure and high temperature seals in the entire plant. Our first major customer had a maintenance manager who came from the nuclear navy. He was aware of how good this product was, and he replaced the seals in the entire steam plant with prefabricated Grafoil. At the time, it was the largest order we had received. By 1983, we had sold more flexible graphite than any other master distributor.

As our business grew, I was, again, looking for financing. This time I had more contacts and a business track record. I decided to go for an SBA guaranteed loan. My loan officer was my accountant's daughter. In 1980, we received a $150,000 loan that was enough, at the time, to build the business. This was the time when interest was in the twenty percent range, which caused serious hardship for many businesses, but we were still profitable. We dealt with this rate for a short time, but the interest rate was not sustainable for long. After about one year, the interest returned to a more normal rate of ten to twelve percent.

Our customers were electric utilities, refineries, and chemical plants. Most of their plants were quite old, with a lot of obsolete equipment. We uncovered an opportunity to replicate old obsolete pump parts. These obsolete pumps were extremely expensive to replace, so replicated parts were a cost-effective alternative. We developed a tool to measure the worn part and draw the reconstructed part. We established a reliable supply chain from pattern makers, to foundries of various metals, and to machine shops. This business was highly profitable, particularly when we could get repeat orders or orders for the same part from multiple customers.

We were also doing well in the manufacturer-representative business. Ironically, Monsanto Enviro-Chem asked me to represent them, in particular, to help them sell one of the systems I had originally designed. I found a project that fit perfectly at a manufacturing plant of oil-impregnated brick used as liner for steel furnace. This project confirmed that it was the right decision for the right reasons that I did not accept my promotion. After we completed this order, I resigned our representative agreement. I do not believe Monsanto Enviro-Chem ever sold another system of this type.

We developed an expertise to handle some complicated projects, mostly around the design and installation of the equipment we sold. This was quite helpful in selling equipment because most of our customers did not have an in-house qualified engineering team. It also helped to increase our revenue and profit. However, the chemical industry went through a short-term decline in the early 1980s, and capital expenditures were seriously cut back. Most of the projects we were working on were postponed, and some of the companies we represented were having financial problems. The companies we represented started to look for ways to improve their business, and they started to offer project management services. This put us in direct competition with the companies we represented, which was not acceptable. It became clear that we needed to cut back our process equipment project activity.

Eventually, we exited the manufacturer-representative business, and one of our salesmen started his own company. He took over representing some of the equipment lines. To replace the revenue losses, in 1984 we acquired a local distributor in the power transmission and conveyor systems. We also expanded to the Kansas City market.

One of the companies we represented was Dresser Industries, the world's largest manufacturer of high-pressure safety relief valves. These valves must be checked and calibrated at a regular frequency. Dresser started a certified valve repair shop program. In addition to selling new valves, we became the exclusive repair shop in the Midwest region. We used our own engineering to build the most efficient repair shop that could compete with our customers' in-house maintenance shops on cost and reliability. This business turned out to be a huge winner for us.

Our business had grown, and so had our cash requirements. Losing the steady flow of progress payments for the process equipment sales and projects management further increased our cash needs. In 1985, we stretched our financing requirement beyond the SBA loan limits. We were quite happy with this bank and had been with them for some time. My original loan officer left the bank and moved to Los Angeles. Her replacement, Chris Griesedieck, and I got along well and eventually became good friends. But soon after, he also left the bank for another local bank. As we needed more funding, we eventually exhausted the willingness of our bank to extend financing to the level that we needed.

During the first ten years of the company's existence, Zoltek became the premier industrial distributor and industrial services company in the St. Louis region. Our annual revenue increased to over $12 million and the business was quite profitable. Mary and I were the first two employees and by this time, the company had grown to about thirty employees. Our sales staff was young and new to the industry, unrestricted by prior experience, and was able to look at the business and at new opportunities with an unconventional approach. We could rapidly react to changes and the needs of our customers, and our customers learned that they could depend on us.

We spent a lot of work and social time together, and we had a lot of fun in the process. We had classic annual sales meetings. Initially we had dinner meetings in town with wives and later, trips to Lake of the Ozarks. We played poker, and the sales guys were doing their best to beat me, but I always won. Mary used to get upset at me for taking their money. I tried to explain that I could not let them win because they would rather lose trying than by my trying not to win.

On one of the trips, we took a cruise on the lake. A bachelor salesman and the waitress on the boat were getting too friendly. I decided to take charge as the captain of the boat and performed a wedding ceremony. We needed a wedding band, and one of the married salesmen offered the use of his wedding band for the ceremony. Before the ceremony was over, somehow the wedding bend ended up in a huge waste container full of shrimp hulls. I can still see the owner of the wedding band diving in the waste container head first searching desperately for it.

Once we had an exceptionally good year and we decided to have the sales meeting in Las Vegas. Everyone was all excited and tried their hand at gambling. I warned everyone not to spend any more than they can easily afford. All turned out okay, and nobody got into trouble. We had a great time. They were all impressed, however, when I paid for the entire meeting with cash from my winnings.

The tenth year of our business, 1985, was a significant year for Zoltek and also in my personal life. All successful businesses at one point would reach critical mass when opportunities for growth expand spontaneously, and we were at that level. With a solid business plan, good sales, and technical team, adequate financing, and a solid customer base, the growth of our existing business seemed assured. I was confident that we were poised for sustaining growth, and, in anticipation, we built our headquarters building. We acquired the land at a low cost in a complex transaction. We also acted as our own general contractor to keep construction cost low. We built a highly visible distinguished building in St. Louis that overlooks the I-270 and I-70 intersection.

Once again, I was back looking for financing beyond what our bank was willing to do. I followed Chris to his new bank to finance the acquisition of the land for our new headquarters building. This was a fairly easy deal to get approved, but we needed to support our acquisition, including some real estate and the construction of our headquarters; all of this was in addition to funding the ongoing business activities. Our total loan requirements were approximately two million dollars for business operations and an additional $2.5 million for real estate acquisition. This loan amount was within a reasonable ratio for the size of our business and collateral, but our business was not familiar to bankers, which always made financing more complicated.

For a short while, we managed to finance the real estate and the business operations at two different banks. This approach sounded like a good idea, but banks generally did not want to split the collateral. Once the headquarters building was finished, we were looking to consolidate our financing at a single bank. By that time, Chris changed to a new bank that could easily handle our total financing needs, and his manager was also familiar with our business from an earlier relationship. It was a very smooth transition.

We were on a roll. When I returned from a business trip in August, as usual, I met Mary for dinner. It was a hot day and on the way home from dinner, I loosened my tie and opened my shirt collar. As I did, I felt a big lump on my neck which turned out to be the first sign that I had cancer. The biopsy confirmed it, but it was not clear what kind of cancer it was. We suspected it was thyroid cancer, but it was not confirmed until my thyroid was removed.

As I sat in my office in September when I knew I had cancer, but not yet knowing what kind, I was wondering what I was doing at work. I promised myself that if I survived this ordeal, the next spring I would concentrate on becoming a better golfer and find other interests beyond the business. Needless to say, the idea of facing cancer of any kind was frightening. However, if you had to have cancer, thyroid cancer was the one to have because it was easily identifiable and generally confined. In my case, the cause was also identified to be the nuking of my head until my hair fell out when I was ten years old. When the surgery was all over, I felt confident that I would not have any recurrence. Not long after my surgery, I was back on the job as if nothing had happened.

At the same time that I was dealing with my cancer, Fr. Joe had a heart bypass operation. His surgery did not go well, and he was faced with a lengthy recovery. After he got well, he decided that I would need someone to look after me when he was gone. He looked for a priest who would be like himself, but would be my age and would get along with a fallen-away Catholic like me. He introduced me to Fr. George Brennen. Fr. George is a wonderful person, and we got along quite well from the first time we had met and had been friends ever since. He introduced me to his younger brother, also a priest, Fr. Gene. Soon they realized the assignment to look after me was a two-man job, and they have performed their duty together. Our relationship also keeps Fr. Joe's memory alive.

The next spring came, and it was time for me to fulfill my commitment to play golf. I was exposed to golf at the university and played off and on for years, but I never took lessons. While I could hold my own, I never really played well. Fr. Joe was a very good golfer, and he took me under his wing. My game improved some, but my appreciation and enjoyment of playing golf changed a lot. I read a book Fr. Joe suggested and took six lessons at the club. During the summer, I played twice a week after work. By the end of the summer, my score was routinely in the low eighties. With both of us over our health scare, over the next few years, Fr. Joe and I took a number of golf trips to the best golf courses in the U.S. However, I gradually slipped back to my old game.

My friend, Laci, was doing well in diabetes research in Holland and in Sweden. He wanted to come to the U.S. because there were many more resources here, and research was being done at a much higher level. With help from friends, I was able to arrange an interview for him with the right person at Washington University. He was successful in obtaining a fellowship and moved his entire family to St. Louis. He did a wonderful job and gained international recognition for his work.

He now has a very successful business in Hungary, performing drug efficacy testing studies on contract with drug companies. He has collected a sizeable gene bank of diabetic families and uses them for diabetic research. Laci believes he will eventually find a way to prevent the occurrence of Type II diabetes, and I hope that he will.

One of Laci's friends, Peter Kiss, came to the U.S. in the summer of 1988 for a long vacation. He and I met while he was in St. Louis after a two-week driving trip around the U.S. with Laci. He was so impressed that he wanted to come and live in America. He asked me for a job. He was an electrical engineer, and I thought his skills fit our needs perfectly. He joined Zoltek and moved his family to St. Louis. They eventually became U.S. citizens. Peter became a good friend, and he later became Zoltek's Vice President of Engineering. He filled a critical position and was a very important help to me as we entered the carbon fiber business and we were designing our carbon fiber manufacturing equipment.

My accountant asked me to join him in participating in the St. Louis County Economic Council. With Zoltek operations running smoothly and doing well financially, I thought this might be an interesting experience. I got on the board that approved SBA loans. The first deal I was involved with was a request to finance an indoor soccer facility. The principals were two Chrysler engineers who were willing to invest their life savings, but they were turned down by the credit committee. They asked for an opportunity for a final presentation to the entire board.

After their presentation, everyone had a chance to comment and vote. For some reason, it was all negative until it got to me. I gave a very positive analysis and voted yes for making the loan. Everyone following me also voted positively. The loan was made and after that, the entire board started to look at requests more positively. That is when I realized that the process is the same in all financing; someone had to stand up for the deal and others would follow.

Later I was appointed to the Industrial Development Authority Board (IDA) that approved the industrial revenue bonds. Eventually, I was appointed by the County Executive to be the President of the IDA. This appointment also came with the appointment to the St. Louis County Economic Council. In 1988, I was appointed to be President of the St. Louis County Economic Council. This was an interesting diversion from business and gave me an inside view of how the government worked, or should I say, did not work.

I was quite interested in developing international connection to St. Louis County, and that objective defined my efforts while I was president. We organized a trade mission to Beijing, including the county executive and the zoo director. This mission started additional contacts with China, but future cooperation was interrupted by the Tiananmen Square incident.

After I became the president, I decided to pursue the acquisition of the World Trade Center (WTC) franchise. My objective was to use the WTC to support globalization activities in the greater St. Louis region. I also hoped to use this cooperation in international business to unite all the economic development activities in the greater St. Louis region under one organization in order to make the economic development more effective. The director of the St. Louis County Economic Council and I successfully negotiated the acquisition of the WTC franchise. It turned out to be a great success and encouraged us to do more, but we needed source of funds to support our ideas.

I thought we should be able to generate fees if we were providing worthy services. But to the government people, the obvious direct source of funds available would have been to add a small fraction to the sales tax. I then suggested developing a plan to justify the sales tax increase and to help convince the voters. This did not go over well with the county administration, and they just added a sales tax proposal to the next county election without any specifics. It was rejected by the voters.

Next, I suggested that the staff should visit several successful cities to see how they were generating funds for economic development. Their final proposal was not really surprising; the best option was taxes. However, their reasoning was a surprise, even to me. All other means of raising money required accounting for the spending, but there is no requirement to account for how tax revenues were spent. Obviously, this is the root of government spending problems. After several times on the ballot, the sales tax increase finally did pass.

When we made the WTC services available to everyone in the region, we developed a dialogue with all the economic development organizations in the area. We were making significant progress discussing the unification of regional economic development. We actually scheduled a conference, including politicians and staff. But politics got in the way.

When the Civic Progress organization, which is made up of the largest companies in the St. Louis area, found out about our plans, they immediately exercised their influence on the County Executive, to cancel the conference. It has been my opinion that their idea of civic progress was to do good for themselves and, if in the process others benefited, it was an unintended consequence. A unified economic development organization with tax money would diminish their political influence and interfere with their objectives.

When my term ended, it was time for me to return my full attention to business. This diversion from business and my short experience working within the government confirmed to me that there are two kinds of governments: bad government and worse government.

After the China mission, Mary got involved with the St. Louis Sister City program. When I ended my involvement with the St. Louis County Economic Development, Mary was invited to take my place on the WTC board of directors. She was a board member for a number of years and also became the president of the St. Louis Sister City organization. She managed to attract the national sister cities organization to select St. Louis for its annual convention.

I felt good about returning my full attention to business after this diversion into politics. The flexible graphite business started to change. Automobile engine gaskets became a large potential application, and Union Carbide started to concentrate on it. There were new competitors selling flexible graphite at significantly lower prices, as low as one-third of Union Carbide's price. By this time my friend Des Baker had left the company, and we tried to develop a business plan to take a more significant role with Union Carbide, but things did not come together. Soon, most of the people we had worked with earlier were reassigned to different position within or outside the company.

We started to buy from Union Carbide's competitors. We believed the best chance for us to build the flexible graphite business and market it nationally was to establish our own brand name. We introduced *Flexigraf* as our brand name and started a national marketing campaign. When we built our headquarter building, part of it was designed as a warehouse, and we moved all the Flexigraf related equipment and inventory into this building and moved the rest of the business in the facility that housed the power transmission acquisition.

Once our brand name became known in the industry, we were receiving customer inquiries from the U.S. and foreign companies. We received a fax from an Indonesian sales agent, requesting a quote with an unusual set of instructions. We were asked to quote our standard price, add 30 percent for commissions, ten percent for bribes, and send our proposal direct to the final customer. Our young inside salesman followed the instructions to the letter and itemized the commission and bribe. When I received a copy of our proposal, I was not happy, figuring we would never hear from them again and probably got the agent and the customer in trouble. However, we actually received the order, and we started doing significant business.

I was quite intrigued and curious. Finally, I had an opportunity to visit this agent in Medan, Indonesia. After discussing products and business opportunities, I had to ask the question about the bribe. He told me this was standard procedure for doing business. He proudly told me he once bought a house for a customer. When I asked how he could afford to give such a bribe in advance of getting the business. He explained that he could go to a bank and borrow the money as long as the bank believed the recipient had enough political clout to purchase enough to make good on paying the bribe. The question was how close the person was to the dictator Suharto. Welcome to international business. After this, our business relationship did not last for long.

Our success brought many visitors who wanted to learn our secrets or to work with us to be part of our success. Tom Burke, the sales representative for Toyo Tanso, a Japanese graphite company and potential flexible graphite supplier, came to visit us. He offered a low price for a trial order. I immediately gave him a sizeable order. He and his Japanese boss were on their way to California to see our competitor when they stopped in St. Louis. It turned out that Tom's manager proudly told our competitor that they had just received an order from me. My competitor immediately went to Japan to make a preemptive deal with Toyo Tanso. He purchased the entire available inventory and contracted to buy the entire next twelve-month production capacity from Toyo Tanso. He hoped to prevent me from buying at the same low price and planned to profitably resell it to Zoltek.

His maneuver was successful and when I contacted Toyo Tanso, they had nothing left to sell to me. I then contacted Hitachi, who was also producing flexible graphite to establish them as our primary source for our *Flexigraf*. I needed to know the price our competitor was paying to Toyo Tanso to be sure I could negotiate with Hitachi. To find this out, I met with Tom in New York. We had dinner and drinks at Rumms bar until Tom told me what I wanted to know.

During the evening, he asked me what I was looking to do in the future to top our success with flexible graphite. I told him that I was interested in producing our own product instead of reselling other companies' products. He asked me if I would be interested in carbon fibers. The answer was "Yes." At that time, I was thinking about carbon fibers as a high-value sealing product, complementing and enhancing our existing flexible graphite business strategy. He promised to investigate the possibility of a carbon fiber company might be for sale and, if appropriate, to provide the introductions for me to make direct contact. The company turned out to be Stackpole Fibers, Inc. in Lowell, Massachusetts.

In 1987, Mary lost her father to a massive heart attack. He was a picture of health and everyone was shocked. Her mother, similar to mine, continued to live in the family house. She had a good executive secretary position and was in reasonable financial shape. Since we lived in St. Louis, Mary could assist her mother if she needed help.

I maintained contact with my family by visiting them in Minneapolis and had my mother come to visit us, sometime with my brother's older son, Árpád. My mother was doing reasonably well. She made peace with some of the Hungarian friends, and she continued to stay in contact with some of her colleagues from the hospital. She also considered buying a home in Florida. Mary and I took her to look at houses, and she actually signed a contract on one in Naples. However, she changed her mind when she returned to Minneapolis. I think that she was worried about what would happen to my brother.

My brother got a job at Univac after completing his electrical engineering studies. He worked in quality control until Univac closed the plant in the early 1980s. After Univac, he was having trouble finding a new job. I helped him write his resume and gave him some suggestions, but he was unable to get a professional job and settled into doing manual labor, like being handyman, doing lawn maintenance, and plowing snow. I am not sure he ever felt comfortable in a professional environment. When Mary suggested that his wife, Kinga, should go to school and learn a profession, my mother got very upset. She was worried if Kinga could get a good job, she might leave my brother. Mary and my mother never really got along after that conversation.

As Mary always said, jokingly, that we have no kids because she is still raising me. Although there was a lot of truth to this, I know she missed having kids. But all of the sudden, several nieces and nephews were born. Mary took interest in the kids and enjoyed them. In time we lost imminent contact with most of them as they either moved away from St. Louis, or we lost contact because some rift in the family.

Recognizing the Carbon Fibers Opportunity

Tom followed up on his promise to introduce me to Stackpole Fibers, Inc. This company was a subsidiary of Stackpole Carbon Company of St. Marys, Pennsylvania, a privately owned company. Stackpole was looking to sell the carbon fibers business and had charged its president with finding a buyer. Tom set up a meeting and accompanied me on my first visit to the company in Lowell.

We met the Stackpole Fibers, Inc. president to inspect the plant facility and to meet with the company officers to discuss the possibility of acquiring the company. When we arrived at the plant, we received a very strange and cool reception. We were ushered into a conference room after a very quick tour of the plant and met with the management team. We were given a slide presentation with minimum information, mostly negative, about the company. It was clear they were not really trying to make the company look desirable to acquire.

I called the president a week later to indicate my continued interest in learning more about the company. I again received a cool reception, and he suggested a meeting in the Boston airport. During this meeting, I got a lot of complaints about the owners, but no new information about the company. They gave me hints that the company's military customers were highly upset and might decide to take over the company for national security reasons. It became clear that the parent company wanted to sell this business, but the president, who they trusted to give it his best effort, had his own agenda.

The company was a sole-source supplier of the carbon fibers specified for several military fighter jet brakes. His hope was to make the company look so unreliable under the current ownership that the government would take over the Stackpole Fibers subsidiary and essentially hand over the business to the current management. It was clear that we were going nowhere with this person and that he could not be trusted to follow the owners best interest.

Before I left Boston, I made a few phone calls. The executive office of Stackpole Carbon was located in Boston. I called there and was connected to Tom Dole, the corporate counsel, who was quite interested and cooperative. After exchanging information, I was convinced this company might be the company I was looking for; it had a unique product with high potential, and I could possibly afford to buy it. I also called Arnie Huntington of Goodrich, the most important customer, who confirmed that their business depended on Stackpole since they had no qualified second supplier. I also called a few other existing customers to verify their commitment to the company. They were all depending on the company for supply and were very supportive about the possibility for new management to take over. This all started to look promising, and it was clear I needed to work with Tom Dole, not the president of Stackpole Fibers.

After some serious thinking and analysis of the information I had received so far, I was ready for a serious discussion and to make an offer. Mary and I were going on vacation to Europe in late September, and I arranged to meet Tom Dole in New York. We met in the TWA Ambassador Club at New York LaGuardia Airport at 11:00 AM and had a handshake on a deal by noon.

The company had annual sales of just under $2 million, but it had a unique technology and single-source program qualifications in aircraft brake application that was quite valuable. I felt I could develop its upside potential. I offered $750,000 for the assets of the company. I indicated that it would take me ninety days to get the financing completed. However, I added that if they left the current management in place for the next three months, there would be no company left to buy. I proposed that we needed to take the company over on November 1, 1987 and schedule to close the final transaction on February 28, 1988. It was an unusual offer, but we had a handshake agreement, and the deal was done.

Before we went to lunch, we tossed a coin to see who would inform the current president. Based on my conclusion during my initial contacts that he could not be trusted, I was not looking to keep him on board. I was happy to win the toss and before we ordered lunch, I called him.

He was quite surprised to hear from me.

I told him, "I have good news and bad news; the good news is I just bought the company, and the bad news is you do not have a job."

After lunch, I took a taxi to Kennedy Airport to meet Mary and take the flight to Paris together. As I waited for her in the bar, it all hit me; I just took on a huge risk, and I would need to start running this business immediately after I returned from vacation. I also had to get the financing arranged, but had no idea how. By the time we returned home, I overcame my buyer's remorse and was ready to deal with the new carbon fiber business. I am not sure Mary shared my enthusiasm for the acquisition, but again, she did support what I wanted to do, understanding that she also shared in the risk because all our loans would be personally guaranteed by both of us.

While I was on vacation, Stackpole Carbon hired a new CFO who took over the completion of our transaction. Of course, he could not believe that we did not have a single piece of paper with a signature on it, and the payment terms were something he had never seen before.

After a lot of negotiations, we came up with a contract that was no different from our verbal agreement. However, he insisted on some proof of financial commitment. We agreed on a letter of credit. I had one week to come up with it, but still had no idea how.

Our existing bank already refused to increase our credit line to make this acquisition. My original plan had been to show positive results with the newly acquired company for two months in order to convince the bank to change their decision, but the need for an immediate letter of credit changed that plan.

The pressure was on; we had one week to produce a letter of credit for $750,000, or the acquisition would be in jeopardy. I called my accountant on Friday before I boarded the plane in Boston. He had talked to the CEO of the largest bank in St. Louis, and he had arranged for me to meet a vice president on Monday morning. Over the weekend, I prepared a complete presentation of the acquisition, Zoltek's financial condition, and financial forecasts for the next three years, including the new acquisition.

When we met Monday morning, the banker opened the binder and briefly looked at the presentation and said, "It is always so nice to see a presentation prepared by an accountant and not the business guy."

Little did he know that my accountant had not even seen the presentation, much less prepared it! After a few minutes of discussion, he told me that he would review the presentation, and he would call me. I knew that it was never good to look anxious when looking for money, so I just shook hands and left, hoping he would call soon. He called me the next day to meet for breakfast with him and a colleague on Wednesday.

As usual, I was late. When I drove up to the front of the restaurant, he was waiting outside instead of sitting at a table having coffee, like most business people would. I also assumed he was bringing a big shot with him, but I saw a young guy who looked like he was still in high school. At that point, I figured he was not really serious, but just came for breakfast to pretend that he really had considered the loan. I did my best not to act cynical and to try to be convincing about the acquisition. When we parted, he again said that he would call. He actually called that afternoon confirming that the bank would produce the letter of credit and the loan.

He asked me, "When do you need the letter of credit?"

"Friday would be okay," I said, still not acting anxious.

He had it delivered to my office by Thursday afternoon. It looked to me like I had swept him off his feet, and I was proud of it. We moved our account to his bank within a week, hoping we had found the large bank that could easily support us through our expansion.

After the acquisition agreement was complete, the manager of another division of Stackpole Carbon, Joe Demendi, who was about to become a significant fibers customer for a new product line of high-temperature bearings for jet engines, found out about the pending sale. He was really upset. He was concerned about continued supply since the primary component for all his new products was a carbon fiber fabric produced by the fibers division.

One day when I was in the Lowell office completing the final due diligence, he called me. He was in a state of panic. The more he talked, the more I realized that he had a heavy Hungarian accent. Finally, I cut in and asked him if he was Hungarian. When he confirmed it, I called his attention to my name. As he realized I was also Hungarian, he relaxed and gave me a verbal commitment to supply him with all the carbon-fiber fabric we could produce. This product sold for $175 per pound with a huge profit margin. Within a year, we made more profit off this business than what we had paid for the whole company.

As poetic justice, at the first closing before we took over the company, the Stackpole Carbon Co. CFO went ballistic when he discovered the plant received over $50,000 in raw materials the day before we took over and that he was stuck with the bill. We took over on the first of November 1987 as planned.

I spent considerable time with the carbon fiber business. The president, who I fired, convinced the key sales and technology people to leave the company, in hopes that we would fail. So I went through a rapid learning curve on the technology and our market potential. I quickly established good relations with our existing customer base. It was clear that every customer was happy to see the change in management. I was glad all the old management was actually gone from the company.

We also started to promote our fibers in the sealing market as we originally planned. However, it quickly became clear that the existing products and customer base represented a much better business opportunity, and it also presented much higher priced products coupled with a much more stable business model. Most of the existing customers were specifying our products as single source, and the qualification of a competitive product was expensive and time consuming.

The carbon fibers we were producing and the applications they were used in were unique. The high temperature and frictional properties were the critical properties required for most of the applications our carbon fibers were used.

The process for manufacturing carbon fibers evolved over many years, but the basic concept has stayed constant. The object was to convert synthetic fibers to carbon fibers by heat treating the fibers at a temperature high enough to drive off the non-carbon components.

The initial synthetic fiber used for raw material was rayon. These fibers were acceptable for the initial applications in the space exploration area, such as rocket nozzles and re-entry tiles on spacecraft. However, there were two serious limitations for rayon-based carbon fibers going beyond these high temperature applications. The carbon fibers were low strength for structural applications, which were fast becoming the primary use for carbon fibers. And as rayon fiber was heat treated, it lost eighty percent of its weight, which caused the cost of the finished carbon fiber to be permanently prohibitive for any large application, aerospace or commercial.

In the early 1980s, acrylic fibers became the best performing and most cost effective raw material for carbon fiber production. Acrylic fibers were lower cost synthetic fibers and because its molecular structure was more linear, it produced much better structural properties and just fifty percent weight loss. The primary carbon fibers producers at the time were eight global chemical companies with some form of acrylic fiber technology. They were all doing the same thing, producing continuous fibers for accentuating the finished mechanical properties. However, acrylic-based carbon fibers have different thermal properties, which make them unfit for the high-temperature ablative/friction applications, like aircraft brakes and rocket nozzles. Stackpole Fibers had developed a process to use the acrylic fibers in such a way to simulate the properties of the rayon-based fibers.

Before the acrylic fibers could be heat treated to produce carbon fibers, they had to be oxidized to make them stable during the heat-treating process. The oxidized acrylic fibers behaved just like the base acrylic fibers and could be converted into different textile format quite easily. For our process, we used textile type of acrylic fibers as precursor, which were considerably lower cost than the special acrylic fibers used by others. These oxidized acrylic textile products were heat treated in batch furnaces up to 1600°C, converting to specific carbon content. These fibers were reasonably easy to substitute for the rayon-based carbon fibers.

The carbon/carbon composite process was developed by a small company named SuperTemp back in the 1970s. The process to produce carbon/carbon composite is quite complex, time consuming, and expensive. Goodrich eventually acquired the company and started producing various high-temperature materials for the space program. From this beginning, the aircraft brakes business developed, and it became, by far, the largest use for this technology. And we were in the best position to be the leader in this market.

Carbon/carbon composite aircraft brakes had huge advantages over metal brakes. The finished product was less than half the weight of steel and much more heat resistant. The weight reduction and heat resistance were clear advantages for aircraft brakes. The two most important performance properties were: friction (i.e. breaking performance) and wear resistance that determined the brake's economic value. For friction performance in aircraft, the rejected take-off (RTO) scenario was the most critical and dangerous. This meant that an airplane must be able to stop before the end of the runway if a pilot decided to abort take-off after the airplane had reached take-off velocity. Another important benefit was that the breaking performance of carbon brake discs does not diminish with increased temperature, while metal brakes would soften, and their braking performance would diminish dramatically as their temperature increased.

Metal brakes also had to cool down before an airplane could take off again, but carbon brakes did not have this restriction. These performance properties improved the efficiency of airlines by having rapid turn-around schedules. The wear resistance was an equally important factor for their economic value. Because the initial cost of carbon brakes was so expensive, airlines were looking for an economic solution to control their cost. Eventually a pay per landing concept was developed, i.e., pay a fee to the brake suppliers each time an airplane landed. This idea caused the friction and wear performance to greatly impact the financial performance of the aircraft brake manufacturers. These critical requirements, and the safety implications that went along with aerospace applications, made it extremely difficult to get new carbon fibers qualified.

When we acquired the company, we had single-source qualification for all U.S. fighter jet brakes. Our customers were the brake producers, Goodrich (now United Technologies) and Bendix (later Allied Signal and now Honeywell). We also had single-source qualification for the C-5 transport plane through Goodrich. There were two big new pending business prospects. First, the original fifty C-5 transport airplanes were built with metal brakes, and they were to be retrofitted with carbon brakes. Second, the Boeing 747-400 was to be the first commercial airplane to use carbon/carbon brakes. Goodrich paid $50 million to be the single source for B747-400 program. They were planning on using the same configuration as the C-5 brake, which exclusively used our carbon fibers.

A French company, Carbon Industrie, located outside of Lyon, France, developed a three-dimensional process for the production of aircraft brakes, and Boeing liked it. They told Goodrich that since they had paid the $50 million to be single sourced, they could keep the contract, but had to negotiate a technology license from Carbon Industrie to produce the new type of the three-dimensional brakes.

All of the development for these new brakes was done in Europe, and the fibers were supplied by a British company, RK Carbon, which later became part of SGL. When I first visited Goodrich, they were in the process of completing construction of a new facility in Pueblo, Colorado, just for the production of the B747-400 brakes. At that point, our fiber had not been tested in the new process. We needed to catch up.

Based on my initial understanding of the technology and our position in the market, I decided the aircraft brake application was our best and quickest business potential.

Another pending application, the rocket nozzle liners, was in the process of changing from rayon-based to acrylic-based carbon fibers. When the initial rockets were designed, only rayon-based carbon fibers were available commercially. However, the production of rayon creates a lot of pollution, and the EPA had earlier forced the only source of the rayon fiber precursor to shut down. At that time, our fibers were the only acrylic-based carbon fibers ever successfully used for this application. I was confident we would be selected as the primary source for this application. Instead, the government gave Hercules Chemical Co. an $80-million contract to find another potential supplier.

The rocket nozzle business was a different story from the aircraft brakes. Very quickly it became clear that Zoltek would not be admitted into the defense contractor cabal. Although there was a real problem with the supply conditions and our product was tested and approved by Jet Propulsion Laboratories (JPL), we were unable to get any information or interest to discuss this business. Obviously, this was going to be a difficult situation.

One more interesting technology came with the business. Stackpole Fibers was issued a patent on March 1, 1988 for a special carbon fiber application for manufacturing radar-absorbing material that would enable the development of significantly improved stealth technology. The assets acquired by Zoltek included ownership of this patent. We had high hopes for this product; a patent-protected and high technology enabling product could command a high price in an exclusive market.

Stealth technology has several components, but the most important is to avoid radar detection of the airframe. This is accomplished by absorbing the radar signal on the surface of the airplane rather than reflecting it. Our patent made a connection between the process of carbon fibers production and achieving the desired carbon fiber resistivity. We also developed the composite fabrication process needed to achieve a desired level of the composite resistivity.

There were two problems that needed attention. First, when I reviewed the patent, I realized that the specific claims were not clearly defined. We needed to improve our claims to clarify the unique nature of the patented invention. There was an opportunity to improve the patent definitions within two years after the original patent was issued, so I started to complete this reissue process on my own because the original inventor went to work for a competitor before I completed the acquisition. The reissue application was filed on February 20, 1990. The patent examiner took a long time to approve our reissue application. After providing additional information, our patent attorney and I personally met the examiner in May of 1992 and received final approval of the reissued patent.

Second, to achieve the specific resistivity in the carbon fiber, the carbonization process needed to be interrupted at a defined temperature. We found that over time, the conductivity changed, indicating that the carbonization reaction continued. We needed to develop a process to stabilize the conductivity by terminating the reaction. Working with an MIT researcher who was funded by the U.S. Air Force, this additional step was in the final development stage. The MIT researcher submitted a report to the U.S. Air Force on the joint development project. The Air Force immediately classified the work as "secret."

We started to produce development quantities of several products covered by our patented technology. I had discussions with Boeing, and we had high hopes for very significant and profitable business. However, this product was part of the airframe and a true aerospace application. That we might not ever be considered qualified to do business with the aircraft designers concerned me.

The plant in Lowell was a mess in many ways. The facility was in a rented warehouse, which originally was a foundry. Installation of not-easily-movable process equipment in a rental property was a very bad idea because the landlord gained total control to set the rent. The equipment was very poorly designed and in seriously poor condition. We had ten badly designed and low-capacity oxidizing ovens, ancient textile equipment for yarn production, and one functioning vacuum furnace. We needed to make significant investment to bring the plant up to a reasonable standard. The lease term was coming to the end, but I was not about to renew it. We needed to move.

We surveyed our employees about moving. Essentially, no one was willing to move, and no one was willing to stay with the company if we moved more than one mile. So, the decision was easy; we would move the plant to St. Louis, where we thought we could find better employees and have a better chance of obtaining the required financing. Ultimately, only four employees out of about fifty chose to move to St. Louis.

Our products were, and still are, sold under the trade names PANEX® carbon fiber and Pyron® oxidized fiber. Our products were not suited for high performance composite reinforcement applications because the filaments were discontinuous and twisted into a yarn, causing a significant reduction in key mechanical properties, tensile strength and modulus (stiffness), in a composite. The prevailing reinforcement carbon fibers were almost exclusively used in aerospace applications. They were too expensive for anything else.

As I was getting acquainted with the business, it occurred to me that we should be able to produce carbon fibers with the same basic mechanical properties from our Pyron (oxidized fiber) as the aerospace fibers. If we were able to produce such a carbon fiber, we could significantly reduce the cost and selling price of carbon fibers. While this fiber may not meet all the strict specifications of the aerospace applications, we could produce it for significantly lower cost with the same properties as aerospace carbon fibers for commercial and industrial applications.

After I studied the carbon fiber process, I designed a pilot plant in Lowell with the help of our maintenance manager. We used whatever high-temperature piping and heaters we could find in our warehouse. Within forty-eight hours, we had something that would give us an initial idea of what kind of properties we could expect.

We used our Pyron® as feed to the pilot plant and ran six different samples with different conditions. Out of these samples, two met or exceeded the prevailing aerospace fiber properties. The difference was in the number of filaments in our tow bundle (320,000 filaments) versus the aerospace fibers, which were fairly standard at a significantly lower filament tow (12,000 filaments). Once applied in a composite, there was no difference in the composite properties.

Either we were really good, or we were lucky. We were now confident we could produce continuous filament carbon fibers! Now we could develop our plans to introduce an entirely new concept in the carbon fiber industry: the commercial grade carbon fiber. For applications from golf club shafts to wind turbine blades to automobiles, we could supply carbon fibers that had the same mechanical properties as the best carbon fiber on the market at a fraction of the cost.

Our plans for a small carbon fiber business changed dramatically and quickly. We had originally imagined, when we decided to acquire the carbon fiber business, a small specialty carbon fiber operation complementing our flexible graphite sealing business. This progressed to a specialty carbon fiber for aircraft brakes and rocket nozzles and, finally, to entering the composite reinforcement carbon fiber business. In the process, we would completely revolutionize the carbon fiber composite industry.

Based on these findings and my analysis of the business, it was time to develop a strategy to build a successful and significant carbon fiber business.

The short-term strategy called for escalating the existing carbon fiber business into a significant, profitable, and growing business as quickly as possible. However, nothing could happen without the appropriate financing to support the business strategy. For the short-term, we needed financing to move the Lowell plant to St. Louis and to continue our proprietary design of the continuous-carbon-fiber processing lines. We established the following strategy:

- Move the plant to St. Louis, modernize it, and significantly increase its capacity.
- Gain a significant majority of the global aircraft brake business.
- Exploit our acquired technologies and solidify our new customer base.
- Develop the stealth technology business around the B-2 bomber.
- Develop continuous carbon fiber technology for optimizing mechanical properties of composites, the carbon fibers must be continuous filaments.
- Develop long-term sustainable financing to support our business model.

For the longer term, we knew that bringing affordable carbon fibers into the commercial applications would revolutionize the industry. What we tried to do had been done before when glass fibers were introduced. It took glass fibers 50 years and for the boating industry to adopt it before it started to grow exponentially. We were in a similar position since carbon fibers' performance had been demonstrated in a number of critical applications for over 30 years, and we were becoming very optimistic about creating a dramatic increase in demand as we made carbon fiber dramatically more affordable. For the long term, our strategy was the following:

- Design process equipment for low-cost carbon fibers production.
- Develop or acquire our own precursor acrylic fiber technology and facility.
- Develop plans to rapidly expand our production capacity.
- Establish a viable marketing plan for carbon fibers.
- Develop a strategy to change the value chain, the incremental

value-added processes from carbon fiber to composite, to lower the finished composite cost.

The difficulty of this strategy was typical of any revolutionary change in an industry when there is no established roadmap or examples to follow. This was further complicated by the significant capital-intensive nature of the product and no sufficient internal source of funding was available from other established product lines. This strategy looked overwhelming for a company of our size.

We did have our industrial service operation to provide the engineering capabilities and our equipment design and installation talent. My plan was to maintain the business level of the industrial business and grow the carbon fiber business as fast as we could. Zoltek was about to change dramatically.

On the personal side, my family in Minneapolis was not making progress. As time went on and my brother stopped looking for a real job, my mother became even more defensive and protective of him. As I got more successful, my mother seemed to resent it because she thought I was lucky and my brother should have been the one to enjoy my success. Mary really resented this.

I could never forgive my brother for dominating my mother's life in so many negative ways. I was always willing to financially help my mother, but I knew if I gave her any money, it would end up with my brother. Whenever I asked her if she needed anything, she would assure me that she was okay.

Once she told me that she and my brother were having problems keeping up with the tuition payment for my brother's younger son, Attila. I called the Catholic high school and paid off all the delinquent tuition and paid in full all the way through graduation, but I asked them not to reveal the source of the payment. The next time I called my mother, she told me there was a Santa Claus, but she immediately realized I was it. I don't know if she ever told my brother.

My brother's older son, Árpád, was not getting along with his parents. After he finished high school, he came to live with us in St. Louis. We encouraged him to go to college, and Mary worked hard to get him admitted to Southeast Missouri State University. It was a difficult task, but she succeeded. We enrolled him and moved him into the dormitory. We were happy that we were able to turn his life around.

We were wrong. He almost flunked out in the first semester, and he did flunk out the second semester. He actually failed campus orientation; obviously he slept through the entire semester. He did not care. Mary was so upset that less than twenty-four hours later, he was on a Greyhound bus, going back to Minneapolis.

After a few months, he called to ask if he could move back to St. Louis. Mary told him it was okay with us, but he needed to get a job, get himself his own apartment, and establish his own life. She helped to find an apartment for him, and he started to work at Zoltek. Later, when we built the Abilene plant, he moved there and worked in the plant until 2010, when he moved back to St. Louis and is still working for Zoltek. He now regrets not taking college more seriously.

After Mary's mother retired and all the kids moved out of the house, living in the large house became more difficult and expensive. We bought a condominium in Clayton for her to live in. With the proceeds from the sale of her house, Social Security, and pension, she was in good financial position and Mary continued to look out for her mother.

Mary was busy with her travel agency. We lost contact with most of Mary's siblings' children as they either moved or we lost contact with their parents. In 1990, Mary's favorite sister, Joan, had a baby girl named Marta. Mary and Joan always got along great, and we were able to see Marta a lot. Thanks for Marta's parents, Joan and Ken, who were willing to let her spend quality time with us, she has become just like part of our family.

Initial Challenges of the Carbon Fiber Business

The first order of business was to solidify and build our aircraft brakes business. At the time of our acquisition, we had a commanding share of the military aircraft brake business, a business that was quite stable because there was no other company that produced competitive fibers that were qualified for the military programs. However, commercial airplanes, which were beginning to change to carbon/carbon brakes, represented a much larger potential, and we were behind our competitor.

Carbon Industrie, which later, after several acquisitions became Messier-Bugatti, just developed a process to make preforms by needling the oxidized fibers into a thick slab and then cutting them into disk shape and then to carbonize them in the same type of batch vacuum furnace in which we had produced our carbon fibers. This method produced a three-dimensional brake that seemed to offer some advantages, which Boeing preferred for the B747-400.

I realized this new technology promised to be a game changer and could have a significant impact on our future business. We needed to establish a relationship with Carbon Industrie immediately. Like Zoltek, they were newcomers to the aircraft brake business, but generated a lot of interest in the market.

In 1989, there were two companies using the same Courtaulds acrylic fiber precursor, RK Textiles and Zoltek. The owner of RK Textiles was a prior Courtaulds employee, and the Courtaulds salesman actively promoted his business over Zoltek. It was easy for us to establish equivalency and to duplicate the performance with the same Courtaulds precursor, and it was little problem to get qualified. Goodrich did acquire the technology license and built a new plant in Pueblo, Colorado to produce these brake discs. We had enough oxidized fiber capacity to become a viable supplier to Goodrich. It takes a minimum of nine months to go through the production and testing of the brake discs for qualification. Fortunately, Goodrich was loyal to us because we had stabilized the supply and price of the existing products, and they honored the prior commitment to use our fibers. By 1990, our Pyron fiber was qualified by Goodrich and soon after, we were supplying our fibers for part of the B747-400 airplanes.

I met Dick McMurry, the manager of the Goodrich carbon business, at the 1990 composite show in Reno, Nevada. After dinner, I went to the craps table. As I was rolling the dice, the guy next to me gave me some encouragement. This guy was Dick McMurry. Someone realized that we had not met and introduced us. I enthusiastically shook his hand and told him I had been trying to meet him for some time. He told me that he did not engage with suppliers, and that was the end of our conversation. At about 2:00 in the morning, I went to the keno parlor to relax before going to bed. Dick was also sitting there, and we began a conversation. We got along great and ultimately, we became friends, and Zoltek became his largest supplier.

The second largest aircraft brake manufacturer was Bendix and at that time, they were supplying the majority of carbon/carbon brake discs for the fighter jet programs. They had a different way of producing the preforms by using finished carbon fibers produced by Zoltek. They were quite upset with Stackpole Fibers and had difficulty accepting that

Zoltek was not going to be like Stackpole. We needed to establish a new relationship with them to differentiate us from the prior management to maintain their business and to work with them to develop their version of the brakes for commercial aircraft. Goodyear and Dunlop, the other two aircraft brake producers, were on the fringes and were no factor in the market.

After the B747-400 brakes entered service and demonstrated their exceptional performance, all new wide-body Boeing and all Airbus aircraft specified carbon/carbon brakes. Goodrich had a preferred position with Boeing. But Airbus was coming on strong in the airplane market, and they looked to be a larger potential customer in the long term. Airbus designed their brake system with Carbon Industrie and they preferred working with them. The commercial aircraft brakes business started to grow rapidly.

If aircraft brake business was to be a primary market for us, Zoltek needed to be active at all of the brake manufacturers and prove to be a reliable supplier the industry could depend on and trust. To capture and maintain a dominant position in this market, we needed to expand our capacity. But it became clear that, for the long term, we needed to differentiate ourselves with our own precursor and develop our precursor capability to differentiate us from our present and potential future competitors. If we were successful, and in order to maintain long-term dominance, eventually we also would need to establish a second carbon fiber production facility.

Prior to our acquisition, Stackpole Fibers had worked with DuPont Orlon fibers with some success. When I contacted DuPont, I was told that the technology had been sold and that several licensees were active around the world, but there was no licensee in the U.S. They also told me that the Hungarian licensee was their best. Peter Kiss was traveling to Hungary in 1992, and I asked him to visit Magyar Viscosa Rt. (Hungarian Rayon Corp.) to evaluate their technical abilities and get some samples of their acrylic fibers. He was quite impressed with what he saw. Although I believed that he was somewhat influenced by his loyalty to Hungary, this company definitely warranted our consideration.

We tried to establish our carbon fiber as a ready-to-go replacement for the rocket nozzle application. Since our fibers had already been tested and approved by the Jet Propulsion Laboratory (JPL) for this application, we expected to receive business fairly quickly. However, the $80-million contract the U.S. government gave to Hercules Chemical Co. to find another supplier that could equal our fiber's performance made a quick change impossible. It also became clear that for the rocket nozzle application, Zoltek would not be accepted by the U.S. aerospace and military contractor cabal.

Keeping us out of this market had to cost the U.S. government at least $500 million. First, they were required to complete a costly qualification of a new fiber that would take years and millions of dollars to complete. Second, while the qualification work was in process, they were forced to purchase a ten-year inventory of the qualified rayon fibers, at a hugely increased price, from a rayon producing company that had already been shut down by the EPA. Later, based on a national security claim by NASA, the rayon producer was ordered to restart. All of these expenses were unnecessarily incurred while we were struggling to survive. It really made one wonder how dishonest our government really was.

While we were kept out of this market in the U.S., our fibers have been used to manufacture the French Hercules rocket nozzles.

Once our technology to produce stabilized specific-conductivity carbon fibers for the stealth technology was declared "secret," our board of directors was required to get secret clearance. Since Mary and I were the only two directors of the company at that time, we were required to obtain secret clearances.

It took me about sixty days to receive my clearance, but Mary was having difficulty. After about six months, Mary was called to the St. Louis FBI office for an interview. She got really upset and demanded to know why her husband, who was born in Hungary, a communist country, and was a naturalized citizen, obtained secret clearance so fast meanwhile she, born in the U.S., was having so much trouble. She was told that she fit a profile for a spy, marrying a foreigner as a cover, and then traveling in communist countries. She had traveled with me to Hungary, and we both had traveled to China on a trade mission with the St. Louis County Executive, not exactly a spy mission. After this confrontation, she finally did receive her secret clearance.

We were also required to store the process definitions and the production parameters in a safe or locked filing cabinet. We could not move the files to St. Louis until Mary and I both received our secret clearance. Only our security officer was allowed to open this file. In the middle of the organized chaos of the move from the Lowell plant, an FBI agent came to the plant unexpectedly and demanded that our security officer open the filing cabinet to check if our documents were still there and kept safely. When our security person opened the locked cabinet, the FBI agent confiscated our files and left. Quite a reminder for me of my experience in dictatorial communist state!

Although I tried to get our files back for several years, I never received any response to my inquiries. Later I found out that Zoltek and I, personally, were under some sort of surveillance. I realized we would never get any business from the government or their favored aerospace contractor cabal. And I was right.

After about two years of learning the technology, securing our existing customer base, and expanding the business that came with the acquisition, we were ready to build an entirely new business around the concept of lower cost commercial carbon fibers. Based on this vision and our initial success in demonstrating its viability, we needed to finalize our plan.

Almost as big or possibly a bigger challenge was the financing to support all our plans. Throughout the history of Zoltek, financing was a huge task. However, the carbon fiber manufacturing was a highly capital-intensive business, far beyond the business we were originally planning. Financing our carbon fiber business was obviously going to be a far bigger challenge than I expected. In mid-1989, I met with our banker to discuss our future plans and the possible move of the plant to St. Louis. This move needed significant additional money, and I outlined our financing requirements to support our plans.

At the same time, the manager of our accounting firm, Price Waterhouse, had recommended to Southwest Bank that Zoltek would make a good potential customer. Southwest Bank had been recently acquired by an investor group led by Andrew (Drew) N. Baur and Linn Bealke. The bank was staffed largely with a number of bankers who had worked with Drew at different banks. Their focus was on supporting small businesses to help them grow.

Before I considered a new bank, I wanted to try to work with the bank that helped us acquire the carbon fiber business. However, our banker was quite negative about it, which at first seemed illogical when he told me that we were more profitable than the bank itself on a percentage of revenue bases. During our discussion, he revealed that the reason they had made the original loan was part of their defensive strategy to load the bank's portfolio with as many high-risk credits as possible in order to make a potential takeover of the bank more difficult. I guess the reason was not my impressive presentation as I originally thought.

Linn Bealke, the Vice Chairman, and Bob Witterschein, the Executive Vice President of Southwest Bank, came to visit me at Zoltek. We had a much longer meeting than what we had planned because we got along so well. None of us could see the future or how the three of them, including Drew, would one day become my mentors and best friends.

We did not discuss any specific needs for financing, thinking I was still in discussions with our current bank.

Since our current banker was not willing to expand our credit as an option, he suggested that I should consider a sale-lease-back of our headquarters building instead of offering it as collateral for the business loan. I did not like the idea, but was willing to listen.

My banker and the real estate investor of his choice came to see me. They talked in circles for a while. They were trying to sell the sale-lease-back concept just a little too much, and I was not accepting their arguments for many reasons. Finally, it became time to find out what exactly they had in mind.

I asked the real estate person, "Okay, let's walk through the deal you are talking about. You will buy the building from me, and let's say you pay me $2 million more than I owe the bank. I will repay the bank and keep the $2 million."

He responded with an enthusiastic, "Yes!"

So, I continued, "Then you will charge me rent based on your cost and some profits."

"Yes."

I again continued, "The largest part of your expense will be the interest you will pay."

He confirmed, and I asked, "Will you get one hundred percent financing? What interest rate will you be paying?"

He confirmed the one hundred percent financing and continued, "The interest rate will depend on Zoltek's financial statement."

That was all I needed to hear. Our banker was willing to lend money to the real estate investor based on our financial ability to repay the loan, but not lend directly to Zoltek.

I looked at my banker and said, "It is obvious my problem is not the financing, but I need a different banker."

That was the end of that banking relationship.

Immediately after this meeting, I called Southwest Bank to confirm my interest in continuing our discussion and to initiate a specific loan request. We immediately started the loan approval process. Linn and Bob approved the loan, but I had one more hurdle to overcome.

I had to meet Drew on the golf course before they could confirm the final approval. This was the first time that I was introduced to Drew, and the four of us played a round of golf. Fortunately, my golfing skills were not the determining factor because if they had been, then my loan would have been rejected. Drew did not like my golf game, but we got along well, and he liked my attitude and honesty about golf, which he interpreted to be the same as it would be in business.

Within a short time, we moved our existing account and loans to Southwest Bank and stayed with them for twenty years, until Southwest Bank was acquired, first by Marshall & Ilsley Bank (M&I Bank) and later by Bank of Montreal.

Dealing with Southwest Bank was refreshing compared to the previous six banks we had dealt with over the prior fifteen years. I felt confident that the financing would become available as we proceeded with the plant relocation and modernization. However, in the middle of the project, our additional capacity needs and development of the commercial carbon fiber concept increased our financing needs. Not surprisingly, Bob had problems with our additional loan request.

The plant building was to be constructed on a developed site owned by the University of Missouri named Missouri Research Park and leased to Zoltek for seventy-five years. This kind of arrangement was not common in St. Louis. We quickly worked out most of the details for the building valuation and the bank's financial interest versus the University's. But financing the equipment was more difficult. Bob suggested getting the equipment appraised to determine the collateral value. This would be an expensive and time-consuming task and, in the end, it would not be useful. So, I told Bob to assume the equipment had the same value as a boat anchor and see how that would work. In a few days, Bob called me with his answer. He figured out that the value was in the customer supply contracts, not in the equipment. The equipment was needed to fulfill the contracts. The numbers worked well with this scenario, and Bob approved the loan.

In 1991, with the financing issue behind us, we began the construction of the plant facility in the Missouri Research Park. We also started to build a significant amount of inventory to support customers during the move. At the same time, we started to redesign the equipment with the goal to quadruple the capacity. As the production runs for each process was completed, we moved the equipment to our industrial service building in St. Louis. We decided to utilize our own staff to do the repairs and reconstruction. This, of course, strained our staff and disrupted our existing business, but our people worked well together and did a fantastic job.

Being part of the University of Missouri Research Park had its advantages. The plant construction could begin almost immediately since the University was the permitting authority, exempted from the County's exhaustive permitting process. We were moving on schedule with the building construction and as soon as the roof was on the furnace area, we started to move the equipment into place. This equipment installation work was done by a non-union contractor. The next morning, there was a union picket line at the entrance of the Park. I was able to negotiate to remove the picket line, and we used a few union workers to assist with the equipment installation.

All was going well again when the local fire chief insisted the University needed to get his approval on the buildings within the Park. Since we were the first tenant, Rick Finholt, the University's Director of the park, thought that if I participated in the meeting, things would go better. The fire chief took issue with our office doors, which were sliding glass doors. He claimed they were not in compliance with the building codes. He was wrong, but stood his ground. I thought interjecting a little humor would lighten up the conversation.

I said, "Chief, you need to consider that the people in these offices will be responsible for operating the plant, and I hope they will not be too stupid not to break the glass door in case of fire." This tested the chief's humor beyond its limits. Fortunately, just about that time, an alarm went off, and the chief had to spring into action.

When we left, Rick and I had a good laugh, and Rick vowed to never allow me to attend a meeting with the chief again. We did put in the glass doors, and the chief and I got along well later.

The move from Lowell to St. Louis did not go smoothly. With delays in financing and construction, we were unable to complete our move from Lowell before the end of the lease. Our landlord was a bad actor, so I went to Lowell the week before the lease expired. We were almost done, but we were finishing the production runs and still had a few truck-loads of inventory and equipment to move. We needed an extra month. I was concerned and before going back to St. Louis, I met with our Boston attorney on Friday afternoon to discuss what might go wrong with the landlord.

At about 3:00 Saturday morning, June 30, 1991, I received a call from the production supervisor. There had been an explosion at the Lowell plant. Fortunately, no one was hurt but the furnace, along with some other equipment, was destroyed. Also, lots of inventory was damaged. Later, we determined that there were two people working at the plant, one operating the vacuum furnace and another running some textile machines at the other end of the plant. The maintenance manager, who was always very friendly with the landlord, showed up for no apparent reason and told the furnace operator to go to the bathroom for ten minutes. While the operator was gone, it appears that he opened a safety valve that caused water to be sucked into the furnace, which was at 1650°C. The furnace blew up in seconds.

This caused further delays and extra cost, but the bigger problem was the possible disruption in our ability to supply our customers. The intensity of our activity increased significantly. We did have about six months of finished inventory, which was not enough. We also had some inventory that had water damage, but could be salvaged. A significant amount of the equipment needed to be replaced, not just moved. This increased our cost as well as the time to complete the project.

The cost of the plant escalated further when we added the housing for the continuous process line. With the damage to the equipment caused by the explosion in the Lowell plant and the resulting delays and the increased cost of the equipment repairs, the cost of the move also escalated. At the same time, our engineering staff was stressed out with managing the project, while they were also working on redesigning the equipment as it arrived at our shop. Our costs were uncontrollably escalating. It became impossible for us to manage our cash flow.

I was the acting CFO, and we did not have a professional accountant on our management team. I realized that, as our financing became more complex, we needed to have someone who our lenders and future potential investors would have confidence to represent our financial position. Coincidentally, our Price Waterhouse audit manager, Cheryl Rene, had come to me and told me she wanted to leave the accounting firm to work for an operating company, and Zoltek was her choice. She was an excellent accountant, and I liked her a lot. She came to work for us and did a great job.

By the spring of 1992, parts of the new plant were ready for start-up. The redesigned oxidizers had quadrupled their capacity. The vacuum furnace was damaged beyond normal repair, but we needed to save some critical components to be able to claim that it was repaired, not replaced. If it were new, we would have had to go through a lot of testing to maintain the product qualifications. In addition to replacing the existing vacuum furnace, we built two new furnaces. We planned to install two more furnaces later. We also designed a significantly larger capacity furnace, which we planned to install for the airbag business. We also installed a complete textile plant to produce yarns and fabrics.

Our start-up was not as smooth as I had hoped. We made some decisions to expedite the project that did not turn out well, and we were forced to make changes that took time, but had no design issues. There was nothing that we were unable to correct in a reasonably fast manner. However, we had huge problems with the oxidizers. We could not run for more than a few hours without a fire. Fires are the common hazard of the process, but they happen rarely during normal operations. Our production supervisor in Lowell, Bob Waraksa, moved to St. Louis. His process knowledge and operations experience were critical in training our new operators and managing our start-up process.

Southwest Bank did everything to support our needs, but with our cash flow running out of control in the middle of the construction project, we were pushing the bank beyond reasonable limits. At one point, we were $400,000 overdrawn at the bank. I certainly do not recommend doing this, but I was desperate. Bob was my main daily contact, and he called me to let me know that Drew wanted me to come to the bank to discuss the problem. After a short discussion and assuring both of them that there was no serious or fundamental problem with the business that we could not handle, Drew approved an over-line loan to cover the overdraft. Bob prepared the paperwork and asked me if the extra $400,000 loan amount was enough.

I told him, "Yes."

We completed the paperwork on Friday, and Bob went on his annual mandatory two- week vacation during which he was not to contact the bank.

Monday afternoon, Cheryl came to my office to tell me that the bank had called to tell us that we were already more $20,000 overdrawn, and they wanted us to deposit money to cover it.

I asked her, "Are you hiding some cash I do not know about?"

She said, "No."

"Then we can't deposit any money today, but as we will receive payments and our checks will be cashed each day, the overdraft amount will change," I said.

"So," she asked me, "what do I tell the bank when they ask for deposit each day?"

"Tell them, 'okay,'" I said.

I am sure this challenged Cheryl's professional conduct standards, but she had faith in what I was doing, and she was loyal to the company. So, this daily process continued on for the two weeks while Bob was on vacation. By the end of the two weeks, we were overdrawn by $250,000. When Bob came back from his vacation, he was disturbed. I got a call.

Bob said, "Zsolt, you are confusing having checks with having money!"

Before our project was all over, we required another $400,000.

Years later while playing golf with Bob, he told me that he had figured out all our relationship issues over the years, but he did not understand why I said that the over-line was enough when it clearly was not.

I asked him, "The day we met Drew, would you have approved an $800,000 loan increase?"

He said, "Hell no!"

So, I asked him, "Then what is your question?"

We both had a good laugh about the whole episode. But at the time it all happened, it was not a laughing matter for the bank or for the company.

While we were struggling with our start-up and restoring our business, Southwest Bank was thinking about going public. The possibility of our loan having to be downgraded was a real concern because it could cause serious problems for the bank's plans. There was no way we could fix our financial position without additional financing from another source. By all measure, our financing needs were beyond what we could reasonably expect any commercial bank to cover, even as good as Southwest Bank was.

Just about that time, a new small investment bank, Pauli & Co., was getting started in St. Louis and the principal, Chris Pauli, claimed he could actually take us public. At the time, we had not fully developed our vision of how we would revolutionize the entire carbon fiber industry. We were more concerned with solving the immediate problems and had just started to develop our long-term strategy. We were in a very difficult spot. An initial public offering (IPO) option appeared to be a viable solution.

The plant was still not fully operational. We had every engineer working on the equipment problems. I also moved the engineering vice president to the plant manager position. In the middle of these problems, I went on a vacation that I had promised Mary for some time. I called in every day from Hawaii to get a report on the past twenty-four hours and discuss plans for that day. Things were just not improving.

When I returned, the first thing I did was to visit the plant. When I went in the plant manager's office, I noticed that his desk was covered with religious displays, all looking for God's help. I certainly did not have a problem with his religious conviction, and I agreed that we needed some help. But it became clear that we were down to our last hope: divine intervention. It was time for me to take direct control of the situation. Unfortunately, our plant manager could not overcome his frustration and in spite of my reassurance, he decided to resign.

Going Public – ZOLT Traded on NASDAQ

It was very unfortunate that at the moment when we were trying to sort out our financing options, we did not have the luxury of choosing among many. The most likely option became the IPO, so we decided to go forward with the public stock offering in June of 1992.

Going through our IPO was a learning experience. The first step was to prepare a prospectus. Drafting of the prospectus was a group project, including the investment bankers and their lawyers, along with the company representatives and our lawyer(s) at a bare minimum. Usually there were some other people who added nothing to the process but bill time.

To begin the preparation of the prospectus, we had to define what would be included in the new public company from the private company, which was entirely owned by me personally. The business, itself, was clearly the prime asset. However, our headquarters was in a separate corporation, intended to provide rental income for Mary and me after retirement. We also had just started negotiations to acquire a carbon fiber line from Courtaulds in Coventry, England, to be modified to become our experimental line. The stealth patent had just been reissued according to my recommendations, and its value was not yet clear. For a number of reasons, the ownership of the patent was intended to be split between the company and me. I decided to include everything to maximize the asset value of the public company, with one exception. I personally retained the fifty percent ownership in the stealth patent and included fifty percent in the public company to avoid future conflict of interest.

The required contents of the prospectus were well defined, a description of the company, its business plans, and its historical performance. All information needed to help to convince investors to buy the company shares. This I could understand, but there were many legal constraints and the "risk factors" that served as warnings to investors of potential negative outcomes and risks. As a first-time participant in the public financing process, the preparation of the prospectus was strange experience. However, I realized that selling shares needed to be on a low profile, and everyone needed to be protected from potential claims from shareholders in case the company does poorly or fails.

The prospectus writing did not go smoothly and took far longer than it should have. I hired the law firm used for the Stackpole acquisition contract preparation. Unfortunately, they were inexperienced in the public financing area, and it showed very quickly. I got an emergency call from the attorney working on our deal.

He started by saying, "You have a problem."

I said, "I thought we were working together, so *we* have a problem."

As it turned out, we had missed a public hearing when we were building the Missouri Research Park plant, which was partially financed with an Industrial Revenue Bond. He was technically correct, but the government's lawyers had confirmed that financing without a public hearing was approved by the State. Our lawyer decided to prove them wrong instead of going forward.

After wasting much time, I asked him to propose language for how to handle this in the prospectus. He proposed the following:

"***Bond Default:*** The Company misappropriated $2 million …." In plain English, I stole the money.

Obviously this was not only unacceptable to me, but the investment banker would not even consider an offering with this language in the prospectus. Our investment banker suggested a new lawyer, Tom Litz. I immediately contacted him, and we met to discuss our situation. Tom was able to deal with this issue and asked me if I had anything else. I told him about the plant explosion. He thought he could take care of that as well. As long as there were no other issues, he was ready to take over. So, after more than a month delay, we were getting ready to go forward with a new team.

While the offering was on a temporary hold, I followed up with Courtaulds on the offer to sell their carbon fiber line to Zoltek. Courtaulds had entered into the carbon fiber business early in the 1970s. They had been one of the early producers of carbon fibers, but everything about their plant was inefficient and expensive. When Mitsubishi Chemical decided to enter the carbon fiber business, Courtaulds offered to sell them their carbon fiber products at a discount from the prevailing carbon fiber market price if Mitsubishi did not enter into production. This was not a good deal for Courtaulds, and they decided to exit the contract by turning over their plant in Sacramento, California to Mitsubishi Chemical and demolishing the Coventry, England plant if Mitsubishi Chemical let them void the sales contract. By the time I went to Coventry, the plant was already shut down, and they were in the final stages of decommissioning before the demolishing was to start. We needed to make a decision fast.

After reviewing the line design with our engineering team, we decided to use the hardware, but we needed to design our own control system and replace the electric motors. I returned to England within a week and made the deal to acquire all the ovens, furnaces, and winders. I also acquired auxiliary equipment that I thought we could use. All these, fully disassembled and loaded on a ship, for $150,000. We then needed to design an addition to the MRP building, which was still under construction, to house the line.

Once Tom Litz was on board, we were able to modify the project to include the commercial carbon fiber concept and continue the IPO preparation. After the prospectus was completed and while the preliminary (the Red Herring) version of the prospectus was getting printed, we prepared the shareholder presentation. The presentation format was less rigid, but still limited about potential future outlook. It was generally used as the outline for the verbal sales presentation. A hard copy was very rarely left with the potential investors.

We had many discussions about how to present our story, what assets to include in the public company, what stock symbol to choose, and a number of other options. In a normal process, a company would use some private financing to reach a level of performance where the existing business and demonstrated strategy could support the highest possible revenue and profit projections, thereby maximizing the initial public offering share price. We were not in a good position and looking back, we were way too small and too disorganized to go public at that time.

I also had to select a board of directors. There were a number of criteria for the selection of directors. In my case, the major concern was that there were way too many risks inherent in our business strategy, and a possible failure would reflect poorly on prospective board members. The initial board members were friends and local associates in the composite world: friend and banker, Linn Bealke; old friend, Jim Betts; local business executive, Charlie Dill; and composite associates, Jim Dorr and John Kardos. I, of course, continued, but Mary resigned from the board. The initial directors, with one change when Jim Dorr left the board for health reasons in 1999 and was then replaced by John McDonnell, supported me for the next fourteen difficult years. They not only gave me moral support and business advice, but Linn Bealke, John McDonnell, and Charlie Dill joined me in making significant personal investment when we really needed it.

While we worked on the IPO preparation, we were making progress on the plant start-up. It is not unusual to experience equipment problems, training issues, and process adjustments, and we were able to deal with most of them. There was nothing out of the ordinary that would be difficult to fix. However, the fires in the oxidizing ovens continued to be our biggest problem. We were getting further and further behind on our shipments and recovering the required inventory levels. Just as big a problem was that we could not represent to potential investors that the plant was operational. This could blow up the IPO. It was getting critical.

The most serious problem-customer was Goodrich. Fairly quickly we were able to catch up with the military program because we were able to recover some inventory from the Lowell plant. Our turn to begin shipping our annual share for the B747-400 brakes contract to Goodrich was coming up, and we were not ready. Everyone in the company was under extreme pressure.

Dick McMurry and his wife came through St. Louis on their vacation. We were going to have dinner, but first, Dick wanted to check our progress in starting our plant. When he realized we were having problems, he confronted me about how much trouble we would be causing with our late deliveries. I assured him that I would do everything not to fail him. I also predicted we would become his best supplier. He was not happy, but he did believe me and promised to give us time to solve our problems. But Dick never confused friendship and business, so we cancelled dinner. Our business relationship turned out well for both of us, and we remained good friends.

Finally, in September, we finished the investor presentation, and we were ready for the road show. This was where the company would make its investor presentations and answer questions. The investment bankers lined up group meetings and one-on-one meetings with more significant potential investors. We made the first presentation to the investment bank sales team, so they would know what potential investors heard when they would call with questions. If all went well, the road show could be done in as fast as one week, but we were not that lucky.

Our investment banker suggested that in order to demonstrate we had management depth, we should include our industrial business and our carbon fiber sales managers in the road show presentation. They also asked for our accounting manager to be there for support. For a thirty-minute presentation, three people were way too many, but we went along with the recommendation. We started out in Los Angeles. At the first breakfast meeting, there was only one person there, and I am sure he had come for the free breakfast. Our presentation did not go well at all. When we were finished, I asked our banker representative why there was only one person at the meeting. He claimed that it was because our presentation was so badly done.

I agreed with his assessment of our presentation, but I asked, "How is it that so many people knew it was going to be so bad since this was our first presentation?"

The silent answer was clear; if anything went wrong, it was going to be the company's fault, not the banker's.

After the first meeting, we got a call that our investment banker's key sales person had died the night before. The bankers huddled and with some delay, we continued to San Francisco. The lunch presentation in San Francisco was delayed to allow the bankers to regroup and contact the investors to confirm delays of the meetings. We did a little better with the presentation until our industrial business manager, standing at the podium jiggling the change in his pocket, proudly claimed that his group was the cash cow for the company. One of the investors asked how much cash the business was generating. He had no idea and called on Cheryl Rene for an answer.

While Cheryl knew the answer, she correctly claimed that she was instructed by the bankers not to answer specific questions and turned the question over to the investment bank representative, who was not ready or able to answer any financial details. That is all one of the potential investors needed; he stood up and said, "Good luck," and walked out. I do not believe he invested in Zoltek in the IPO, but in later offerings, he always participated.

The next morning, we went on one-on-one meetings at investors' offices. These meetings went better. I did all the talking for the company, and these meetings involved more spontaneous discussions, not the structured presentations. At one point, the banker's salesman said that the investor we were about to meet had taken a significant loss on the last deal.

I asked, "Why would he see you after that experience?"

His answer was quite revealing. "No one knows which deal might be a big hit, and he does not want to miss a possible home run."

In other words: Greed! That explained a lot about the entire process.

The following week, we went to New York. The results were not much better. It looked like the deal was dead, but we had too much time and money invested to give up. The bankers continued to call people and tried to put an optimistic face on the possible outcome. We were still having start-up problems, so, to some extent, a delay was welcome.

After about two weeks of no activity, an eternity during the offering process, I got a call from our banker that he wanted to make one more attempt. He lined up some investors for lunch at the 21 Club in New York. I told him I would not take the whole crew and just go by myself.

I had set a goal that the oxidizer ovens had to have been running for at least forty-eight hours without interruption before I would represent to the investors that our plant was running. We reached that benchmark the morning I went to New York. This helped for me to appear more confident and convincing in my presentation.

The lunch meeting was quite interesting. There were more people there than we expected. After the meeting, people were much friendlier and treated me as if I was one of them. Both of these were good signs, and there were enough indications to buy the desired number of shares. The offering was completed that day.

The last and most important step was the pricing, which takes place on the last day of the road show once a sufficient number of buyers make their commitments. We were trying to sell shares at $12.00 per share, but the demand for shares was not strong. So, the transaction was completed on November 6, 1992, at $4.00 per share. We sold 1,100,000, about one-third of the company. The company's share of the proceeds was $4,070,000. Based on standard accounting rules, the fees and costs of an offering were deducted from the gross proceeds, and they were not visible on the company's financial statement.

The money we raised was quite disappointing, but enough to continue the active projects and pay down part of our loans. Also, just as important, we became a public company. The final version of the prospectus was printed, and it became the permanent offering document. After the initial public offering, the market value of Zoltek was $16,800,000.

Becoming a public company almost exactly five years after entering the carbon fiber business changed everything for Zoltek. Financing had been a major problem all along, but to achieve the revolutionizing of the carbon fiber business would be impossible without a ready source of capital. Being a public company was the only long-term option we had to assure the availability of capital. Also, as a public company, we enjoyed a lot more visibility, which was essential to execute on our strategy. But nothing was free in the world and being a public company came with significant costs and lots of work.

With the IPO behind us, we concentrated on business. Our capacity in the new plant increased by a factor of four, and we were able to become current with customer shipments within a few weeks. At that point, we were ready for additional business from our existing product line and customer base. We were also ready to develop and refine our commercial carbon fiber strategy and begin making it a reality.

Once the IPO was completed, the work and responsibility of being a public company had just begun. By regulations, the company had to publish a quarterly report (10Q) and an annual report (10K), all on a timely basis. The preparation of legal documents and financial reports was also a group effort, involving company representatives, lawyers, and auditors. In addition to dealing with auditors and lawyers each quarter, the company needed to communicate with investors.

This was where Andy Wilson, my "scribe" as I liked to call him, came into the picture. In addition to the SEC required reports, there were the quarterly earnings (press) releases and the glossy annual reports. These involved subtle legal considerations, as well as the need to present the company in as positive a light as possible. When all was going well, it was much easier to prepare these reports than when the company was having problems. In our case, we had many ups and downs, so our reports were difficult to prepare, but we did an effective job in presenting a positive view of our business. Our annual reports were high quality in content and appearance. We used our annual reports to communicate to the shareholders our unwavering confidence in our long-term strategy and ultimate success

Usually a day or two after the quarterly press release was sent out (almost always after the market closed), we would conduct a quarterly investor call. This was where friendly and unfriendly analysts and investors questioned the management in an open forum. These calls usually lasted for an hour, and depending on how the company was doing, it could be quite cordial, or it could be rancorous. Additionally, there was a need for me to talk constantly with individual investors, current as well as potential future shareholders.

One might think all of this was just too much trouble. However, for companies like Zoltek that required significant capital investments, being a public company was the only viable financing option.

What we did not know at the time was that the small size of our offering (i.e., the number of shares, just over one million, available for trading) exposed us to unscrupulous manipulation of our stock price. Almost from the beginning, our own investment bank's brokers were calling our plant engineers to engage them in improper conversations in order to conjure up some basis for either positive or negative rumors that would increase or drop the stock price to create trading profits for themselves. For example, one morning, a broker called an engineer at MRP. The engineer said that he could not talk right then because he was in a meeting with an EPA representative. By that afternoon, the rumor was that the EPA was about to shut down our plant.

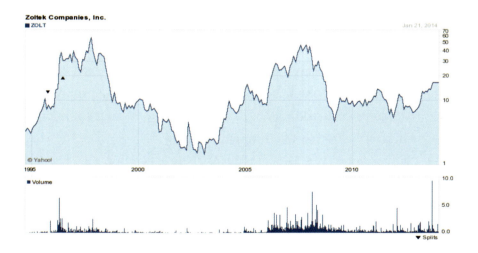

(Please note the share price on this chart is on a log scale)

These kinds of rumors were used to induce the selling or buying of a significant number of shares, enough to move the share price significantly. On a good rumor, the price would increase, and they would sell the shares, sometimes with huge gains, and then after they sold the shares, they would put on a short position and start a negative rumor. With only one million shares available for trading, it takes a very small amount of trading to cause large price swings.

Later, when we had around thirty million shares, which is still a relatively small number, the more sophisticated short sellers took over. Such manipulation caused confusion to legitimate shareholders and very negatively affected the company's ability for orderly public financing. This problem followed us all the way to the end.

The IPO was a temporary fix for both Zoltek and Southwest Bank. We, for the moment, cleaned up our financing situation. However, as we proceeded in developing and executing our strategy, we needed to rely on sufficient bank financing for a period, complemented by profits from our existing carbon fibers business. The parent company of Southwest Bank also successfully completed their IPO.

For me, personally, the IPO was a mixed blessing. It was certainly a gratifying achievement to create a highly productive company and take it public. I was also happy to remove the Zoltek loan as a potential obstacle to Southwest Bank's IPO. Although I always believed that it was necessary for Zoltek to have access to public financing. I was not yet prepared to deal with the work and communication requirements that came with being a public company. I had a lot to learn.

Mary

Mary with her mother and father

Wedding party—bridesmaids: Mary's sister, Patty (center),
Judy (left) and Vicki (right) – the two who introduced us in 1967.
Groomsmen from left to right: Mike Duffy, Dennis Fitzgerald and John Standal.

Mary meets my grandmother on her first trip to Hungary in 1969

Mary with Aunt Irén and Uncle Ede

Mary on cruise in 1983

Vacation in France

Vacation with friends, Jim and Diane Betts

Marta visits Mary at her travel office

Marta with her mother Joan, Mary and grandmother, Mary—celebrating Mother's Day

The Gallagher girls heading to Ireland

Marta and I

Father Joe with nieces Marta, Megan & Molly

Marta with her parents—Ken and Joan

Mary goes gray!

Marta and Mary

Mary and I with St. Louis County Executive, Gene McNary and his wife, Susan, on China Mission

Golf in Augusta National; Drew Baur, Jack Baumstark, Linn Bealke and I

Jack's and my answer to Drew's instructions on how to behave at Augusta—"If you want to play golf, wear either a jockstrap or pants, no shorts allowed. Only members can wear green jackets."

Linn and I relaxing after golf, which Linn usually won and before Gin game, which I usually won.

Bob Witterschein, who told me "You're confusing having checks with having money".

Drew and I—our last trip to Budapest together, on way to the bank golf trip to Scotland.

Peter Kiss and his wife, Ria, with Mary and me

Best friend, Laci and I

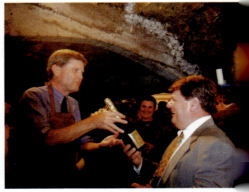

Friend and Board member, Jim Betts, bottling champaign in a wine cellar restaurant in Budapest

Section 5
Beginning of Commercial Carbon Fibers

Refocusing Zoltek

During the IPO process, we made the decision to enter into the production of continuous carbon fibers for composite reinforcement applications, like golf shafts, automobiles, and wind turbine blades. As we completed the IPO, Zoltek had three ongoing categories of business activity: the original equipment and services business, the newly acquired carbon fibers business, and the still-to-be-developed reinforcement-carbon-fiber technology business. Up until this time, we had operated Zoltek as a single entity, but it had become too much to handle and way too complicated for the size of our organization.

After we committed most of the company's resources and financing to the carbon fiber business, the equipment and services business suffered. The redesigning and refurbishing of the carbon fiber process equipment took too much time and energy away from their business, and their revenues declined significantly, approximately twenty-five percent, over the prior four years.

In 1993, in order to rebuild the division, we separated the Equipment and Services Division from the rest of our business. I appointed our star salesman/sales manager to run the business, and we moved all the people involved with the equipment and services business into the same location. With no more distractions, the work to repair and recondition the equipment that we had moved from Lowell was completed, I was expecting this business would recover quickly.

The best salesman did not necessarily make a good manager, that was certainly our case. The Equipment and Services Division stayed dormant, and people were unhappy with the new management arrangement. We started to lose key people, and the business needed my attention, but I could not allocate enough time to turn it around. I did make some personnel changes and removed the manager. I gave him a second chance to head up sales for the *Flexigraf* product line.

But by 1994, the damage was done. We lost one key sales person, and another was about to leave. The two of them, Bill Pfitzinger and Terry Hickey, approached me and expressed interest in acquiring the business. Selling this business was certainly a viable option because our carbon fiber revenue was starting to grow rapidly enough that we could replace the equipment and service revenues in one or two years.

After some consideration, I decided to go forward with a transaction with Bill and Terry. I am sure we could have found a buyer who would have paid substantially more for the business, but it was the best option for our employees and customers to sell the business to them, which we did. They were able to continue the business without any interruption and kept the team together.

Once the equipment business was gone, the *Flexigraf* business did not really fit with the carbon fiber business and our sales manager was not making any progress. The following year, we also sold the *Flexigraf* business to the same group. We essentially transferred these businesses at book value to give their company a good chance to succeed. I still meet with the two of them at least once a year. It is gratifying to see that most of our old employees are still there, and they have continued to build on our earlier success.

There was only one difficult issue. My brother-in-law has worked for the company, but he was negative and vocal about the carbon fiber acquisition, which caused a lot of distraction. After we sold the equipment business, he was in an awkward position and needed to find another job. I let him keep his Zoltek stock options and, I recently learned that Fr. Joe also gave him the shares he bought on his own. Unfortunately, consistent with his negative view of the carbon fiber business, he quickly sold his shares. If he would have waited two years, our shares had appreciated tenfold. Of course, I was blamed for this mistake, and this situation had caused a rift for Mary and me with him and the rest of her family.

The carbon fiber plant move to St. Louis was essentially completed and we were getting close to stabilizing our existing customer relationships. The lengthy problems we were having with the oxidizers ultimately turned out to have an amazingly simple solution, and we were in full production mode. Bob Waraksa, the production supervisor from Lowell, handled the training and filled in as plant manager until I could find a permanent plant manager. I handled the aircraft brake business and the existing carbon fiber customers. Our sales manager for carbon fibers was responsible for generating new business and to begin to look for potential commercial carbon fiber applications.

The continuous-carbon-fiber-production was new to Zoltek. There have been a number of carbon fiber companies with virtually unlimited finances and deep technical expertise, which had failed miserably in developing a cost effective carbon fiber production facility because the process was much more difficult and dangerous than it appeared on the surface. Ignoring these difficulties, the Zoltek team, without any prior knowledge of carbon fiber technology and minimum financial strength, but with lots of energy and confidence embarked on this project.

By this time, Peter Kiss was managing the engineering team. Peter was an excellent equipment designer, and I was pretty good at chemical reaction process technology. Peter and I made a good team. Based on our experience with the batch process for carbon fibers manufacturing and studying the available literature, I oversaw the process chemistry and definitions. Peter dealt with the process control technology and the equipment design. Our first task was to modify the Courtaulds equipment to a million pounds per year production pilot line. We did that while we were constructing the MRP building. Once the MRP building was completed, the engineering team was responsible for the installation of the pilot line, which was already on its way from the Courtaulds Coventry, England facility.

While the pilot plant construction was progressing, my first order of business continued to be solidifying our relationship with our aircraft brake customers. Our largest customer was Goodrich, and we were doing well with them, but we still had some work to do. Carbon Industrie was making fast tracks with their three-dimensional process for preforms. A group of companies, Bendix, Goodyear, Dunlop, HITCO, and Carbon Loraine were active in the aircraft brake business to various degrees and with limited success. I worked with all of them.

Goodrich represented the quickest and highest potential business. The C-5 Transport brakes were produced in Santa Fe Springs, California. The first person I called before the acquisition was Arnie Huntington, the purchasing manager for this plant. He lived up to his word, and we maintained our qualifications, and remained their single source supplier. His positive response had been very helpful, and we worked well together. He was helpful in teaching me to understand the pending Boeing B747-400 technology and its business potential. I was a regular visitor to this facility. After our initial meeting in Reno, I also had the opportunity to get to know Dick McMurry well.

Goodrich was building a new plant in Pueblo, Colorado for the B747-400 brake program. Once the plant construction was completed, Dick moved there, and the center of power for Goodrich carbon brakes moved with him. I also switched my own attention to Pueblo. Before he moved, he hired a replacement manager, Orel Kiphart, for the Santa Fe Springs facility.

As with any new and complex plant, Pueblo had its startup problems and a number of personnel changes. It was hard to get anything done, but slowly the plant normalized, and the qualification of our fiber began. By early 1992, we were at the position to start selling full production quantities of our fibers. Goodrich requirements were projected to explode, which was the reason for increasing our capacity when we moved from Lowell. Actually, we quadrupled our capacity of the Pyron production, which was enough to cover all of Goodrich's requirements for several years. Dick wanted to have two suppliers, and he wanted to split sixty/forty. Initially, we were to get the forty percent share.

One day in February 1992, I met Dick in his office, wearing a coat and tie. It was a beautiful day, and Dick looked disappointed as he told me I was not dressed for golf. I told him I could change that. We headed for the Pueblo Country Club. I bought a golf shirt and rented clubs. This turned out to be my best customer golf game ever. We played for $1 a hole. It took me a few holes to get into the game and lost the first three holes, but won the next thirteen. We changed the bet to $5 a hole for the last two holes, which I lost, a perfect ending by beating Dick handily, but did not win any money from my customer. I became such a regular visitor that for a while, I joined the Pueblo Country Club, and Dick and I played just about every time I went to Pueblo.

In 1994, Dick was promoted to the Troy, Ohio, headquarters, and Orel was promoted to replace him in Pueblo. I called Orel to congratulate him and told him I wanted to see him after he had a chance to settle into his new position to discuss long-term plans.

On my first visit, Orel and I played a round of golf. When we returned to the clubhouse, I told him my assessment of the brake business and its fiber supply. First, as the aircraft brake business grew, Goodrich would need to have a reliable supplier with stable competitive pricing. Second, if he maintained the sixty/forty supply share with two suppliers and expected each to supply its share continuously, it would be very costly for the suppliers, and it would naturally lead to higher prices. I would prefer to get the forty percent share at the highest price I could get, not the sixty percent at a competitive price. He asked me to give him my proposal, which I prepared that evening. What I proposed was a minimum eighty percent share of Goodrich requirements. The next day, he lined up a meeting with his management team to present my proposal.

In a week or so, I received a request for proposal with the exact terms and conditions I had proposed. I assumed he sent this to my competitor as well, which really upset me. In about two weeks, he called me. He wanted me to see him right away and meet at the Colorado Springs Airport. When I got there, he told me that upper management had authorized him to negotiate a one hundred percent supply agreement if I wanted it and was able to meet their supply needs. We came to an agreement and before the year ended, we signed a ten-year exclusive supply agreement. For the duration of this agreement, Zoltek was able to maintain stable prices and never missed a shipment.

Bendix was the second largest customer and potential. They had most of the fighter-jet brake business, and they were very unhappy. The previous Stackpole Fibers management delayed shipments and steadily increased prices to a ridiculous level. Initially Bendix did not even want to talk to me, and they were looking to establish a second source of supply. After I assured them that I was not like the previous management and had lowered the price to a reasonable level, they finally were willing to talk. It took several months, but we gained their confidence and won their business. We still supply one-hundred percent of the fibers for their fighter-jet business.

But, for whatever reason, our attempts to expand into their commercial aircraft brake business development just never went smoothly. They were trying to compete with Goodrich and Messier-Bugatti with a similar, but more complex process. We supported their development by carbonizing their preformance, but every time something went wrong, they tried to find a way to blame us. Bendix was trying to have all the manufacturing steps, except the final chemical vapor deposition, done by their suppliers. Bendix was its own worst enemy. Their purchasing department sent out a request for proposals for every step of the process, and they were going to use different suppliers for each step. I considered this to be a completely impossible system for maintaining any kind of quality control and accountability.

To make matters worse, the purchasing manager was trying to give the business to his favorite vendors, and Zoltek was not on that list. At one point, a quality engineer came to our plant, and we caught him writing down details of our carbonization process from our process log book. We asked him to leave and did not allow him to return to our plant. Impossible to believe, but he called me a year or so later to ask for a job. When I told him it was out of the question, based on what he had done, his excuse was that his management had instructed him to do it.

In the middle of all this turmoil, Allied-Signal acquired Bendix. On his first visit to Bendix, the new CEO made a number of management changes, giving us hope for the future relationship. But we never got any part of their commercial aircraft brakes business at that time. They have been quite unsuccessful in capturing a significant share of this business. Eventually, they combined with Dunlop, also a difficult company to work with, and they somehow won the A-380 program. Today they have only about eight percent of the commercial aircraft brake business.

As hard as I tried, I could not change their attitude toward Zoltek. They continued to refer to the shabby treatment they had received from Stackpole Fibers. It was unfortunate for both our companies because we could have saved them a lot of headache and money and at the time, their business would have been highly appreciated by Zoltek.

As it turned out, they continue to be unsuccessful in getting a significant share of the commercial aircraft market. Since then, Honeywell has acquired Allied-Signal, and we recently started working with them again.

The next major potential customer I needed to get to know was Messier-Bugatti. Their plant, which was the Carbon Industrie facility, was located outside Lyon, France, and their headquarters were in Paris. I have not met them and had never done business with them before. They did their product development with our European competitor, and I did not think they knew much about Zoltek. I started to visit them on a regular basis. They were always very nice to me, and I enjoyed our visits. It was impressive to have fine wine for lunch at the plant; it was the French way of life. I met Bernard Malassine, a very nice and interesting man, and he was receptive to Zoltek becoming a supplier. He later became the U.S. representative for Messier-Bugatti, and he promoted the idea within the company to utilize our fiber for their U.S. business.

Messier-Bugatti was always concerned about our financial position. I finally fought back and told them they should worry more about Courtaulds keeping the acrylic fiber business going with all the financial problems they were having. If they went under, the whole industry would be left with no supply of qualified precursor. I promised that we would have our own precursor before that happened, so it would be to their advantage to start working with Zoltek.

Two favorable things happened. Messier-Bugatti was successful in getting the Boeing C-17 contract, and Bernard moved to the U.S. to build a new plant in Walton, Kentucky. At that point, Bernard initiated the qualification process for our fibers, which were still made from the Courtaulds precursor.

In addition to the aircraft brake business we developed a miscellaneous specialty and smaller potential applications. We also supplied Stackpole's two divisions with fibers at a highly profitable level.

Another new business was the milled fibers used in the automobile airbag applications. The first airbags were based on what they called pyrotechnic technology. They were actually operated by a rocket fuel explosion. Carbon fibers assisted in the uniformity of the fire and held the resulting char together. Our customer was TRW. They had built an underground plant in Mesa, Arizona, to assemble the propellant cartridge. The plant was operated completely with robots to eliminate injury to workers in case of explosion during the production of the propellant. Our batch-processed fiber was the perfect fiber for this application.

This was a highly profitable business for Zoltek, particularly because we were using the remnants from the Goodrich preform process. It was much more efficient to carbonize and provided for high-volume production, significantly reducing our cost. One of our competitors finally caught on to what we were doing and told our customer, TRW, that we were using reprocessed fibers that were curly. Theoretically, he was correct about recycling, but the fiber was never altered by Goodrich, and we had traceability and quality documentation.

The purchasing agent called me to ask if our competitor was telling the truth. I told him if he could find a single curly 150-micron long fiber, I would take all of our fibers back. He said that is what he wanted to hear, and that was the end of it. Unfortunately for Zoltek, the pyrotechnic style airbags became obsolete very quickly, and the need for carbon fibers ended. But it was fun while it lasted.

While we were selling the batch-processed fibers that we called Panex-30, we were working diligently on the technology for and the design of the pilot line for the continuous carbon fiber process.

We did reaction kinetics studies of the oxidation process and studied the chemistry from precursor to the finished carbon fibers. Through this effort, we developed the process control concept and Peter, with his engineering staff, began the design of the process control software. Simultaneously we also started the hardware design that would facilitate a more open and safer process. At the same time, our objective was to be able to build production lines at a fraction of the prevailing capital requirements.

The Commercial Carbon Fiber Concept

It did not take long to realize that the carbon fiber industry, as it then existed, would never be competitive for commercial applications. Also, as it became more and more obvious that the government/aerospace cabal just would not do business with Zoltek, we needed to look for other opportunities. The commercial market was clearly where we had to go. It was obvious that the price had to come down, but how? In addition to price, the business models for aerospace and commercial applications were quite different.

The chemistry for aerospace carbon fibers and commercial carbon fibers was virtually identical, so the savings had to come from lowering the processing cost and the capital equipment cost. The required cost change we were seeking was dramatic. The generally expected selling price in a commercial application, to effectively compete with other materials, was $5 per pound ($11 per kilogram), which was about eighty percent lower than the prevailing price of carbon fibers in the 1980s. This difference could not be overcome by operational improvement or sales volume. It would take an entirely new concept that the incumbent companies had not been willing or able to embrace. This goal was a very tall order for any company and should have been all but impossible for a small company like Zoltek.

We started with a blank page and built up from the very beginning of the process to the end. First, we needed to define the product we were to produce. Clearly, we could not reduce cost this dramatically and still make an identical product. Therefore, we concentrated on the critical product performance: tensile strength and modulus (stiffness). For production efficiency, we widened the variability range and increased the strand (tow) size to 50,000 filaments versus the prevailing 12,000 filaments configuration. We also introduced the "commercial-carbon-fibers" name to differentiate our products from the "aerospace-carbon-fibers."

The manufacturing process started with the acrylic fiber precursor. The precursor fiber had a significant impact on the final carbon fiber properties and the cost. However, the basic chemistry and the general process of textile acrylic fiber and precursor fiber were quite similar. In textile applications, acrylic fiber was a substitute for natural wool, and the manufacturing process simulated the natural wool properties, which would not do well as a precursor. However, the process could be changed inexpensively to improve the textile acrylic process to produce credible precursor. In our initial carbon fiber process development, we started with the Courtaulds precursor fibers, which were far from ideal. We had already started to look for a way to develop our own precursor with better properties.

It was a stroke of luck that Courtaulds decided to exit the carbon fiber business and that they were dismantling the Coventry, UK, plant. The precursor polymer was manufactured in Grimsby, and the polymer was shipped to Coventry, where the finished acrylic fiber was produced. I was not interested in the precursor production equipment because it did not meet our concept. But the carbon fiber line was perfect for our pilot line. While it was not exactly what we were designing, it was close enough for us to easily modify it. It was also a full production line, so we could get into production immediately. By 1994, we were doing trial runs of continuous carbon fiber production on the pilot line using a modified Courtaulds precursor.

The carbon fiber produced from the Courtaulds precursor had reasonable mechanical properties, but poor handling and way too many broken fibers. This was a result of their process and equipment problems. We helped to make improvements, and we were learning what we would need to do to develop a better quality precursor for our own use. In the meantime, we started to produce and sell these developmental carbon fibers into the thermoplastic compounding business that required short fibers, cut to one quarter inch long or milled to 150-micron. This was our first commercial reinforcement carbon fiber that we introduced in the market. We called it Panex-33.

Another significant difference between the commercial and aerospace carbon fibers markets was how fast the commercial applications could develop and how quickly the market size could grow. An aerospace application took years to develop and testing could take many more years. In total, it might take a decade or more from planning a new airplane to the first flight. But commercial products could be developed and introduced in the market in a few months and ramp up rapidly. We needed a strategy to support this difference.

Once we had demonstrated that we were able to produce carbon fibers with the required mechanical properties in a continuous process, we took the next step. Our engineering team developed the equipment specifications and began to design our unique process equipment.

The design objectives were: safe operation, low capital cost, ease of operation, and six-month-or-less installation time. Ultimately we were successful in designing our equipment at a cost as low as ten percent of what other carbon fiber producers had spent on a line, and we were able to add lines in six months that would take our competitors eighteen months or longer to install.

An earlier version of the below graph was presented in our 1994 annual report to represent the concept behind our commercial carbon fiber strategy. We used this chart both for financial presentations and for marketing. The key concept was that the successful utilization of carbon fibers in commercial applications was definitely price sensitive.

When we made our strategy known to potential customers, there was immediate enthusiasm. Besides gaining new business in thermoplastic reinforcement applications, we initiated a number of development projects. We established ten application categories with specific strategies in each. These categories were: Sporting Goods, Transportation, Automotive, Alternate Energy, Infrastructure, Marine, Construction, Friction, Industrial, and Electronics Applications.

There were two additional significant differences between the aerospace and the commercial markets that the reduction in carbon fiber price by itself would not resolve. First, there were a number of processing steps between carbon fiber and the finished composite product whether it was used in an airplane or in a golf shaft. Each step was generally performed by a different company, and the intermediate product was marked up significantly in each step. The problem was that the added cost was not nearly as big a deterrent in aerospace as it was in commercial applications.

Second, several products made with carbon fibers were exorbitantly high priced, either because these had a significant performance advantage or simply because of the marketing hype associated with carbon fibers. I would be the last person to begrudge someone making significant profit on carbon fibers, but if the high prices limited the size of the market, it would hurt the democratization of carbon fibers.

A *Wall Street Journal* reporter called me one day and asked my comments relating to these issues. He was questioning me as to why carbon-fiber bicycles cost as much as $3,000 when carbon fibers were available at such low prices. I tried to explain that they did not need to be so expensive, but that the bicycle manufacturers were taking advantage of the unique properties of carbon fibers, and a small percent of bicycle buyers were willing to pay for it. I was trying to get him to rethink his article to point out that the bicycle producers should be able to sell their product much cheaper, but he would not have any of it. So, I finally told him that we, meaning the carbon fiber manufacturers, just like to screw with the bicycle makers. That is what he wanted to hear, and he was gone, and that is the only comments from our lengthy discussion he put in his article. I certainly thought it was funny and had a laugh about it, but on the serious side, I knew we needed to develop a plan for how to deal with these issues.

I was convinced by two of our directors to pursue a government supported development contract with the Advanced Research Projects Agency (ARPA), which was a government agency supporting the aerospace industry. Among our partners were McDonnell Douglas, Naval

Research Laboratory, and Washington University. Our project was to demonstrate the use of our Panex-33 in a low-cost process to produce aircraft floor panels. It was an interesting project because commercial carbon fibers would be perfect for many aircraft interior applications. After winning approval by ARPA for our project and before we received the contract, we were summoned to a meeting to Washington D.C. for a special project review by a newly employed project director.

It was a standard operating procedure at ARPA, like so many government agencies, to hire people who failed in private business. This new project director was a perfect specimen. He headed up a failed carbon fiber business with one of our carbon fiber competitors. We were familiar with this bad actor, and we knew he was going to try to derail our project.

It was a memorable meeting. Seven of us from the project team gathered at the ARPA headquarters in a tiny meeting room. This guy came in angry, dressed in a pink shirt, which turned out to be a major mistake. He gave us thirty minutes to make our case. We decided to have one of our team, who had a well-prepared presentation about the project, to start. As soon as he began, in mid-sentence, he was interrupted and in no uncertain terms, this flunky told him he had no idea what he was talking about. After a few minutes of his venting, our presenter started back right at the word where he was first interrupted. This went on for twenty minutes. At that point, our flunky became quite agitated, and his pink shirt was turning red from sweat, and his face was turning purple. He told us that none of us had any idea what we were talking about. He then went down the line insulting and dismissing everyone in the room.

I was the last one, and he told me I knew nothing about carbon fibers. At that point, I had had enough. I said, "You called us here less than twenty-four hours ago, and I prepared a presentation, which I worked on until 2:00 in the morning. So, at this point, I do not care what you think, but you will sit there with your mouth shut and listen to my presentation!"

He was stunned, but kept his mouth shut as I made my presentation. His face was getting more and more purple with rage, and he was really sweating. His pink shirt became red from his shoulder to his belt. When I finished, the meeting ended. We never heard from him again, and we received the contract. And we successfully completed the project. Zoltek received some compensation for our work that was helpful in reducing our carbon fiber line start-up cost. More important, we did gain some important visibility in the composite industry.

During 1994 and 1995, we had a great number of potential customers who came to see us in order to discuss various applications that could become economically viable if our price objectives were met. Qualification, testing, and production planning for developoping a new application take significant time. In 1995, enthusiasm was high, and our carbon fiber sales were growing significantly as a percent of prior year revenue. But our carbon fiber sales in 1995 were still at only $13 million.

Zoltek's stock price, however, reflected this newly won enthusiasm, and there was a general expectation of significant and instantaneous growth. We decided to split our stock three for two, and the share price reached $25.83 per share, approximately $160 million market capitalization in the fourth quarter. This price represented $38.74 per share pre-split or almost a tenfold increase in three years after the IPO.

Although I was always optimistic about the potential for carbon fibers and Zoltek's long-range value, the market value was overly aggressive, considering that we were not yet finished with our strategic objectives and had only one experimental production line running.

The Hungarian Acquisition

One of the most important components of our strategic objectives was the development of our own acrylic fiber precursor. Early in our entry into the carbon fiber business, it became clear that the precursor would be the key to achieving our low-cost objective. It took little over two times the weight of acrylic fiber for the unit weight of carbon fiber. In other words, any savings in precursor cost were doubled in the cost reduction of carbon fiber. While we were developing the process and design of our unique carbon fiber lines, I concentrated on looking into the precursor situation.

The popularity of acrylic fibers in the textile market had been steadily losing ground, which should have made conversion from textiles to precursor production an attractive business proposition. Stackpole Fibers had tested DuPont's Orlon as a potentially viable precursor and had successfully oxidized it. That was a good reason for me to start my investigation with DuPont. I also reviewed the only other two available U.S. producers of acrylic fibers: Monsanto and American Cyanamid. Monsanto's acrylic fiber did not work because their basic chemistry was incompatible with the carbon fiber process. The only other U.S. option, American Cyanamid's Santa Rosa, Florida, plant, was in process of being shut down, and there were many environmental issues that eliminated them as a viable option.

After Peter's earlier report, I contacted DuPont again to find out more about Magyar Viscosa Rt. (Hungarian Rayon, Inc.). They confirmed that the Hungarian company was considered to be their best qualified licensee. DuPont actually hired the Hungarian team to commission the plants of the Indian and the Indonesian licensees. With this endorsement, I targeted this company for acquisition and to develop our precursor production. This facility also would offer the opportunity to establish a foothold in Europe. An additional strong point was that I was familiar with Hungary, its culture, and its language.

In the spring of 1994, I contacted the general manager of Magyar Viscosa, György (George or Gyuri) Pászty, to arrange a meeting. My initial purpose was to evaluate the management and the facility and to assess what it would take to acquire the company. I met a few of the managers, including György Bakos, the CFO, for dinner and spent a full day at the plant. I was reasonably impressed, but there were complications with which I needed to get more familiar.

The communist system started to break up in May 1989 when Hungary allowed several hundred East Germans to take refuge in the West German Embassy and allowed them to leave for Austria. By November 1989, the East German people were freely allowed to cross the gates of the Berlin Wall to West Germany. The final blow to European communism was when the Berlin Wall completely came down in 1992. By 1994, the privatization of industry, the means of production owned by the government, had already started in some of the communist countries, including Hungary. I was convinced that the Magyar Viscosa plant was destined for privatization, and we could acquire the company at an affordable price.

When I returned to St. Louis, I had a lot to think about. The DuPont acrylic plant was in fairly good condition. It was moved to Hungary from Ireland five years earlier and only started up in 1992. The company used "Mavilon" as its brand name. The plant had a

25,000-metric ton acrylic fibers capacity. There was another acrylic plant, based on technology from SNIA, an Italian acrylic fiber company. This production unit, with 10,000 metric tons of capacity, was in not quite as good condition and employed a different technology. If we could convert both to precursor, these plants' combined capacity could produce approximately 17,500 metric tons of carbon fibers, which, at that time, was about equal to the entire world's existing carbon fiber production capacity. That was the good news.

The bad news was that the plant also included several other, unrelated operations. There was a nylon plant, a cellulose facility, and several plastic processing operations. They all had obsolete technology, quality that was not suitable by Western standards, and there were too many employees. The original facility had started as a brick manufacturing plant. In 1942, it was rebuilt into a rayon fibers plant, which was then shut down in the 1980s. Later, nylon was added, and the last major addition was the acrylic fiber plants. Other than the acrylic facilities, the plant was in very bad shape. There were other problems resulting from the communist idea of making the industry and citizens interdependent for a variety of services, such as water, sewage treatment, and steam for residential heating. The company also owned a number of apartments and a small hotel, all in disrepair.

The company was owned by the Hungarian State Property Management, but it had gone into bankruptcy two years earlier. A number of banks and large venders were owed over $60 million. After recapitalization, the company had emerged from bankruptcy in 1993 as a shareholder-owned company. In the recapitalization process, the State Property Management Agency ownership was reduced to 50.1 percent, and the State Development Agency owned ten percent of the shares. Part of the debt and significant account payables were converted in part to shares and in part to long-term debt. In total, there were eight banks and three supplier companies that owned the remaining 39.9 percent of the shares. The largest owner was Central-European International Bank (CIB), which owned 25.74 percent.

It would have been easy and certainly justifiable to walk away from this situation. However, with no precursor of our own, our entire long-term strategy and possibly our company's survival would be questionable. With political changes moving rapidly and with the likelihood of Hungary quickly becoming part of the European Union, Hungary had a great potential to be the European base for Zoltek. All considered, I decided to go forward in a two-prong approach; first, to get to know the management and the people at the company and second, to try to work the privatization and the financial deal on my own.

I felt confident that, with my Hungarian background, this would be the best European option for us. I also must admit, the idea of introducing carbon fiber technology to Hungary gave me personal satisfaction.

After the first couple meetings with the Magyar Viscosa upper management team, it was clear that they were dedicated to saving the company, which had just come out of bankruptcy, and less than one year later, was close to returning to serious financial trouble. They had lived under communism for almost fifty years, and suddenly the world was changing. They lacked the experience to work within a free economy, one free of government support and control. The idea of being part of a publicly traded U.S. company was a huge mystery to them.

Their primary markets for the company's products were the Hungarian textile industry, and over fifty percent of their products were exported to East European countries and Russia. Their annual revenue was $45 million, but the business was losing money. Their markets were rapidly changing. Privatization of the textile industry in Hungary was counterproductive. Instead of strengthening the industry, privatization facilitated the shutdown of the textile industry as European Union imports became readily available at competitive prices. The management team did not have an answer as to how to save the company. Zoltek was the only identified possible savior. However, they were more interested in financial support than buying into the carbon fiber concept. So, my job was to convince the management that abandoning their current business for the new technology of carbon fibers was the right path to saving the company.

On the financial side, the CIB Bank held the majority of the non-government shares and the most significant loan position, so they were the most critical to making any deal happen. The State Property Privatization and Management Agency, as it came to be known, was equally important with their 50.1 percent ownership, so I concentrated on these two owners. The total capitalization value on the company's books was $43 million debt, and the shares (converted debt) were valued at $24 million. Initial attempts to negotiate a reduced payout were summarily rejected because the bank had already taken a major haircut during the recent recapitalization. Negotiating a reasonable deal that we could afford was not going to be easy.

By the fall of 1994, I had met with the management group a number of times as I frequently traveled to Hungary. Although I knew some Hungarian, I had lost the ability to speak it fluently. I decided that I would speak English and make the Hungarians suffer, but I was grossly outnumbered and realized that I could learn Hungarian faster than any of them could learn English. Quickly, I developed a good relationship with the executives and started to have meetings with the entire management group. On each trip to Hungary, I met the upper management, about twenty-five people, and occasionally the expanded management team of about seventy-five people, to get them familiar with Zoltek and the carbon fiber business. These meetings were painful.

They would usually give me a blank stare when I told them about carbon fibers and Zoltek operations and how they would fit in. The team was knowledgeable about their respective technologies and their existing business, but they struggled to understand Zoltek. They were even struggling to understand how their business could run as a private company. They definitely could not comprehend the concept of abandoning the majority of their current products and markets.

I was making slow progress, and I had a long way to go. I ended up spending a lot of time with the general manager, Pászty György, who did speak near-perfect English, and the CFO, Bakos György, who spoke absolutely no English. My plan was to convince them that the company needed to change so that they would be able to prepare the rest of the management to be ready when Zoltek took over. Each time I was in Hungary, I also met with as many people as possible from the banks and the privatization agency. I started to include Bakos György and the financial team at some of these meetings in order to make sure the banks became aware that the company, as presently organized, was not sustainable and that a new financial crisis was around the corner without new technology and management.

The privatization agency was just as difficult. The privatization process was not well defined, and there was a rush to acquire premium Hungarian companies and use whatever influence the buyers could exercise to put themselves into a favorable position. Foreign accounting firms, law firms, and consultants flooded into Hungary. As an individual, trying to get the attention of agency management was nearly impossible. Magyar Viscosa was not a highly desirable company to acquire, so I did not have to worry about someone with more influence walking away with the company, but nobody in the agency believed this company was a high priority. Finally, I submitted an unsolicited offer, which caused the agency to hire one of their consultants to prepare a bid document.

In the middle of my discussions, the National Property Agency (AVÜ) appointed a new president, Bartha Ferenc. He also assumed the position of Commissioner of Privatization. It just so happened that I had met him at a party with my friend Laci about four years earlier when he was the President of the Hungarian National Bank. I immediately contacted him and from that point on, it was clear that we would be able to make a reasonable deal with the government. Now, I could concentrate on the CIB Bank.

I met with Ferenc a number of times. Once he asked me to come alone, and he introduced me to a Hungarian friend of his who was living in Switzerland. Ferenc suggested that his friend and I meet for coffee and discussion. When we did, he asked me if I wanted to buy Magyar Viscosa for a very low price. Of course, I said, "Yes," and asked him what his idea was. He promised he would contact me after I was back in St. Louis. He did actually call, and I asked him to send me a fax defining his proposal. I never heard from him again. Later, I realized it was probably an under-the-table proposal, which I would not have accepted, but getting a written documentation was not going to happen. I was still sure that I would be able to arrive at an acceptable price for the AVÜ's ownership share, but I first needed to conclude an agreement with the banks in order to move forward.

Between trips to Hungary, our engineering activity continued on the design of our carbon fiber lines, and we were learning more and more about the continuous carbon fiber process, but our carbon fiber revenue still only came from our batch-processed Panex-30 products. All of a sudden, there was an announcement by a Dallas company, Keiser Industries, that they had signed an exclusive contract with Russia to import unlimited low-cost carbon fibers. They also claimed that there were shiploads of Russian carbon fibers on their way to the U.S. Needless to say, this possibility was very disturbing and would have undercut our strategy.

In the spring of 1994, while I was stewing over this unexpected development, I received a call from a company called Diamond Fibers. They wanted to see me to discuss nickel-coated milled carbon fibers. It turned out they were a group of Russian immigrants who claimed that there was a process developed in Russia that could nickel-coat milled carbon fibers at a high production rate and low cost. They asked me to join them on a trip to Russia to visit their partners. I jumped on this opportunity.

This trip was interesting for several reasons. I wanted to see Russia and how people lived, wanted to assess their carbon fiber capabilities, try to understand the level of their composite technology, and learn about how Russia is dealing with the changes that would be certain to come after the rejection of the horrible communist system.

Personally, I had hated Russia all my life for what they had done to Hungary and my family, but I was anxious to see it. We arrived in Moscow's relatively new airport. It was quite dark and unimpressive. We were picked up in a small bus with three bodyguards. We stayed in central Moscow in the Moscow University hostel. My room was quite uncomfortable, basic, and unkempt. Being with several Russian natives gave me the opportunity to see more of Moscow than I could have otherwise.

Moscow was built in three major concentric circles. The central circle, where we spent most of our time, was the best Moscow had to offer. The Kremlin, where the center of the government resides, was an old complex originally built in the fifteenth century on the shores of the Moskva River; it was impressive. I had seen films of troops marching in front of the Kremlin during my youth. The parade route, which was about a mile long, had a unique design; it started at the St. Basil's Cathedral, rising to Kremlin's entrance and Lenin's Tomb, and declining to the other end of the Red Square. When troops marched and military equipment rolled past the front of the Kremlin complex, this design effectively gave the impression of a never-ending military strength. While there were some beautiful buildings in central Moscow, they were mostly built long before the Communist Revolution.

My hosts proudly proclaimed that the outer circles were built by war prisoners, which was Russia's version of modern-day slavery.

The people looked even poorer than we had been in Hungary. The state showcase department store, GUM, was full of merchandise, but not many buyers. Clearly communism had not helped the Russians any more than it had other oppressed countries communism created. Russia was changing, but more slowly than Hungary. The ruble was almost worthless, and the street exchange rate was as much as one hundred times the official rate. I wanted to exchange some dollars, and one of our bodyguards accompanied me to the central subway station. We quickly found someone who wanted to change a hundred-dollar bill, and I foolishly pulled out my money clip that had a number of hundred-dollar bills. All of the sudden, my bodyguard's shoulder bag became an AK-47 ready to fire. Russia was a dangerous place because people were desperately poor.

We went to a Moscow University laboratory for a demonstration of the nickel coating process. We were welcomed by a person of undeterminable age, white as a sheet with absolutely no hair on his head or arms. Everyone else stood in a corner and stared at him while he demonstrated the process to me. It was a fluidized bed unit, and he was unable to start it. The idea was to suspend the carbon fibers in hot air and inject nickel carbonyl, a very dangerous chemical, to decompose and coat the fibers with nickel. As the coating increases the weight of the fibers, they fall. In principle it worked, but the huge difference in weight of the fiber and the coated fiber made the process physically impossible. When I explained this, he pointed to all the samples on a shelf he was able coat with this process. I asked him what they were, and his answer was that they were crushed rock, coated with uranium. That explained his physical appearance, and I wished I would have brought a Geiger counter with me. We left the lab as fast as we could.

The next day we went to a military complex about seventy-five miles west of Moscow. It was a closed city, and we were told that I was the first Westerner ever to set foot in the complex. They had a fibers research facility and, among other things, they were developing basalt fibers, which are produced from lava rock. The main reason for the trip was to witness a demonstration of their process to turn carbon fibers into silicon carbide fibers. This was the kind of fiber involved with our F-22 stealth fighter. So I was quite interested.

They were working with a pilot plant that I figured needed to be redesigned and simplified, but the process was interesting and had a good chance to work. I was actually thinking that we might want to duplicate it. It was a complex process, and I did not think they could start it without some modifications that would take longer than a day to complete. We went for lunch, and they assured me that the process would be running when we returned.

The restaurant was in a building that had one small door and virtually no windows. The table was set very nicely with several small bottles that looked like soda, but which I later found out were vodka bottles. Immediately people were offering toasts and drinking shots of vodka. At about 4:00 PM, we all realized the effort to start the process was hopeless. We had a final toast and exchanged signed ruble bills, which in Russia represents friendship and the hope of meeting again. I had the impression that a lunch like this was not unusual for the Russians, and I rode back to Moscow with four Russians, all of whom had passed out.

Finally, we met with NIIGrafit, the State graphite research institute. This was our sponsoring organization and, more to the point, this organization, we were told, controlled the Russian carbon fiber industry. Some of the individuals in the Institute were also supporters of the Diamond Fiber group. This was my opportunity to find out about the Russian carbon fiber capabilities and the Keiser contract.

From our discussion, it was my suspicion that there was very little carbon fiber production. We discussed future cooperation, and they were interested in the possibility of NIIGrafit acquiring a carbon fiber line from Zoltek. I met the person who signed the agreement with Keiser. He explained to me that to a Russian, a signed contract meant nothing; a deal was honored by a handshake. Keiser was not about to get any carbon fiber from Russia.

Magyar Viscosa had an office in Moscow with two employees. They were responsible for sales in the Russian market. I asked them to make direct contact with NIIGrafit's carbon fiber plant in Balakovo to arrange a visit and to see if they had any inventory to sell. I also asked them to see if there was another carbon fiber plant anywhere in Russia and to contact Nitron to investigate if we could buy ACN directly from them, bypassing their agent, ICD, who was the only major supplier that did not participate in the recapitalization of Magyar Viscosa after the bankruptcy. They found the chemical industry research institute's plant that claimed that it also produced carbon fibers.

In September 1994, I returned to Russia for the second time. György Bakos and I visited the Moscow office that was located in the Hungarian government compound in central Moscow. With their help, we visited the specific chemical plant in the outskirts of Moscow that housed the carbon fiber facility. We met all the top Russian carbon fiber experts and saw the carbon fiber production facility. The plant was totally shut down, and the electricity was disconnected. We visited the carbon fiber operation with flashlights. At best, it was a pilot plant, and they were experimenting with the production of rayon-based carbon fibers. I determined that we had nothing to be concerned about competition from Russian chemical industry.

The NIIGrafit plant, named Himvolono plant, was located in Balakovo, a city of about 200,000 people in the Saratov Province on the Volga River, about one hundred miles from Volgograd (Stalingrad).

The Nitron Plant was located about one-hundred-fifty miles from there, in Saratov, a major port on the Volga River and the capital of the Saratov Province, with a population of about one million.

We visited both of these operations. We flew from Moscow to Balakovo, then to Saratov and back to Moscow on a chartered flight. This trip was quite an experience. When we arrived in Balakovo, we were met by the management team at the airport, which did not have a viable terminal; they seemed very anxious. It was a closed city during the communist era, and every road intersection leading into the city had an unmanned machine gun bunker.

The Himvolono plant was constructed in three concentric circles with machine gun-equipped guards that looked more sinister as we crossed the inner circle gates. The plant looked like a rusting abandoned junk yard. The carbon fiber facility was in the center of the plant among their most valued treasures. We saw one typical line which was a table-top size line. They had sixty such lines that, in total, produced less than one of our lines. We did not have to worry about them competing. We found out that their precursor came from the Nitron plant, which made our trip to Saratov more interesting.

Their business collapsed, and the future seemed hopeless. After some discussion, we made arrangements to buy some second quality carbon fibers that we could mill and complement our own capacity. It was a profitable business and helped us to increase our availability for a very short time. We discussed a number of ways to work together, including that they would like to sell their carbon fiber plant to Zoltek. This, of course, was of no interest to me. We just could not arrive at a long-term mutually beneficial way forward. They graciously treated us for lunch at their guest house, and they accompanied us to the airport. As our airplane taxied away, I could not help but to feel sorry for them as they waved goodbye with a look of losing their last hope, clearly realizing that they would not see us again.

The Nitron plant was a mess. Steam was leaking everywhere and in the winter, when Saratov was very cold, the steam would freeze and cover the plant, making it look like a giant igloo. We were guided by a fifty-year-old engineer. He was quite knowledgeable, pleasant, and spoke English well. He told us he was retiring within a month, the first opportunity to collect a pension, because there was no future for the company. The precursor plant was not running because they had no orders.

We met the plant manager, who was also quite knowledgeable and professional. He explained that ICD had gained control over the company by gaining control over a small Moscow bank that controlled Nitron's money. ICD was not providing enough money to maintain the facility, and he needed to sell some inventory directly to customers to get cash in order to keep the plant running, and he would be happy to sell direct to us. We arranged future direct purchases of ACN, which was the primary purpose for our visit.

This trip opened my eyes about how Russia had changed from the communist system. The first indication of what was about to come happened while Mikhail Gorbachev was still the president. In August 1991, while he was on vacation outside of Moscow, he and his family were put under house arrest for three days by a group of military officers. During the coup, several billion dollars disappeared form the government bank accounts around the world. And when the coup ended, a number of military officers were killed or committed suicide.

After the communist system broke down, dictatorship turned into anarchy. The communist dictators and thugs became the oligarchs. When communism finally collapsed, the old communist hierarchy went to work to steal the country's productive assets and treasury.

For centuries, Russia had been controlled from Moscow, which was even more prevalent during the communist system, and the general population had accepted it as the way of life. This system facilitated people in power's grabbing control of the financial system, the nation's natural resources, and the huge number of vertically integrated industries. This system made the Russian form of privatization unique.

It seemed there were three favorite methods for taking control of significant national assets. One method, that I actually saw happening, was through the banking system. If someone or a group could take control of a bank in Moscow, they were in position to control the companies that were funded by that bank.

Another method was based on an effort to turn state-owned companies into privately owned companies by giving shares to the employees. This may have been a good concept, but it completely failed. The recipients of these shares had no idea of the value, and most people were desperate for cash to live on. These shares were acquired by the deposed communist bosses at a tiny fraction of their value with stolen money. Some of these were also funded by western investors. For a while, a very volatile stock market developed in Russia where these shares were sold to mostly western investors at or near their true value.

The most bizarre method was for management of state-owned companies to sell their companies as if it was their own and pocket the money.

There was no one in control of the government. During the communist system, the powerful communists lived like royalty, but if they fell out of favor, they were lucky to escape with their lives without any financial gain. When the communist thugs realized that they could abandon the communist propaganda and steal the country blind and be able to keep what they stole, they easily abandoned communism.

What resulted was a chaotic free-for-all with competing groups resorting to every kind of force, including murder, to gain control of government assets. The end result was the oligarchs had billions of dollars that they hid outside of Russia, including in the USA, while the common people were still suffering as before. Russia was still a living hell when I went there.

My visit did confirm that there was no Russian threat to our strategy and business concept. We also assured a direct source for ACN. Now I was ready to complete the acquisition of Magyar Viscosa and start the development of our precursor. With my concerns about Zoltek's carbon fiber business eliminated and growing at a fifty percent annual rate, we were running out of installed capacity; we needed to finish our development work and start building carbon fiber capacity.

By the spring of 1995, I was a regular visitor to Hungary. I enjoyed my visits to Budapest and by this time, these visits were more relaxing, so between business meetings, I was able to reconnect with some childhood friends. I spent a lot of time with the Magyar Viscosa management and started to lead discussions on how to change the company. I wanted to fully understand their thinking to be ready for change after the acquisition was completed. I became increasingly involved with the Hungarian business, including the purchasing of acrylonitrile (ACN).

When we would successfully develop our precursor, the cost of acrylonitrile, the primary raw material, would have a very significant effect on our carbon fiber cost. At that time there were two sources, Dutch State Mine (DSM) and the Dutch trading company ICD, representing Nitron. But neither one offered competitive prices. Buying direct from Nitron was very helpful.

However, I was still not making a lot of progress with the banks. In mid-year, AVÜ announced a deal to sell five premium hotels to a company in the U.S. for $24 million. This caused a major uproar and a scandal. Ultimately it resulted in Ferenc Bartha losing his position. By that time, I had an agreement with the agency, which was not affected by his dismissal. Shortly after his demise, Ferenc called me for a meeting. He offered his services to help make a deal with CIB Bank. When Ferenc was head of the National Bank of Hungary, the CIB Bank chairman was working for him. We agreed if he could secure an agreement for twenty percent of the loan amount, I would pay him $150,000 in consulting fees. Within days we had a meeting with the chairman. After a few minutes, he asked me if he agreed with our proposal, if we would complete the transaction. I promised that we would, and we shook hands. I was out of his office in less than five minutes.

Now that the acquisition looked real, I needed to bring the deal to a conclusion, I invited the Zoltek Board to visit Magyar Viscosa so that they could see what we were about to acquire. After the plant tour, they were treated to an extravagant thirteen-course Hungarian lunch at the company hunting lodge. The Board had a very positive impression of the management team.

In July, the proposal to the AVÜ was completed, which required the inclusion of a strategic plan for the company after acquisition. This would be reviewed two years later to confirm the validity of the transaction. We submitted this proposal on August 1, 1995. The transaction was approved. With the CIB agreement secure, we needed to raise the money to pay for the acquisition and reduce the existing bank debt we had incurred both in our carbon fiber development work and during the initial installation of our own carbon fiber line. The obvious course of action was to pursue a secondary stock offering.

After discussions with investment bankers to gauge the interest in a stock offering, I returned to Hungary to meet with all the other banks and everyone who had an ownership interest in the company to further define our financing needs. It was a hot summer, and there was no air-conditioning in most offices. It was a miserable time for serious negotiations. I had to take a number of extra shirts and routinely returned to the hotel between meetings to change. I was successful with some of the lesser creditors and owners, but I was unable to get commitments from the other banks. I did make it clear that, in order to complete the pending acquisition, we needed to settle all loans and buy all shares. They still did not realize that the company could not exist as it was, and they were not yet willing to negotiate. This process was taking a lot of time, and I needed to bring it to conclusion.

When I was trying to close the deal, I stayed in Hungary for two weeks and over the weekend, I went to London to meet with an investment manager. He was recommended by Southwest Bank as someone who might be interested in participating in our offering.

When we met Saturday morning at this investor's office, he said, "I understand you are a golfer." I confirmed that I did play golf, but not well. So, he invited me to have lunch and play a round at Sunningdale.

He had a PhD chemist meet us who would quiz me about the carbon fiber technology. We had a nice lunch and found out that there was a tournament, and we were not going to be able to get on the course until after 5:00 PM. So we proceeded to have more conversation over a number of vodka Pimms. Finally, around 6:00 PM, we went to play the round of golf. I was teamed with the local assistant pro, and the investor and his expert were playing against us. I was not a good golfer under normal conditions, but even worse after talking business and drinking vodka all afternoon.

On the way back to the clubhouse, the expert asked me, "Now Zsolt, what are Zoltek shares selling for?"

"$28 per share," I said.

"Now, how many shares do you own?" he asked.

"Two million shares," I said.

In the typical pompous British-style, he said, "By God, you could afford a golf lesson."

That explained what he thought about my golf skills, and I am not sure if they ever decided to invest in Zoltek. However, taking time out to visit them was a nice diversion.

When I returned to St. Louis after this trip, we started to prepare for the stock offering. The first order of business was to make the final selection of the investment bankers. We needed to upgrade from our

IPO bankers, but our options were again limited. It was a fine balance between bankers that could understand our business and those who would have the confidence to successfully complete the offering.

Once the selection was made, there was a lot of work to do to prepare for the offering, including completing the acquisition terms. We needed to complete the final due diligence and develop the pro-forma financial information that consolidated the two companies. Our accounting team spent a lot of time with the Hungarian team to understand the financial information. All this was more difficult than normal because we had a limited number of people who were proficient in both languages.

I returned to Hungary during the due diligence process to be sure there were no changes or problems surfacing. I also planned to meet with the ICD representative to complete my negotiations for ACN long-term supply. We had a full tank of ACN at a high price while the market price was actually falling rapidly. I intended to negotiate a significantly lower price of this inventory or ask them to remove it from our tank. György Pászty, György Bakos, and I had lunch before they drove me to the airport for the flight to London. I had this feeling that something was wrong, but could not figure out what. On the way to the airport, I told them that I would not get out of the car until they told me what was wrong.

Finally, they came clean: the ACN tank was empty. They were unable to pay for the ACN, but needed to keep the plant operating. They assured me that the $3 million payable to ICD that was on the financial statement reflected the missing ACN, so there were no financial reporting issues. This made the problem less of an issue for the acquisition, but made my negotiations more difficult. I was able to negotiate a lower price for the "existing" inventory, though not as low as I planned, on the condition of a long-term supply agreement at competitive pricing. We signed the agreement and within ninety days, ICD declared bankruptcy. It seemed that the Russian plant manager circumvented ICD's and the Moscow bank's control and had sold enough inventory directly to customers, to get money to operate the plant, to bankrupt ICD. I directed our accounting department not to pay ICD and to prepare a claim to recover the prior overpayments we had made to them for years. In the end, we settled for $600,000, which was twenty cents on the dollar.

We still did not have an agreement with all the Hungarian banks, but we were ready to start the stock offering process. The investment bankers needed to see the plant to give them confirmation that the plant was actually there and to give them the confidence to convince investors of the value of the company. I decided to combine the three tasks: the final negotiations with the banks, the due diligence plant visit by the investment bankers, and finish the writing of the prospectus.

The investment bankers, the accountants, and the lawyers traveled to Hungary. We all stayed at the Budapest Hyatt, and we rented a large conference room where we set up to draft the prospectus. On the first day in Hungary, we visited the plant and had an extended lunch with the management team.

On the second day, we started the writing of the prospectus. I arranged a formal lunch and invited representatives from all the banks. Before lunch, I introduced our investment bankers and, in Hungarian, informed the bank representatives that this was the last chance for them to agree to the same settlement as the CIB Bank had already agreed to. I also warned the banks that without our acquisition of Magyar Viscosa, it was likely the company would soon declare bankruptcy again. However, this time it would never start up again. I outlined the terms as thirty percent of the total debt and share value, which was contingent on all the other banks accepting the same terms in order for our offer to go forward. After the CIB Bank representatives confirmed our agreement, I told them I needed their answer by the end of the day. I looked over to György Pászty and György Bakos, who were turning white from fear. The bankers were speechless, and we all had a friendly and polite lunch.

After the lunch meeting, we continued drafting the prospectus. About two hours later, Pászty and Bakos found me. Their color had recovered some but they were very upset. They told me that we could not talk to bankers like I had, and it was all over. As I was trying to assure them that all was well, the first bank called to let me know they agreed with the proposed terms. By the end of the day, all but one of the banks had agreed to the terms. The last bank, which had refused to consider my offer, wanted to negotiate a better deal. I went to see them the following day. The bank had been acquired by an Italian bank, and the bank chairman wanted to negotiate. After refusing to change my offer, I let them talk. Once I felt they were worn down, I pretended reluctantly to agree to an additional $50,000. That made them happy, and we shook hands on the deal.

As I shook the chairman's hand, I asked, "We were talking liras?"

He almost passed out when I told him I was just joking. That made him happy.

Now we were ready to complete the transaction and accelerate the offering. We had a very difficult story to tell; the acquisition of a company with $45 million in annual revenue to produce the raw material for a carbon fiber business with only $12 million in revenue did not make sense on the surface.

We presented a five-year outlook. The carbon fiber business was a developing materials business with the strategy of low cost carbon fibers to be used in commercial markets. We projected that our annual carbon fiber revenue would reach over $50 million. We presented the Hungarian company as an independent profit center that would develop the acrylic fiber precursor for Zoltek and in five years, sell or close down all non-acrylic product lines.

For the longer term, we needed to explain that the carbon fiber business would grow large enough to require all the acrylic fiber capacity the Hungarian company had to offer. When we achieved this goal, our carbon fiber capacity would reach 20 million per year or approximately £150 million in annual revenue.

On our road show, George Pászty presented the Magyar Viscosa story, and I presented the Zoltek carbon fiber business. We were hoping investors would understand our short-term strategy and would continue to support our carbon fiber concept.

The offering was reasonably successful. We completed the offering on November 17, 1995. We raised almost $24 million by selling 1,900,000 shares. The share price at the time of the offering was $13.73 per share ($41.19 per share pre-two for one and three for two splits). In just three years, Zoltek shares had increased to a value over ten times the IPO price. This represented over $90 million in market valuation. At this time, Zoltek market valuation was reasonably reflective of the company's financial results and near-term prospects.

The acquisition was completed on December 6, 1995.

Uncle Édi was very happy and enthusiastic about the possibility of the acquisition. He was an important part of my connection to Hungary, and I am sure he would have been pleased to see the completion of the acquisition and the rebuilding of the company. Unfortunately, he had died before the acquisition was completed. I used to meet Uncle Édi for dinner and discussions every time I was in Budapest, but after he was gone, I lost a good friend and with it, lost much of my contact with my Hungarian family. Uncle Édi wanted to maintain our relationship, but others did not understand my relationship with my brother and resented my Hungarian business interests.

Post-acquisition, one of the financial consultants to the Hungarian government landed at the University of Virginia's Darden School of Business. He asked me to work with him to prepare a case study on this acquisition. It was an interesting project, and I had the opportunity to present it to the class and be interviewed on film for future classes. The students were asked if the transaction should or should not have been done. The result from the students was split, but overall, they were in favor of doing the acquisition.

After the acquisition and the offering, Mary and I headed for Hawaii for a well-deserved vacation. We have taken vacations in Hawaii a number of times since the first time we went on our twentieth anniversary in 1988. We enjoyed it so much that in 1993, Mary was ready to look for a place to buy. We settled on looking for a place on the Big Island, the island of Hawaii. The market was slow at that time, and we were able to buy a place at Waikoloa on a golf course and have been enjoying it ever since.

Over the years, we used this place for numerous family trips, occasional golf trips with friends and for business, like management and directors meetings.

Building the Carbon Fiber Business

With the Hungarian acquisition complete, Zoltek became a much larger international company with over two thousand employees. The acquisition brought many possibilities, but also many significant challenges. I spent a lot of time traveling to put the Hungarian acquisition together, and it looked like this schedule would not lighten up anytime soon; I needed to take a break. Our two-week vacation in Hawaii gave me an opportunity to relax and to start planning how to accomplish all the things we needed to do.

In order to get the entire company to work together, I decided to initiate a plan with the goal of becoming a world-class carbon fiber company. Not to mimic the communists with their endless five- and ten-year plans, I decided on a five-year program that I called ZOLTEK-2000. The goals were to build enough installed capacity to manufacture 35 million pounds (15,750 metric tons) of carbon fibers annually, targeting a $5.00 per pound selling price, while keeping our cost at $3.50 per pound, and to begin manufacturing enough precursor in our Hungarian plant to fully support our carbon fiber production. All of it assumed that the ACN price stayed at or below $1,000 per ton.

In the spring, Mary and I hosted the Hungarian management team and their spouses in New York for a long weekend of fun and business discussions. My intention was to make them feel good about becoming part of an American company, present the five-year plan, and to have a serious discussion of the future of the company in a relaxed environment.

We all had a nice time, and everyone appreciated the opportunity to see New York and enjoyed the sightseeing, wonderful dinners, and the theater. It was interesting that after we saw the *Phantom of the Opera*, they all agreed that the actors were lip-synching, not actually singing in their own voice. I was not sure why they thought so, but obviously they thought nothing of accepting that the production would be a total fake; it would not be unusual in the Hungarian communist system.

Mary and I had a cocktail party each evening before dinner. At the specific starting time, the bell to our suite rang and when I opened the door, all fourteen people were standing there. Even though I made fun of it the first day, it never changed for the entire weekend. Also, during our business discussions, I could not get a freewheeling discussion started. There was no individual initiative or distinction in the group. This is the result of the communist system, and I realized this attitude was prevalent in the entire organization and would be a problem for initiating changes in the company

My five-year plan summarized the goals and to achieve these goals, I set out three primary objectives for both the U.S. and the Hungarian operations:

First, for the U.S. operations, we needed to complete the design of the continuous carbon-fiber lines and install the first line in order to prove the concept of a modular design, which would enable us to install multiple lines in six months or less at a cost of $5 million per one million pounds of production capacity. This target compared to the competitors' cost of up to $75 million and twenty-four months or longer to install similar capacity.

Second, we needed to get our production facilities in place. We were still fine-tuning and expanding our St. Louis facility. We were adding capacity, and we were planning to move our textile processing to our new Hungarian plant. More important, we had yet to develop a carbon fiber plant in the U.S. It should have been an easy decision to locate in St. Louis, but we were being targeted by the unions, and I was determined to never have unions in any Zoltek plant. We were also having problems finding employees willing to work in a manufacturing environment, and we expected this situation would get worse with the additional requirements of the continuous carbon fiber process.

Third, we needed to continue expanding the market for our existing carbon fiber business, particularly the aircraft brake business. In addition, there were many other friction applications relying on the technology we had initially acquired. We needed to become active in the primary carbon fiber market with the fibers produced on our pilot line and to capture as much short fiber business as possible. Most important, we needed to promote our commercial carbon fiber concept in the industry and get very active in application development with identified potential new customers.

In Hungary, first, we immediately had to start our precursor process development to have it available by the time we were ready with the new carbon fiber lines. My plan was to first convert the DuPont acrylic unit to precursor production and continue running the SNIA process for textile customers until we needed to convert the entire acrylic fiber business to precursor production. Hopefully this would happen before the textile acrylic business totally collapsed.

Second, we wanted to exit from production of the plant's other products in an organized way and reduce the number of production workers before it became too expansive. The second largest operation after the acrylic fibers was the nylon fiber business, which had many problems, including poor technology, low quality, and a very limited market; it just had to go as soon as possible. There were some smaller operations that had the potential to be maintained for some time, if that would ease the pain and cost of changing the company. I knew this was a difficult and emotional task, but it had to be done.

Third, we needed to introduce carbon fiber production to the Hungarian facility. We planned to immediately transfer our Pyron textile production from the St. Louis plant to utilize the Hungarian textile expertise, both the people and facilities. We also planned to bring a team of our Hungarian workers to train in the operation of our carbon fiber pilot line. We needed to employ as many people as practical from obsolete operations in the carbon fiber business activities.

We began 1996 with great energy and enthusiasm and even more important, very successfully. We completed the installation and conversion of the carbon fiber line acquired from Courtaulds, and we began the carbon fibers production, utilizing the Courtaulds precursor. Once we made our plans public and introduced an eight-dollar per pound carbon fiber price point, we were inundated with inquiries and new product development projects from a wide range of customers. We received attention from the carbon fiber industry, as well as from the financial community after the Hungarian acquisition and completion of the secondary offering.

One of the unexpected outcomes was a call I received from a law firm in Chicago. One of the bankers that we had interviewed for the offering told his brother-in-law, a patent attorney, about the status of our stealth patent. The firm offered its services to monitor the use of our patent by the defense industry in an effort to collect royalties.

This was a welcome call because I had given up on building a business based on this patent, as I had done with other business with the U.S. government and the defense industry in general. Our high hopes for business coming from this technology were dashed when the FBI raided our secret files gestapo-style and confiscated our process documentation.

By that time, we had already sent out notices of infringement, but we were not getting acceptable responses. Bringing in legal support was an encouraging prospect to actually be able to collect some compensation for the use of this very important stealth technology. We agreed with the law firm to assert claims and to initiate a lawsuit on a contingency fee basis against the U.S. government and its contractors.

The patent was registered to Zoltek Corporation, but the ownership was divided equally between the company and me personally. Unfortunately, against my instructions, the law firm initiated the suit only in the name of the company, not jointly with me. I did not insist on correcting it because it did not seem to be as big a problem at the time as it turned out in the end.

We very quickly confirmed that the B-2 bomber utilized the carbon fiber and the composite fabrication process directly defined in our patent, but Northrup Grumman had purchased the carbon fibers from a foreign-owned company. The F-22 was also utilizing our patented technology by using ceramic (silicon carbide) fibers. The contractors, as standard procedure, had been directed by the government to violate our patent, and the U.S. Air Force gave them our technology. The government thought they could bypass our patent by buying the fiber from Japan. Actually, the fiber production I saw in Russia was just like the fibers that Lockheed Martin bought from Japan. We could have easily produced this fiber in the U.S. if we had been given the opportunity.

We never received any business from Northrup Grumman or Lockheed Martin, while other companies, all foreign, were paid many millions of dollars. We had never been compensated for the use of our technology either by the U.S. government or any of its contractors.

Our carbon fiber sales had been increasing by over sixty percent annually for the previous five years, and we were on track to do it again. But we were still operating at a very low level, around $20 million in annual revenue. But we were reaching our full production capacity. The continuous carbon fiber line design was going well, and it actually accelerated after the Hungarian engineers got involved. Installing the new capacity and bringing in new business was getting more critical. Timing was everything!

The Hungarian operation started out at full speed. Their traditional product sales increased about twenty-five percent, and their technical staff immediately began supporting our carbon fiber design group. The Hungarian company became cash flow positive from the start. They were able to build a carbon fiber production building that would house four million-pound-capacity production lines. My goal for the management team was to develop a systematic reduction in employees and an orderly exit from their traditional businesses. The significant initial success was a mixed blessing. While it was good for the financial performance, it caused the management team to falsely believe that there was a future for their old business model.

We all were more focused, and the company was doing well. I was very optimistic about the future. In May, I was invited by Drew and Linn to join the Southwest Bank board of directors. This was a hugely appreciated gesture on their part and indicated to me that they were confident that financially we had turned the corner.

As my confidence in the business success grew, Mary and I began to feel that our financial risk was under control, and we were more relaxed. Although our lifestyle did not really change, we did buy the condominium in Hawaii. In St. Louis, our house was in a neighborhood that we really liked, but it had some serious problems. Our options were to either tear it down and build a new house or sell it. We decided that tearing down and rebuilding would take a long time and require two moves, so we elected to buy an existing home. We bought a larger home closer to the county's central district.

Until this time, I was managing all functions in the company, which was demanding enough when it was only in the U.S., but now, with the Hungarian facility, my schedule got more difficult. I got into a routine to be available for part of the business hours to all operations. When we were limited to U.S. and Europe, it was challenging enough, but later, when we added Asia to our business, my schedule became more demanding. I was always available to the management or the customers. It became a twenty-four-hour job. I kept this schedule for two decades.

Of course, I could not do it all by myself. I needed to build a management team. I did have a good start with a core group in St. Louis, and Hungary had an experienced management team. I needed to round out the team and get them to work together. It was not an easy task, and I only partially succeeded. There was some friction between people in St. Louis over who had the most knowledge and who had contributed more to the success of the company. In Hungary, the management's acceptance of and reaction to the new privately owned and managed company, as compared to the old government owned and operated business, presented significant challenges. To get everyone working together was my challenge.

There was enormous demand for performance on the management team; therefore, it was not surprising that we had an unusually high turnover rate. Fortunately, most of the turnover was among the new hires, which was better than losing members from the experienced team, but all turnovers were costly in time and money. On a positive note, we maintained a core group who either stayed for a long time or at least for several productive years.

There were a few important long-term contributors who formed the backbone of the company. For example, for nearly 20 years, Peter Kiss, Engineering Vice President, helped to bring the U.S. and Hungarian engineering teams together and energize them to successfully manage all their projects. Mike Westcott, with the longest service to Zoltek among the team, progressed from managing the St. Louis plant to Vice President of Quality. George Bakos, who was the Hungarian CFO at the time of the Magyar Viscosa acquisition, provided critical support throughout the following twenty years, first to me and then to the Zoltek Zrt. (Zrt means a closed, shareholder-owned company) general managers who followed.

However, building up the rest of the top management team did not go well. The first position I wanted to fill was the Chief Operations Officer. Orel Kiphart, the manager of the Goodrich plant at Pueblo, approached me with the idea that he would like to work at Zoltek. Orel was not exactly the kind of person or the type of manager I liked, but he did appear to be in command of the Pueblo operation. He was also the person who put our one-hundred-percent supply agreement together. I felt that I owed him an opportunity. Before I could confirm any offer, I told him that I insisted on talking to the president of his division.

I met the division president for dinner in Los Angeles. When I told him that I was considering offering Orel a position with Zoltek, he seemed to be happy about it and offered to pay his relocation expenses. I immediately realized my original impression of Orel was correct, and I was about to make a mistake; no one would pay to relocate an employee to a job with a new company unless he was very happy to see the employee leave. Orel did not fit in and never gained respect at Zoltek.

During the secondary offering that financed the Hungarian acquisition, the investment bankers convinced Cheryl that she should be Zoltek's CFO. I was reluctant because she was a great accountant, and she liked to control the financial reporting, but she seemed not to be interested in the other CFO functions, like managing financing, investor relations, and planning. Finally, I did promote her, but as I expected, she just did not want to do the traditional CFO functions.

However, she was the best accountant we ever had at Zoltek, and I wanted to be sure she would stay with the company. As I tried to push her more into the CFO functions, I tried to have her hire some additional accounting help, but she resisted. I argued that it is easier to find a reasonably qualified accountant than a person knowledgeable of the company who can take over the CFO functions. I finally offered her the newly created position of Chief Accounting Officer, but she decided to leave Zoltek for a plant accounting position next door to our Missouri Research Park plant.

By that time, we really had to have a CFO, and Cheryl recommended her replacement. He was our accountant's husband. He did not last for long, but unfortunately long enough to ruin our computer system. Next I hired a person recommended by one of our directors. I trusted this director's judgement and accepted his recommendation. In some ways, he seemed to be the right person for the job, although he also did not have CFO experience. He did not work out well.

About mid-year of 1996, we were ready to start building the continuous-carbon fiber lines. To do so, we needed to raise a significant amount of money. Starting the second quarter with our quarterly results showing huge profitable growth, enhanced by the Hungarian company sales, our share price started to climb. We took the opportunity to split the shares two for one in May. We were hoping that the higher number of shares would reduce the manipulation of our share price, which would help the company to obtain reasonable long-term financing and also reduce our shareholders' investment risk. Soon after the stock split, I started to organize another stock offering to finance our expansion.

In my effort to build the executive team, I organized a three-day planning meeting with the three operating managers at a Lake of the Ozarks resort. I had George Pászty, the President of Hungarian operation, Orel Kiphart, and our new CFO attend. Those three days were the most painful and unproductive time I ever spent with three people. There was very little in common among the four of us, culturally, socially, or intellectually.

On the way back to St. Louis, we stopped for breakfast at McDonald's. During breakfast I tried to sum up the results of our meeting with as many positive comments as I could muster. During the conversation,

I told the CFO that the next day we needed to start a project that the accounting department has been neglecting. He told me he would not be able to because he would have the State of Kansas tax auditor in our office.

Since we had no tax liability of any kind to Kansas, I asked him, "What the hell are you doing, wasting your time with that?"

He was offended and on the way out from the restaurant, he said, "Because you do not respect the accounting department, I am going to resign."

By that time, I had no patience and I told him, "That is fine with me."

I did not think any more of this conversation. He and Orel drove back together and finally, when Orel came in to the office, he was alone.

Our new CFO refused to come in to the office. That evening we had a scheduled board meeting. Our CFO had called his board contact to complain and by the time I arrived at the board meeting, the whole board looked to be panicked. We were about to start our offering, and they thought losing our CFO would be looked upon negatively. However, by that time, I had already discussed it with our investment bankers, who had never been impressed with the CFO, and they were quite happy to proceed without him.

But the board pressed to try to get him back anyway. I was not about to ask him to return, but our board member called him. After that call, the CFO called me to offer to return. I told him I would consider his return on a three-month trial basis. Without responding, he just showed up at his desk the next morning as if nothing had happened.

With the stock price then in the thirty-dollar range after the split, which I felt was an aggressive valuation, we did have some concern about being able to complete this offering successfully, even though we upgraded our investment bankers to Merrill Lynch as our lead underwriter. We started out with great energy, which was severely dampened when the SEC investigation started. (See the story in the Prologue) It seems that a short seller claimed that we did not actually buy the Hungarian plant. After we met with SEC and convinced them that our company was for real, the investigation ended. Once the investigation was behind us, we completed the work on the offering documents, and we were ready to start the road show.

We had named our CFO in our prospectus, so I felt I needed to take him along on the road show, against my better judgement. Not surprisingly, he became more of a problem than a help. He said some dumb things in his first presentation to the investment banker team, and he was told by our lead banker to stay on the script and let me handle the Q&A. He acted insulted and became a robot for the rest of the road show.

There were times it looked as though we were not gaining momentum. We even extended the road show to London, without taking the CFO, hoping to attract European investors. Just as in a loan approval process, someone had to take the lead and in an offering, one investor had to commit to purchasing a significant number of shares, like ten to twenty percent of the offering. We were running out of the high-roller prospects, and I was losing my enthusiasm.

We were down to the last few possibilities. One of the principal investors did not even see us, but sent his daughter in his place. She was about twenty-five years old and did not seem to be interested in our presentation and had very few questions. Nevertheless, I did my best to get her involved in the discussions that followed the presentation. To all our great surprise, that evening she committed to 500,000 shares. She led the deal and set the price!

We completed the offering on September 18, 1996. We raised over $60 million by selling 2,000,000 shares. We were suddenly in great financial shape. Finally, we had all the resources we needed to take a giant step forward in the execution of our strategy. At that point, Zoltek's market value was approximately $450 million. This was clearly an aggressive valuation particularly because we had stated many times in a variety of presentations and publications that our goal was $200 million in gross carbon fiber revenue over the next four years. I started to be seriously concerned about our share price running away from a reasonable valuation because it makes things much more difficult for the company to live up to such high investor expectations.

Three months to the day after he returned, our CFO resigned. Within a month after that, Orel also left the company.

At this stage of Zoltek's business development, with too many uncertainties, it was quite difficult to find and attract top management talent. It seemed that hiring people we knew from previous relationships should be more efficient. I realized that invariably anyone trying to get a job through directors was a flawed process. I also realized that in general, getting directors involved with the hiring process was a mistake.

By any measure, our financial performance in 1996 was great. We successfully completed two stock offerings that provided over $90 million. Our carbon fiber sales grew fifty-eight percent, and with the addition of revenue from the Hungarian company, our total revenue increased by four-hundred-forty-five percent to $60 million. Our net profit increased by over 200 percent. Zoltek's share price increased from the low of $6.50 to a high of $39.00.

The next two years were pivotal for Zoltek. We had reached a point where our carbon fiber sales required our full capacity, and growth would only be possible after we built the new manufacturing facilities. But we needed to show improved performance. We could stretch our carbon-fiber capacity with some incremental steps by finding some carbon fiber in Russia that we could recycle into milled products. We also recycled some of the aircraft brake production waste. However, real growth would only come after the new production lines were running.

Generally, after a significant offering, the lead banking firm would assign an analyst to issue research reports to keep investors informed. In addition, several brokerage firms who recommend a stock would usually assign an analyst as well. The analysts' reports are considered to be independent and carry more credibility than the company's own reports. If investors really knew how ignorant most of these analysts were, and even more important, how their reports support their company's trading plan and not the reality of the subject company's situation, they would be shocked. The sell or buy side analysts, and many times their reports, are conflicting, and if shareholders knew the analysts' objectives, it would destroy their confidence in the system.

I tried hard to work with these analysts to explain what our company was doing and what the Hungarian expansion meant to our business. My concern was that our carbon fiber revenue was much lower than the Hungarian plant's traditional products and eventually, our carbon fiber revenue would increase, but our total revenue would look stagnant as we exited from the traditional markets.

Unfortunately, time and again, we would lose analysts because they considered Zoltek a one-of-a-kind company that took too much work to follow. They preferred covering several companies in similar markets, doing research that applied to a number of companies. Without independent credible research reports, the short sellers and manipulators could have a significant negative influence over our share price.

On the surface, 1997 started out well. But I was more concerned than ever. The Hungarian traditional business only increased slightly in the first quarter of 1997 from the fourth quarter of 1996, indicating that sales were leveling off. At the same time, carbon fiber revenue already leveled off because we had reached the maximum production of our installed capacity. We would have a reasonable revenue increase in 1997, but 1998 would be a problem.

Commissioning of the carbon fiber facilities was the most important task. We were earnestly proceeding to locate a facility in the U.S., and we began installing carbon-fiber capacity in Hungary. This project was led by Peter Kiss and was well under control. Peter was a good engineering manager and with his Hungarian background, he could unite our global engineering team. Almost as important, I knew I could rely on him to keep me informed if he needed additional information or support. I was able to concentrate on sales and integrating the Hungarian management team into Zoltek.

There were several challenges facing the Hungarian team. They needed to understand and buy into the commercial-carbon-fiber concept and downplay the initial success of their traditional businesses. Their most important task, of course, was the development of the Mavilon precursor. We showed some quick initial positive results, but the quality of our initial products was not much better than the Courtaulds precursor.

We needed to accelerate our efforts in order to have the precursor ready by the time we were going to start up our new carbon fiber lines. We did not do much to exit from the traditional businesses during 1996, and now we needed to start a deliberate and systematic exit from the obsolete traditional products. Even though we were enjoying record sales, I was convinced that it would end soon.

The Hungarian plant was located in a small town on the south shore of the Duna River called Nyergesujfalu, with about seven thousand inhabitants at that time, and at least one person from almost every family worked for our company. A major lay-off would have been a problem for the locals. However, at the time the wages were very low, but with the entry into the EU pending, I expected wages to rise rapidly. I suggested initiating significant lay-offs immediately after the acquisition, coupled with significant wage increases. My thought was to minimize the negative financial impact on the families, while reducing our employment to a manageable level. I noticed that George Pászty was vacillating about making significant changes. As the traditional business improved, he was even more reluctant to change, and I became seriously concerned.

I traveled to Europe frequently for the aircraft brake business and to build my relationship with the European auto companies. Each time I went to Europe, I also went to Hungary to monitor their progress. We had remodeled the old nursery into a guest house, and that is where I stayed during my Hungarian visits. On the surface, everything looked okay. We were reducing the employee level, but after a closer look, I realized that we rehired most of them as contract workers at a higher cost than we paid them as employees.

There were other hidden problems, and I needed to spend more time there. We had large management meetings in which I kept the team aware of what our goals were and updated them on our progress. There was very little feedback. I invited the management team to the guest house for social time. That helped to get them to open up and communicate with me. I found out a lot about the business as well as management's attitude.

It became obvious that they had many concerns about the way a privately owned business operated. Some people had traveled to visit western facilities and had been to technical conferences; therefore, they had some understanding, but others were lost. At times I requested something to be done that required a modification or demolition of a building, and it was not done. It turned out our Hungaian Vice President of Engineering did not think I had the authority to make the decision without some government official approving it. Our in-house Hungarian attorney thought her role was to instruct me about what the government wanted me to do, rather than to make sure that we were staying within the law while proceeding with what we were trying to accomplish.

A number of the managers did not want to take on additional responsibility. Fortunately, most people were anxious to learn, but it was not going to be easy. If I had not known the Hungarian language, what I tried to achieve would have been impossible.

The top management group operated like a private club with the objective of keeping new members out, so I visited production units individually to look for people who might be ready to move into the upper management circle and to support the carbon fiber production management. I learned a lot and pulled some people out from their lower level positions. I got a firsthand glimpse of how the management operated and the difficulty they had in changing. I also realized the initial reduction in headcount had not come from improving operating efficiency, but from eliminating key specialty maintenance and housekeeping staff. Once they were off our payroll, we had to hire them back as independent contractors. Clearly this was not producing the results I expected.

The plant had almost all metal doors. Everything was locked. When I asked to open some of the doors, all I saw was a mess inside. The place looked like a prison. I asked why they had locked everything, and the answer was that people would steal things if the doors were left open. I suggested that would be great, and we would save the cost of hauling everything away. This comment obviously shocked them because they thought those were treasures. If those rooms were not full of junk, there was inventory everywhere, but there was no inventory control system. The forklift operators would put inventory anywhere there was open floor space.

I met a number of customers, mostly in Hungary and Poland. We had an office and warehouse in Lodz, Poland. The manager was our employee, but acted independently. We attended a textile show and had an opportunity to see a number of customers. I also spent time with the manager, who lived quite well considering the circumstances.

I found out that he liked to gamble and when I joined him in the casino, I was not impressed with his gambling skills. Not surprisingly, we were missing a significant amount of inventory. I had to shut down the operation immediately.

While the Hungarian products business was booming, there were signs of a serious weakness developing in the Polish textile market, which was our largest customer base for our textile acrylic fibers. This further confirmed that we needed to move rapidly toward exiting the textile business.

On the carbon fiber side, the aircraft brakes business continued to be the most significant steady business. We already had a one-hundred-percent supply contract with Goodrich, but Messier-Bugatti was not yet buying from us. Their first big U.S. program was the C-17 transport brake, and we actually qualified for that program. That was our first step in eventually becoming the primary supplier to Messier-Bugatti. I began concentrating on winning their business and visited them frequently. All the people were very pleasant and hospitable. We had serious discussions, but I was not making a lot of progress in actually getting orders.

During 1997, SGL, a German carbon and graphite manufacturer who was not yet in the carbon fiber business, acquired RK Carbon, our only competitor in the aircraft brake business. This gave me the opening I was looking for at Messier-Bugatti. I went to visit Messier-Bugatti's headquarters in Paris.

When I arrived, they asked me, "Zsolt, did you just come from America?"

"No, I have been in Germany calling on the auto companies," I told them.

"How do you think Germany is doing?" they asked, just to be polite.

"I think they are doing well, and they are ready to start a war within minutes after they thought they could win," I responded.

They smiled, and it seemed they all agreed. I reminded them, "You know the first place they like to go is Paris." As they mulled this over, I added, "I wonder how you will like doing business with them now that they acquired your fiber supplier."

At that point, after a few laughs, they promised, "Okay, we will start qualifying your fibers if you promise not to remind us again."

By the end of 1998, we had executed a fifty-percent supply contract. We supplied them from our Hungarian plant, but we were required to produce from the Courtaulds precursor. At that point, we had the majority of the global aircraft brakes business, and my challenge was to qualify our Mavilon precursor.

After the successful offering and the significant increase in our share value, I was asked to make a number of investment presentations. One unique request came from a money management firm named Sustainable Asset Management in Zurich, Switzerland. There were four presenters: Volkswagen, Mercedes, Ballard (fuel cells), and Zoltek. We presented in Zurich and in Munich. There was a BMW board member at the Munich presentation. Within two weeks, he sent six purchasing and engineering people to visit us in St. Louis. This meeting led to an expensive and long, over ten years, development projects with BMW.

We were building carbon fiber lines, both at our newly acquired plant site in Abilene, Texas and in Hungary. By mid-year in 1999, we were ready to start up our new lines, initially with purchased precursor because our own was not yet ready for introduction.

I was quite unhappy about the lack of progress in the precursor development activity. I trusted George Pászty and was convinced that he was on board with overseeing the necessary changes, but sensed there was something wrong. I had a discussion with our Hungarian management about the future. With the resurgence of their old business, they were actually thinking they could remain independent and keep the old business model with carbon fiber as an additional product line.

I could not believe what I was hearing. I told them there would never be carbon fibers sold from the Hungarian plant under any other name than Zoltek, Panex, or Pyron. I also directed George Pászty to immediately change the company name to Zoltek Zrt.

Life at Zoltek continued to be exciting and demanding. Executing our plan was not easy; timing was very critical. We accomplished our tasks on a timely basis, but we were not always in control of our destiny because neither the development of the carbon fiber market nor the longevity of the traditional Hungarian products business was easily predictable. While we were concentrating on the carbon fiber projects, unexpectedly the acrylic fiber business had a significant boom that drove our revenue and profits beyond expectations. Normally, this would be great, but in our case, it was problematic.

My earlier concern was now proving prophetic. Although we tried our best to show shareholders the carbon fiber and the Hungarian traditional products revenues separately, I was concerned that most investors did not understand or pay attention to our message, assuming that all our revenue was coming just from carbon fiber sales. My concern was that the traditional products business boom was not sustainable and that when the market collapsed, our carbon fiber revenue would not expand fast enough to cover the difference, resulting in a significant loss of confidence by our investors.

In 1997, we were enjoying a record year. Our revenue was over $90 million, a thirty-percent increase over 1996. Zoltek's share price continued rising rapidly. By September, our share price was at an incredible $65.75 per share. In just five years, our share price had increased fifty times over the IPO price, and our total market value was over $1 billion.

But I was concerned because I knew that we were in no position to support such high expectations.

It is predictable that this kind of over-valuation also attracts the worst parasites of the investment world, the short sellers. It was reported by the *Wall Street Journal* that as much as thirty percent of our shares were "gobbled up" by the short sellers. When short sellers gang up on a stock, they do everything unethical, dishonest, and even illegal to destroy the stock price.

On a personal note, as our share price continued to climb, my friendly stockbroker suggested that I sell two million of my shares. My ownership in Zoltek was over thirty-five percent at that time, making my personal shares worth over $350 million! Based on my concerns, I did not feel it was morally correct for me to cash in. I believed that our share price was about three times what I estimated the value to be. I felt that it would be unethical for me to make such a profit at the expense of someone who bought the stock in good faith. My broker then begged me to sell at least one million shares. I still refused.

It would be less than honest to not admit that I had some regrets about my decision not to sell any shares when the share price went as low as $2.20 per share a short time later.

Adding to the problems developing in business, there was a very depressing event in my personal life: Fr. Joe died. He had been fighting diabetes for years and finally, he lost that fight. He had been an important part of my life for twenty years, and he was a mentor and a very good friend. Mary and I socialized with him and his friends, and we had taken several trips together. He reintroduced me to the game of golf, and I played golf with him and his priest friends to the point that many people thought I was also a priest. I appreciated all that he did for me, including finding Fr. George to look out for me spiritually after he was gone. I still miss him and every time I see Fr. George, I am reminded of Fr. Joe and the good times we had.

There was no time to think about personal issues and had to concentrate on the business situation. As 1998 unfolded and we were preparing to start up our carbon fiber lines, our sales were not increasing as expected. Application development projects were materializing slower than we expected based on earlier indications from our customers. The quality and performance of our fibers were still way below our expectations because we were still using Courtaulds precursor. The other concern I had was that, while we were ready with the carbon fiber lines, the development of our precursor had stalled. I needed to get the program energized.

During the social events in Hungary, when people started to open up and we were having a good conversation, George Pászty would interrupt, and our discussion would end. The non-responsiveness during expanded management meetings also seemed unnatural. This really disturbed me, and I began developing serious doubts about George. Very disappointingly, I learned that George had instructed the acrylic technology group to develop a polymer that could be used for either precursor or textile fibers. He wasn't sold on the future of carbon fibers and thought the dual-use acrylic fiber would be a safer way to go. Spending a lot of time with George, I tried to bring him around. I was hoping not to have to get directly involved in the precursor technology, but at that point, I realized I would have to pay closer attention.

There were significant differences in the quality of the polymer needed for precursor and the polymer needed for textile applications. Once we focused on higher performing precursor, we realized that part of the DuPont technology would not support the precursor performance we required. We needed to redesign part of the equipment and convert the DuPont fiber spinning process entirely. This redesign represented several months of delay and a significant unexpected additional investment. I had to make the decision that we would no longer produce textile-grade acrylic fibers again.

When George realized that we would never turn back, and he had made a mistake not getting on board with the strategy for the carbon-fiber business, he decided to resign rather than to lead the transformation of the company.

In late 1998, I appointed the head of the acrylic group, Lajos Árvai, to replace George. He was a good engineer, but had very little management talent. Initially his primary assignment was to finish the precursor development, and I assisted him with managing the rest of the Hungarian operation to keep it from imploding. Unfortunately, he was a passive manager when we needed a real leader to guide the company through significant changes.

When Zoltek Zrt's traditional businesses started their inevitable decline, our carbon fiber business had not yet started growing. We gained some new business, but we also lost some business due to the serious setback in the Asian electronic industry. This was the situation I was most concerned about. Initially, our revenue just stopped growing and by the end of the year, our revenue had declined almost ten percent, and our net profit had declined more than twenty-five percent.

As I expected, this financial setback was enough to trigger a serious decline in our stock price. Some decline was certainly expected, but I did not expect it to drop as far as it actually did. By the end of 1998, our share price was lower than $12. There were clear indications that the short sellers had been waiting for this opportunity. Once the stock price hit this low, I knew it would be a long period before we would be able to regain investor confidence.

During the time the stock price was falling, I was interviewed by the *Wall Street Journal*. The reporter was asking me what I thought caused the decline in our stock price. Finally, he asked me if it might be because the short sellers. I learned over time that the reporters usually write the article they want and in order to give it credibility, they call around to solicit some supporting comments. I was irritated and I just blurted out, "Those fucking snakes!" This was exactly what the reporter wanted to hear.

He quoted me in his article after cleaning it up for publication. A reporter from the local St. Louis paper, *The Post-Dispatch*, called our office for an explanation of my comment. I was on a train from Paris to Lyon when I got the call from our CFO, asking me what he should say. I told him to tell the reporter that I was misquoted. The local paper reported just that and the case was closed, I thought.

When I attended the Southwest Bank board meeting after I returned from France, Drew kindly assured me that he was totally convinced I was misquoted because the adjective was missing! I guess he knew me way too well.

Realizing the demand for our carbon fibers was not developing as we expected, we discontinued our capacity expansion and reevaluated our plans. By this time, we had installed carbon fiber lines in Abilene and in Hungary. And we converted one line in Hungary to produce Pyron products for the Messier-Bugatti aircraft brake business.

We concentrated on our precursor development, and it became the top priority. We were getting close to meeting the mechanical properties we had targeted. We discontinued producing the DuPont process acrylic fiber and converted the line to produce precursor exclusively. By this time, the textile-acrylic fiber demand was rapidly declining, making the decision fairly easy. Once we redesigned the production line for precursor, we could never turn back. By doing this, we would reduce the Hungarian plant's traditional product sales by $29 million.

The carbon fiber competitive picture was not working in our favor. Our total capacity was still very small, and almost the entire carbon fiber industry supplied the aerospace market. Any relatively small change in market demand would have a huge impact on application development. Our aerospace carbon fiber competitors became concerned about our obvious long-term presence in the market, but they did not seem to understand our business strategy. With the aerospace market experiencing a serious slump, the aerospace carbon fiber producers dumped their excess capacity on the commercial market. Employing our fibers required modifications to the existing carbon fiber users' process, and the sudden aerospace carbon fiber availability at our price levels served as a deterrent to start using our fibers.

Carbon fibers go through several value-added steps, such as weaving and pre-impregnating with resin, before the final product fabrication. Often the value chain fabricators control the carbon fiber purchase. With the aerospace-carbon fiber being the most accepted product, our ability to penetrate markets was dependent on these fabricators for selection and for the ultimate cost of the finished product. It was time for me to review our sales approach to deal with the value chain issue. I had always been aware this would eventually be a potential problem but did not think it was going to happen so soon. If the demand grew and the intermediate processors needed to add capacity, life would have been much simpler for us.

Zoltek's Board of Directors had not changed since the IPO, except in 1998 when Jim Dorr left the board for health reasons. John McDonnell, the former CEO of McDonnell-Douglas, replaced him. Personally, I was always concerned about the exposure for our Board members. As our valuation became so volatile, the board members could be subject to shareholder complaints that would reflect on them personally. Fortunately, we were never exposed to such action.

Developing the Commercial Carbon Fiber Market

We started 1999 knowing that the Hungarian product sales would suffer a significant decline, and our carbon fiber sales were not increasing fast enough to cover the gap. My worst fears were coming true. I felt that we needed to do something dramatic to change this trend and increase carbon fiber sales quickly. At the same time, we needed to minimize the negative financial impact of the Hungarian operation.

We spent a lot of time and money on application development with our potential customers, but the market was very slow to respond. While the end users of our carbon fibers were anxious to start buying from us, they were actually buying an intermediate product to fabricate their own finished products. The value chain had evolved for the aerospace market in such a way that any incremental added value significantly increased the total cost. The aerospace industry could tolerate these cost increases, but the commercial market could not.

The slumping aerospace market resulted in excess capacity. This was characteristic of the carbon fiber business at the time and each time this happened, the prices dropped dramatically. This made the intermediate product supplier's life easy and instead of learning how to use our fibers, they just followed the carbon-fiber producer's lead and reduced their own prices. A number of customers who were ready to buy from us before we built our capacity were now happy with their old suppliers at the reduced prices.

Almost all carbon fiber applications require a secondary process to get the carbon fiber ready for the final product fabrication. The majority of these processes are performed by a third party. The general business model requires these third parties to mark up the carbon fiber in addition to charging a reasonable price for their actual value-added contribution. With this system, the cost savings of our carbon fiber diminished. Another concern was if the intermediate processor and the final product producer charged too much for their finished product, they would wind up selling less of their product, resulting in lower carbon fiber demand.

Even more of a concern was that the intermediate processor was actually the main contact with the customer. Ultimately the final customer is looking for a more competitive cost and so, the intermediate processor was able to apply leverage to Zoltek by threatening to buy carbon fibers from our competitors. If the carbon fiber demand was expanding, this leverage would not work because the supply would be severely limited. Ultimately, what we needed was to find or develop a major commercial-carbon-fiber user. We were losing control of our markets and needed to rethink our sales approach.

Carbon fiber-reinforced composites derive their fantastic mechanical properties by the synergy created through properties of many individual carbon fibers. The way to accomplish this was to infuse resin into a carbon fiber bundle, woven fabric, or tow sheet in such a way that all the fibers were wetted with the resin. After this step, the impregnated carbon fibers were formed into a specific shape, and then the resin was heat cured under pressure. This sounded simple, but combining resin and fiber could be very difficult. In most cases, this step was done as a separate operation.

For example, "graphite" golf club shafts, the first significant non-aerospace application, were actually produced with carbon fibers. We would sell our fibers to a prepreg producer who would have resin knowledge and the equipment to spread a number of carbon fiber tows into a thin blanket, impregnating it with already catalyzed resin. The impregnated carbon fiber blanket was wound in a large roll with each layer separated by release paper. The rolls of prepreg were stored in a freezer so the resin would not cure until the shaft manufacturers received it.

The prepreg was then sold to the shaft producer. The prepreg was unrolled and die cut. The release paper was removed, and the prepreg was rolled onto a steel mandrel. Each golf club shaft was made up with about 400,000 carbon fiber filaments. The mandrel was inserted in a heat shrink plastic tube and was heated until the resin cured. The shaft was cleaned and ground to a smooth surface and painted. The shaft was then sold to the club maker. The golf club sold to us golfers for several hundred dollars contained about ten dollars' worth of carbon fibers. The golf shaft price elasticity is not affected by the carbon fiber price, but because club brand controlled the market, we had no influence on the golf club market.

Many products, including one-hundred-meter-long wind turbine blades, go through a variation of this process. For us to sell our carbon fibers, we needed to convince the end product manufacturer first and after that, we needed to sell each of the companies in the supply chain on the desirability of using our fibers. This sales process was difficult and with each value-added, step adding significant cost to the finished product, it diminished the benefit of the lower cost associated with our commercial carbon fibers. This problem was compounded when aerospace carbon fiber manufacturers dumped their products in the market significantly below their cost. Actually, our carbon fiber price was below the aerospace carbon fiber producer's depreciation expense and below their incremental cost.

From the early days of developing our commercial carbon fiber concept, I studied the history of the glass fiber business. I always thought there was a lot of similarity between the two products in terms of the application technology and market development.

Fiberglass was introduced in the 1920s and, along with the glass reinforcement, the advanced composite concept was born. Initially there were two manufacturers of glass fibers, Corning Glass and Owens Illinois Glass, both working on the introduction of glass fiber composites. The two companies merged in 1929, forming Owens Corning, when they combined their technology and development effort to accelerate the introduction of glass fiber-reinforced composites. The initial interest came from the military for lighter weight in airplanes. One important application was Radom, found on the nose of airplanes, because glass composites were transparent to the radar transmissions and would be the perfect protection for the radio and radar equipment. These military applications were nice, but not a high-volume business.

After WW II, Owens Corning resumed their concentration on developing commercial applications. I had an opportunity to visit the application development facility in Granville, Ohio. While it had a look of a museum, it was quite impressive. The facility consisted of all types of composite production equipment in operating condition that, in its prime, had the capability to duplicate and troubleshoot any customer's process. I was quite jealous and wished that we had similar capabilities.

Owens Corning also started subsidiary companies to introduce finished products to begin the application growth. Once the application was well on its way, Owens Corning would divest these companies and encourage natural competition in the industry to develop. Probably the best example was what they did with the gasoline storage tanks in retail gas stations. Over a relatively short time, they replaced essentially one-hundred percent of the steel tanks. Both of these capabilities were fantastic business strategies, and I strongly believed that we needed to do something similar. At one point, we started to discuss some form of co-operation, but unfortunately, Owens Corning became distracted with asbestos litigation and any possibility for further discussion ended. Also, we did not have the financial strength or the experienced staff to duplicate such a facility and such a marketing strategy. We needed to come up with our own way of achieving similar results.

As we were preparing to introduce our new carbon fiber produced with our own precursor, it was time to find a way to inform the composite industry about our plans. While we were quite well known in the financial world because our share price performance, until this time we had not been very active in the composite industry. A consulting company had initiated a carbon-fiber-centered annual seminar. The usual participants were companies that considered the use of carbon fibers, but who wanted to know more about the industry. I was asked to speak at this seminar. There were about seventy-five participants, most of them composite engineers from the aerospace industry. I decided this was the best forum for me to introduce Zoltek's strategy to the industry. When I accepted the invitation to speak, I was immediately named as co-keynote speaker.

When it came my turn to speak after the lunch break, there was a problem with the computer equipment used for the PowerPoint presentation. While the equipment was being fixed, and I was standing on the podium, I decided to tell the audience a story:

My wife and I went on a safari to Africa with a group led by the St. Louis Zoo Director. We visited a Maasai village, which consisted of a large corral in the center surrounded by several huts. The animals were in the corral, taken care of by the children. Each hut was built by one of the wives, and the husband took care of the wives.

I looked into one of the huts; it was totally dark and in the center was a post, holding up the flat roof. On the way back to the lodge, our driver proudly told me that the huts are built with dry grass and dung.

He claimed that the wives had learned over time how much grass and dung to pile on the roof to make it last through the monsoon season.

So, I concluded, the Maasai women might have the claim to being the first composite engineers.

No one thought it was funny.

Once my questionable first impression was behind me, I laid out Zoltek's three prong strategy: lower cost carbon fiber, stable long-term pricing, and guaranteed availability. This concept went over much better than my story, and the entire group was energized. I believe that this was the first time many of them realized that the carbon fiber composite business could become a reality in the not-too-distant future. This was what they wanted to hear, and a number of people came to see me after my presentation to express specific interest in beginning to work with our fibers.

There was no question that we were on the right track with our commercial carbon fiber strategy, but like with so many other possibilities, each project required a lot of development work, intermediate products, and a copious amount of testing. It was hard to see how we could possibly do all that by ourselves. While the positive response from all the industry experts was gratifying, I felt a tremendous pressure to do something dramatic to accelerate our carbon fiber composite business.

The year 1999 was turning out as I feared. Carbon fiber sales had only increased by ten percent, but we were accumulating serious costs as we were bringing the carbon fiber lines into operation. At the same time, our Hungarian products sales fell by almost thirty percent without any decrease in operating costs because we were still in the process of finishing the precursor plant and starting production. It was my concern that we would lose our shareholder confidence if our revenue continued to decline.

After a lot of thinking and lessons learned from the glass fiber history, I decided our best way forward was to enter the intermediate products business.

At that time, we were selling our carbon fibers to a prepreg producer in San Diego who supplied the golf shaft producers. They were not doing well financially and owed us approximately $1 million. They decided to sell their company, and we became the most probable buyer. We concluded the transaction fairly quickly, and we were all of the sudden in the composite intermediates business.

We were starting a significant project with Pratt-Whitney to design compressed natural gas tanks for transport ships. We started to work with a filament winding company in Salt Lake City. They were also up for sale, and we decided to acquire them. We completed the development project with Pratt-Whitney, but the transport ship had not yet happened, though it was still under consideration. We also acquired an interest in a company working on bridge projects and earthquake resistant bridge column applications.

The largest acquisition was Structural Polymers (SP), a British prepreg company that concentrated on wind turbine and marine applications. Both of these applications were significant targets for our commercial carbon fibers. This company also had more expertise in resin technology and composite design and testing than all our other acquired companies.

In total, based on the acquired companies' revenues in 1999, we added almost $60 million to Zoltek's annual revenue. This additional revenue would more than overcome the reduction of the Hungarian specialty products revenue and would accelerate the carbon fiber sales enough to maintain Zoltek's growth projections.

However, this move came at a significant financial cost and put a strain on our management team. Financially, we borrowed to the maximum amount of money we could hope for, just to pay for these acquisitions, and everything would have to go smoothly for us to live up to our commitments. With the acquisitions came a significant number of new management and technical people who needed to become part of the team and support Zoltek's carbon fiber strategy.

We divided the company into three business units: Carbon Fibers, Composite Intermediates, and Specialty Products. The Carbon Fibers group was essentially the existing Zoltek carbon fiber business. All of the new businesses and the carbon fiber textile processing that we were already doing comprised the Composite Intermediates unit and was headed up by the president of the British company. The Specialty Products unit consisted of the Hungarian traditional product lines. With this organization and the added new management, we finally had the management team I had been trying to build, as well as extended capabilities with a framework for continued growth.

For change of pace, I took time off for the annual bank golf outing. Two weeks later, I went to Augusta for the first time. Drew was invited to join Augusta National, and he was kind enough to invite me as part of the first foursome he hosted, along with Linn and Jack Baumstark.

A week or so before the Augusta trip, I received a letter from Drew about our trip. In the letter, he warned that we could not wear shorts, so if we wanted to play golf, we needed to wear long pants or jockstraps. He also warned us that we could not wear green jackets because only members were allowed to do so. A few days later, I saw Jack and asked if he also got this letter, which he had. I told him I thought the letter was a little condescending to two fine gentlemen like us. I suggested that we should, at some point while at Augusta, appear in nothing but jockstraps and green jackets. Jack agreed, and we did just that on the first evening cocktails in our cabin.

Drew and Linn were all dressed for dinner and sipping on their martinis when Jack and I appeared in our outfits. The shock on Drew's face was worth the show. It took him a few seconds to connect his letter to our outfit. We all had a good laugh about it, and I do not think Drew ever sent that letter to his future guests. But I did pay the price for this trick on a later trip to Augusta.

With all the acquisitions completed, we were looking for a turnaround year in 2000. We organized an initial team-building conference in Arizona with our new management and key technical staff, including those from the Carbon Fiber and Composite Intermediates groups. The initial meeting went well, and we were optimistic about the future. However, I saw some potential problems with the new companies being overly defensive about their old businesses, and I was not convinced these new managers were totally committed to Zoltek's strategy.

For the first six months of 2000, all was going fairly well. In the spring, at the primary composite trade show in Paris, France, we introduced our new carbon fibers that were produced with our own precursor. Again, it was a big success, and we generated a lot of positive feedback. Our total revenue was recovering, but our share price continued its decline. It finally became clear to shareholders that our revenue growth was not coming from carbon fiber sales.

The acquired companies were not shifting their efforts to sell our carbon fibers fast enough. I worked with all of them to change their business plans. Everyone was quite cooperative, except the managers of Structural Polymers. They were a bit too arrogant and dishonest about their commitment. I had always trusted my instincts about people, but I had realized I had made a mistake with this group.

They truly did not want to change and did not understand that they were acquired to use their infrastructure and composite expertise to advance our carbon fiber strategy, not for their existing business, mostly prepregging glass fibers. I spent a lot of time trying to turn them around. Most of their people were working with the rest of Zoltek and trying to change, but the top managers were not supporting them.

The San Diego operation was supplying prepreg made with our carbon fibers to a company in California that manufactured large sailboat masts. This customer closed its California facility and moved it to

Australia. We decided to transfer the business to SP, since they had a sales presence there. When we were not getting carbon fiber orders, we looked into the reason. We found out that SP had actually switched to buying carbon fibers from one of our competitors. I had to do something to turn them around, so I interviewed each manager and key technical staff individually to see what they were thinking and how they felt about being part of Zoltek. Most of the individuals were happy with being part of Zoltek and fully supported our business strategy.

The top managers, who were the prior owners and personally had the most to gain from Zoltek's success, were the problem. They were arrogant to the level that they acted as if they actually had acquired Zoltek. I made it clear that either they change their attitude, or we would immediately overhaul the management. The following day, I had an all hands meeting during which it became obvious that, after my individual meetings, the top managers had intimidated everyone in the entire management team and had turned them against Zoltek. The meeting quickly became hostile.

I decided the only way to deal with them was to give the top managers a choice: either buy back the company or be replaced. They decided to buy the company, and I gave them ninety days to complete the transaction; the price was $5 million more cash than what Zoltek had paid. They also had to return all their Zoltek shares.

It was recommended that we also ask for a carbon fiber purchase agreement to show shareholders that we had gotten something out of this short-term acquisition. Although this went against my thinking because I was sure we would never do business with them again, but regrettably, I agreed. This decision turned out to be a costly mistake that would come back to haunt us six years later.

Our acquisition strategy did not work well. In reality, I don't think we could have done anything at that time to accelerate the market development. Participating in the value chain was the right strategy, but the companies we acquired were ineffective. Our timing was also too early.

After trimming, consolidating, and integrating these companies into the Zoltek organization, we embarked on the application development effort on our own. We already knew that the existing carbon-fiber value chain, based on the aerospace economic model, did not work for commercial products. For different reasons, the economic model for commercial products value chain based on glass fiber technology would not work either. Developing the correct balance between technology and economics was the key to successfully democratizing the use of carbon fiber composites. We had to understand this and try to change the prevailing dynamics.

We started to register losses, and the overall carbon fiber market was just getting worse. The precursor plant and the new carbon fiber lines were way underutilized because the carbon fiber market prices had no bottom and aerospace carbon fibers were selling at a fraction of their cost. It was impossible to develop new customers for commercial grade carbon fibers in such market conditions.

We embarked on several expensive application development projects with automotive companies, the biggest one with BMW. We also chased many applications, from fire-retardant mattresses to shipping pallets. We targeted likely markets, such as automotive and wind turbine blades, to be the defining markets for commercial carbon fiber composites.

Although I continued to be quite optimistic for the long-term, I realized we were in for a period of struggle. To minimize the overall effect of the slow carbon fiber growth, we slowed down the exit from the Hungarian traditional products. We hoped to maintain base revenues and minimize the financial losses from the Hungarian operations.

Struggle to Survive

In the spring of 2000, just over three years since acquiring the Hungarian acrylic fiber business, we introduced our new carbon fiber at the JEC global composite trade show in Paris. Along with our new fiber, we promoted our long-term strategy. Both were received enthusiastically, but very little changed in the overall market. The carbon fiber manufacturers were adding capacity, and the demand did not grow.

At the time, the total carbon fiber market was very small and mostly concentrated in military and aerospace applications. Any small amount of new capacity would cause meaningful oversupply in the market, and all the producers were trying to increase their market share by dumping their extra production. On the positive side, if any significant application did develop, there would not be enough carbon fiber, and there was no company other than Zoltek that could gear up fast enough to support any new demand.

About this time, the U.S. Air Force was funding a technical committee to investigate how to develop a low-cost carbon fiber. Every U.S. and foreign carbon fiber producer was invited to make a presentation. The only company not invited was Zoltek. One of our board members was aware of the committee, and he was able to get us an invitation. I made a presentation about our ability to produce all the carbon fibers the U.S. Air Force might need at a price point well within their objectives.

A heated discussion followed, as some of the committee members supported Zoltek, and others refused to accept that a commercial-grade fiber would be suitable to produce lightweight vehicles that could be delivered to remote sites by air transport. Once the technical staff agreed that the commercial carbon fibers were quite satisfactory for this application and using aerospace carbon fibers was not necessary, the chairman blurted out that they could just call the aerospace fibers "government fibers" and continue buying at high prices. Obviously his intention was not to find a low-cost fiber, but to justify paying a higher price. This was the typical government attitude. We really needed to find a new defining commercial application in the private sector.

The first non-aerospace applications were tennis rackets and golf club shafts, but these products could tolerate the higher prices. With interest developing in many truly commercial applications, we all thought demand would develop very fast if the cost came down to an affordable level, but it did not happen. After our painful experience of trying to speed up market development through downstream acquisitions, we had learned one lesson: to be a little more patient, which was never my virtue.

In 2000 and 2001, we wrote off our start-up costs, adjusted the inventory valuation, cut back operations in Abilene, and reduced the number of employees in Hungary. We also had to write off the difference in valuation of our shares used for the SP acquisition when they were returned at a significantly lower price when we divested the company. In total, we took huge losses for these years, but we ended up with a solid balance sheet and in good position to maintain a cash-flow neutral operation until a truly market-defining application became reality. We expected this application to be automotive, and with BMW in particular. A lesser possibility was the wind turbine blades, if in fact they were going to be as long and as big as some of the wind turbine companies were projecting.

But our business was just getting worse. Our revenue stopped growing, but our expenses continued to increase. In the case of the carbon fibers, we had started to use our own precursor, but our plant utilization was minimal. We were required to continue using Courtaulds precursor for our aircraft brake customers until our own precursor was qualified, which could take as long as a full year if everything went well. At this time, once again, the aircraft brake business was our only steady and profitable business, and we needed to convert them to using our own precursor-based fibers.

Given our financial position, I had some difficulty convincing our prime customers to commit to the qualification process. My sales pitch was that, for the moment, the aircraft manufacturers believed there were two sources of carbon fibers, Zoltek and SGL. But the problem was that both used the same precursor, meaning that, effectively, there was only a single source. Further, I predicted that Courtaulds would sell the acrylic business, and the new owner would put it into bankruptcy. If this happened and the aircraft brake customers realized this problem, there would be panic. Messier-Bugatti accepted my argument and qualified our precursor for all airplanes. Goodrich was much slower, and their hesitation ultimately cost them a lot of money and market share.

After we exited from the textile acrylic business, the Hungarian traditional businesses continued to decline further. The main product still active was the nylon fiber business, but our market position was weak. We did have a few small product lines of business that still had some strength. I promoted Ilona Tandi to the general manager position in Hungary. She was willing to do the unpopular things like reducing headcount and increasing productivity. She was also very loyal and did everything I asked her to do to keep the team on course with our overall corporate plans.

We tried to maintain our application development activities, even as our operating losses mounted. At the end of 2002, we were out of compliance with almost all our loan covenants. Compounding our problems, Southwest Bank was acquired by M&I Bank. The new bank did not have the same level of trust in me and/or the commitment to Zoltek and requested us to significantly reduce our borrowing. We had no chance for raising money from the stock market, and finding another bank was also out of the question. I started to look at ways to reorganize the company. This was the only time that I thought we might not be able to survive.

There was no clean way to break up the company because by this time, we were so interdependent on each operation. We did shut down the carbon fiber production at the Abilene plant, but otherwise there was very little we could do beyond cutting excess costs. In spite of all our problems, I was still determined that we were pursuing the correct concept and strategy.

Linn and Drew came to the rescue. Linn told Drew about our problems, and Drew decided to take matters into his own hands. He called me to tell me that he knew that I needed help, and he was going to organize a group to make an investment in Zoltek. I appreciated this very much because I would not have asked for such help; I believed that I needed to solve the problem myself and thought it would not be right to expect friends to share in my risk. Drew put together an investment group that included himself, his children's trust fund, Linn, John Mac-Donnell, Charlie Dill, several other friends, and me. We purchased $8.1 million in convertible debentures at $3.50 per share when shares were trading around $1.50 a share. This was a tremendous help and probably saved the company. It did, however, place tremendous pressure on me to make sure my friends would not lose their investment after they had trusted me. It all turned out well for the investors as several years later, Zoltek's share price increased to about fifty dollars.

Our significant losses continued, and our loan was viewed as a serious problem for the bank, particularly since I was still a director. I knew that Drew's loyalty would make it difficult for him to remove me from the board, so in 2003, I decided to resign. It was the right thing to do, and Drew appreciated it, and he was determined to put me back on the board in the future.

During those difficult years, I tried to reorganize the management team several times because we kept losing people who thought our situation was hopeless. Our employee turnover in the most critical positions was excessive. Even a number of the people who stayed started to lose their confidence. Hiring competent people into our situation was not realistic. Most people viewed our situation as a business that had lost its ability to compete. It was almost impossible to convince investors and employees that we were a developing company and that we were looking to change the composite industry.

The singular bright spot in my business life that year was that we succeeded in our Mavilon precursor-based fibers getting qualified in more and more brake programs, and we solidified our leadership in this field and our position as the largest supplier to this market. I single-handedly managed the aircraft brakes business, which continued to be the only solid business we had.

At Zoltek we were working with a number of potential customers on various application development projects with heavy concentration on the automotive market. Among the projects, there were two auto companies, BMW and Daimler-Mercedes, who appeared to be the most interested in developing carbon fiber technology. Eventually, we entered into a multi-year development agreement with BMW to develop the use of carbon fibers in automobiles.

We had serious projects with BMW and during our hardest times, we spent over $7 million supporting specific projects; first, a small roadster and later, the high performance X-5 utility vehicle. We also worked on several smaller component development projects. To entice us to continue supporting these projects, we had signed a contract assuring Zoltek to be the preferred and primary carbon fiber supplier for BMW. This was the reason we were investing so much time and resources to support their research when we really could not afford to.

Wind turbines were the other major market we were concentrating on. The blades were getting longer in order to increase the generating capacity, which would improve the economic viability of this market after the government subsidies discontinued. Up to thirty-meter long blades, glass fiber worked well, but the longer the blades became, they could only prove economical by using the much lighter weight carbon fibers.

We found Vestas Wind Systems to be the most likely first major customer. They were looking at aerospace carbon fibers, but realized the prevailing and projected price at the time would not be sustainable for their long-term cost requirements. We were able to convince them to test our fibers. Our performance was as good as or better than the aerospace fibers they had been using, but they were concerned about Zoltek's financial viability.

Our European sales manager, Tim McCarthy, who was generally a very good salesman, was unable to overcome this concern, and I tried to build his confidence with almost daily phone calls. Ultimately, I had to make numerous trips to Denmark to present our story and give Vestas management my personal assurance that we would be able to supply their requirements. As our financial situation was getting worse, this task became more and more difficult.

We completed the exit from most of the Hungarian traditional products. The real problem was that the carbon fiber business during this period grew very little, and our revenue fell to $60 million from $90 million five years before, putting our entire business strategy in doubt.

In 2004, our share price hit the low point of $1.25, which translated into total market valuation of the company of $20 million; a serious fall in just five years from over $1 billion. I understood the concern from our shareholders, but I never lost my confidence for the long-term and did my best to project this confidence. There were investment bankers who recommended taking the company private and after the market turned around, to go public again and make a huge profit. It was a good idea, but I believed this maneuver would cheat the shareholders who had trusted me. I felt just as I had years earlier when I would not sell stock when I believed the price was way beyond reasonable valuation.

There were also consequences in my private life. Many people praised me when the share price was rising rapidly, but they also personally blamed me when the share price fell like stone. This feeling seemed to be so strong that it affected my personal relationships. A positive outcome from this was that it helped me identify who my real friends were and are. I had and still have many good friends who maintained their trust and confidence in me during these bad times that lasted several years.

Through these five difficult years, we laid off a large portion of our workforce, both in the U.S. and Hungary, and we cut back in every possible area without abandoning our single defining goal of commercializing carbon fibers.

We were at the end of our limit for bank financing for both the U.S. and the Hungarian operations, and we were chronically short on cash. Most of the scrutiny was concentrated in the U.S., while the Hungarian financing was relatively stable. That all changed when we were late on a customs duty payment, and our bank account was directly debited by the government. This shocked our Hungarian bank, and we were immediately put on a workout list. This was purgatory in the banking business. Fortunately, the banker in Hungary assigned to review Zoltek's financial position understood our business and arrived at a positive recommendation. Even so, our banking relationships were still in a dangerously unstable position.

Just in time, after a lot of testing and negotiations, we received a significant initial trial order from Vestas Wind Systems. This gave us reason to believe that in 2004, our business would start to change for the better and we were hoping this troubled period would come to an end.

During these stressful years, Mary and I did our best to project a confident image and maintain our normal lifestyle.

By this time, Mary had ended her full-time travel agency work. However, my travel and Zoltek's international travel increased dramatically; Mary continued to save a lot of money by using her extensive knowledge to minimize our travel costs. After a few years as the computer systems for travel agents shifted from the necessity to be at the office, Mary could use her iPad to do the travel work anywhere. She continued to have an affiliation with a travel agency, but she only used it for the back-up services. She also did complicated travel arrangements for our friends, but discontinued working full-time.

She started to participate on various institution boards, such as the St. Louis Art Museum Friends, St. Louis History Museum Friends, the St. Louis Botanical Garden Friends, and others.

As my own travel became more frequent and more intense, there was less time to enjoy the travel experience; Mary began to cut back on joining me on my trips. Instead we took some actual vacation trips and continued to visit our place in Hawaii. She took a few trips with her family to Ireland and several cruises to celebrate birthdays and special events. Marta joined us in Hawaii several times, sometimes alone and other times with her parents, and it became one of her favorite places.

I used our Hawaii trips to improve my golf. On the way to Hawaii, we had a layover in Los Angeles, and I would call our golf pro to arrange times for lessons. My game was not improving a lot. One day I decided it was time to have some fun with the pro. I went to the pro shop and asked the nice Hawaiian ladies if Peter, the pro, was in. They called for him to come out of his office.

I said to him, "Peter, I want to tell you that you are getting a bad reputation in St. Louis."

Peter said, "I don't see how that is possible. I have never been to St. Louis."

"That may be, but when people ask me where I got my lousy swing, I tell them I learned it from you," I told him.

First, he was stunned, but when the ladies stated to laugh, he realized I was just joking. I think he tried harder after that.

Linn was my banker and board member, but more important, he was also my best friend. He loved Hawaii and he and his wife, Jenny, joined us a few times there. We had great golf games and almost all the time he won. He was a better player than I, but even if I had a chance under normal circumstances, the constant phone calls at critical points were very distracting. There were times I thought he was actually organizing the calls to distract me, and he did not deny it. In the evenings, we played gin, which I won. In the end, most of the time we were even on the money won and lost. We always had a great time.

Section 6
Building Zoltek's Carbon Fiber Business

Breakthrough – The Pivotal Years

The general demand for carbon fibers improved with requirements for the development of three major high-carbon-fiber-content aircraft programs: the A-380, B-787, and B-777ER. The excess industry capacity was absorbed by this newly increased demand. Even more important, the wind turbine business surfaced as the first major breakthrough in commercial carbon fiber applications. And we were in the best position to take advantage of the situation.

The emergence of the wind turbine blade application was the first true confirmation of the divergence of the carbon fiber business between aerospace and commercial applications. Almost more important, the wind turbine-blade application was quite similar to that of aircraft wings, and the use of the different type of carbon fibers demonstrated that our lower-cost commercial fibers could match Vestas' performance requirements at a much lower cost than if they used aerospace fibers. This combination completely validated Zoltek's market concept and truly began to revolutionize the entire industry.

The wind turbine blades were built like and function similarly to airplane wings. In the wind turbine, the wind energy turned the turbine blade, rotating the generator, and thereby converting the wind energy into electricity. Airplane wings were designed to lift the airplane by converting the engine propulsion energy, which provides the forward speed, creating the wind which pulls the wing upward, i.e., lifting the weight of the airplane. Mechanical stiffness and strength, which were provided by the carbon fibers, were the clear necessity for both.

Minimizing the weight of airplane wings was an obvious advantage in airplanes. In wind turbine blades, the importance of weight-reduction was subtler, but it could greatly improve the performance and reliability of the wind turbine. The wind turbine blades were produced in an enormous tool configured like clamshells. Glass fiber fabric was manually laid into the lower and upper clamshell and resin was vacuum impregnated into the fiberglass fabric. In a separate process, the center spar was fabricated with carbon fiber prepreg to a finished composite and laid into the lower clamshell, and then the clamshells were closed. The entire blade was placed in an oven until the resin was cured. It sounds simple, but remember, the blades could be as long as one hundred meters, longer than a football field.

Vestas Wind Systems, the largest wind turbine company in the world, needed to increase the length of turbine blades to improve the efficiency of one of their smaller turbines in a low-velocity wind region in Mongolia. They needed to reduce the weight of the blades and used carbon fibers to accomplish the required design change. The project was so successful that Vestas decided that they would change to carbon fiber composite blades for their entire turbine models in order to improve and upgrade their turbine efficiency and reliability.

After we decided to target the wind turbine application and I had directed Tim McCarthy, our European sales manager, to personally cover the potential customers in this application, he spent a lot of his time at Vestas. They were clearly the most likely company to embrace our carbon fiber technology. However, they were still working with the aerospace fibers to assure an uninterrupted carbon fiber supply. I continued to visit Vestas a number of times to keep the pressure on and to reinforce my personal commitment not to let them down, in spite of our questionable financial position.

We supplied our carbon fibers for testing and after many test runs and a series of successful initial orders, Vestas was convinced that our commercial-grade carbon fibers could match the performance of the aerospace carbon fibers. They also realized that Zoltek's market strategy and our low-cost carbon fibers were the only long-term viable option to support their own strategy. Ole Kristensen, the purchasing director for the blade manufacturing unit of Vestas, realized that there were several carbon fiber suppliers who could supply part of their needs, but he also saw that no carbon fiber company other than Zoltek could supply them at a sustainable price and at the required supply level.

Time was running out, and Ole had to make a decision. He had to convince Ole Barup Jacobsen, the head of the blade manufacturing operation. This was not easy because both of them had to bet their careers on our meeting our commitments. Finally, after I reassured both of them that I would personally make sure they would not be disappointed, we did receive a supply contract in 2004 and by the end of the year, a commitment for at least eighty percent of Vestas' current and future requirements.

Almost simultaneously, we received a contract from Gamesa Eolica, the third largest wind turbine company at the time, based in Spain. Gamesa had a joint venture with Vestas for a few years. Their turbine design came from this joint venture, which fell apart just prior to Vestas beginning the conversion to carbon fibers. Gamesa tried to follow Vestas' lead and introduced their version of the carbon fiber-based design. They were ramping up slowly, and their projected requirements were only a fraction of Vestas' requirements.

As soon as we received a projection of Vestas' requirements, we began the process of restarting the Abilene Plant, increasing our precursor production, and developing plans to expand our Hungarian carbon fiber capacity. Our Abilene plant had been shut down, and the entire company had been in a survival mode for about two years. Restarting the plant and energizing the entire organization became the immediate challenge.

First, we reassigned all the engineers to review the condition of the production lines. Second, we started hiring managers, engineers, and operators. And third, we dispatched a start-up team from Hungary, headed by Tibor Ledvényi. Our design capacity was more than enough to supply the initial requirements of both customers. But starting from no activity to one hundred percent speed was extremely difficult.

Unfortunately, what could go wrong did go wrong. But the ultimate problem that we encountered, and could not overcome, was that Abilene had been the wrong location for our plant. We concentrated on finding a readily available facility, and we failed to foresee several factors: one, the lack of potential operators in the Abilene workforce. Two, the lack of traditional factory working families in the area and the difficulty in training and retaining factory workers who came from oilfield and ranch work. Three, the warning signs that led all the manufacturing companies to exit Abilene before we built our plant, and four, the inability to keep employees long enough to go through training and have them gain enough experience to depend on during the night shift. It was too dangerous to operate the plant with untrained employees. So, after several months of trying, we were forced to look at other options.

We decided that our best option was to concentrate on the expansion of our Hungarian capacity. This was a significant project. We needed to build a building to house the new lines and had to demonstrate that we could build and commission carbon fiber lines in six months, which we claimed we could do, even though it was unheard of in the industry. While we completed the expansion, we operated Abilene as best we could. We also accelerated our exit from all the

Hungarian traditional businesses and reassigned as many operators as possible to the new carbon fiber lines.

We financed the restart of Abilene with additional private placement convertible debentures with friendly investors. But to build the Hungarian capacity, we needed significant funding. Bank financing was not an option. We attempted to do a secondary public offering, but we were not able to attract a competent banker or investors. The most viable and expeditious option available to us was convertible debentures with one or more institutional investors.

We were fortunate to connect with Bruce Bernstein, the managing partner of Omicron Capital. He came to visit Zoltek to discuss our needs. I spent about two hours with Bruce, including a tour of our MRP facility. Our meeting went well and by the time he arrived back to New York, he decided to finance our project up to $50 million. I certainly appreciated his confidence in me and his support of Zoltek's business strategy. We continued our relationship as we built our business in the following three years. It turned out to be a great win for Bruce and his investors and a huge help for Zoltek as we worked through some difficult times.

The convertible debt financing provides the lender the opportunity to convert the loan to share ownership. Zoltek would borrow the money at a negotiated interest rate, and this debt could then be converted within a certain time to Zoltek shares at a negotiated higher price than the prevailing share price at the time of the closing of the financing. In some cases, in order to provide more incentive for the lender, we offered some warrants, giving investors an opportunity to buy additional shares at a later date at a negotiated share price, equal to or higher than the loan conversion price.

While this financing was expeditious, there was a serious negative consequence to this approach, created by the Sarbanes-Oxley Act, which changed accounting from an exact science to fiction. The accountants, who were in no way qualified to do so, were expected to estimate the ultimate price of the stock at the time the investors would decide to convert the loan or warrant to shares. The difference was assumed to be a non-cash interest and "beneficial conversion feature" cost, and the company had to amortize these losses during the life of the loan. This was total fiction, but these non-cash losses could destroy the actual earnings for several years. In 2005, these non-cash financing costs amounted to over $25 million on our income statement.

An average potential investor or shareholder could not understand this accounting or the consequences to the business. Almost more of a concern was that most of our major customers and our potential new customers could not comprehend how we could possibly overcome these huge losses.

During 2004 and most of 2005, we were struggling to keep up with the Vestas and Ganesa demand for carbon fibers. Vestas developed their own process for producing their prepreg. Their process was designed around our carbon fiber properties and format. Using other carbon fibers would have been more difficult and significantly more expensive for them.

However, Gamesa bought prepreg, using our carbon fibers, from SP. Gamesa wanted to control the carbon fiber supply and the prepreg production cost, so they purchased the fiber from us and directed us to ship it to SP. With our fibers being in short supply, Vestas was willing to buy prepreg if it was available to supplement our fiber supply. SP would take carbon fibers from the inventory that we shipped for Gamesa and sell to Vestas, causing problems and disputes with both our customers and resulting in several unpaid invoices from Gamesa. Based on terms of the ill-conceived supply agreement we entered into when we divested them, SP Systems actually sued Zoltek for not supplying them enough carbon fibers, even though they had no orders for additional carbon fibers.

As I had predicted, Courtaulds went through financial problems and in May 2005, the acrylic fiber business, after first being spun off, declared bankruptcy. This immediately resulted in an opportunity to dramatically increase our aircraft brake business. We needed to add more capacity in Hungary to be able to take full advantage of this opportunity.

With all this activity, we needed more people throughout the company. I spent considerable time recruiting a president to take over the management of sections of our business. It was a difficult challenge to bring on a person new to the industry and to our company, while Zoltek looked financially unstable. After two failed attempts, I had to give up for the time being and concentrate on recruiting lower-level management.

By the summer of 2005, we were in a good position and had mostly caught up with the current demand, but projections for the future demand were significantly beyond our capacity. We needed to re-evaluate our long-term business plan. We had proven our commercial carbon fiber concept, and now we had the choice of either settling for a piece of the available market or continuing to build Zoltek into the undeniable leader in the world of commercial carbon fibers, completing the democratization of carbon fibers composites that I envisioned years before.

In making the decision about which direction to go, I called for a special Board of Directors meeting. I presented the two alternates. First option: with the expansion of our capacity and the recently developed rapid growth of our business, we were in very good position to ultimately reach about $250 million profitable revenue with minimum additional financing and few management changes. Second option: complete our current expansion, consolidate and improve our expanded operations, building a strong management team, and embark on an aggressive expansion that could take our annual revenue to one billion dollars or more.

The meeting did not go well. What I expected was to have a lively but constructive discussion and come to a consensus about the direction we should take. Instead, several of the directors expressed serious frustration and unloaded personal criticism and lack of confidence in me. We never actually got to discuss the future plans. I was also disappointed that only one director, Linn, expressed his full confidence and support for the direction I would decide to take.

In a few days, one of the directors insisted that I turn over the management of the company to another of our directors and if I were not willing to comply, he would resign from the Board. This was a ridiculous demand for many reasons, and I refused to consider it. There was no question that this move would have been a disaster, and I encouraged this director to go ahead and resign, which he did.

I was always concerned that our directors had assumed a certain amount of personal and financial risk as our share price was more and more volatile, but now I realized that several directors did not fully understand our business and their associated personal risk, I realized that further changes to the Board composition was inevitable. I also decided it was time to give the Board more access and exposure to our management team.

It was clear that I alone would have to make the decision about the future direction of the company. This decision was not terribly difficult. I could not justify fifteen years of struggle to change an industry and end up just building a small, slow-growing company. Of course, I decided to go for the aggressive strategy.

As we were aggressively pursuing our expansion projects and converting the company to a one hundred percent carbon fibers business, I was preparing our business plans for the next five years. While I was developing my plans, I felt that I was losing my energy and enthusiasm for the future.

It turned out that I was experiencing congestive heart failure. It was a shocking experience, and my doctor was not very encouraging about my future. Getting close to sixty-three years old and facing potentially serious heart problems, from which my father had died at exactly the same age, made me think twice about going forward with an aggressive business plan. It also made me think hard and develop plans to build the management team.

One of the favorite questions at almost every investor presentation was, "What will happen to Zoltek if you get hit by a bus?"

Thinking that I was bulletproof, I would jokingly respond, "I do not really care because I will be dead."

Generally this answer was accepted with a laugh, but now I started to think that it was not all that funny. I needed to develop a succession plan.

However, I recovered in a month or so, and my health was almost back to normal. No one was able to identify the cause of my condition. As I was inquiring what caused my problem, my doctor friend told me, "We do not ask a lot of questions when things turn out well." It seems my illness was caused by a virus.

During the entire time, I did not miss a day of work and once I started to feel close to normal, I was more determined to go forward with a plan to build Zoltek into the undisputed leader in the commercial carbon fiber business, completing the democratization of carbon fibers.

We closed out 2005 with $55 million in carbon fibers revenue. This was twice our 2003 revenue. Our share price also recovered somewhat to $14 per share, and our market valuation was just under $250 million.

Early in 2006, I went to visit my family in Minneapolis for my mother's ninety-first birthday. We spent some time together and had a few meals with the whole family. Things were seemingly normal, and we had a nice time together. My brother had been diagnosed with cancer the prior year and had gone through several surgeries and was still not doing well. This, of course, was a major concern for my mother, given their very close relationship.

The last evening I was there, we were in my brother's living room. His son, Attila, had two small children at the time, and they were running around like little kids do. Although my mother's health was okay, she was not interested and seemed withdrawn. It was very unusual for her. That was the last time I saw her, and she died two weeks later. Although she and I drifted apart over the later years of her life, it was difficult for me to accept that she was gone. My brother was devastated.

As I looked back at her life, it was hard to imagine how difficult her life had been. She lived through two world wars, her young and happy life was disrupted as World War II arrived in Hungary, and she had to bring up my brother and me essentially alone during the horrors that followed the war and during the miserable life under communism.

She found a comfortable life with the family all together in America for only fifteen years until my father died, and she spent the last thirty years of her life alone, worrying about my brother and his family. She lived her entire life selflessly for the benefit of our family. I felt terrible, and I felt that she deserved much more from life.

My brother's health seemed to be doing better, but his diagnosis was not very encouraging. My brother died the next year. I am glad that his health was still looking optimistic before my mother died. If she had lived to see my brother die, it would have killed her.

My brother's life was very simple. He lost his first and only professional job when Univac closed its St. Paul, Minnesota, plant in the early 1980s, and he never had another steady job of any kind. My father had pushed him to finish his degree at the university and try to become successful in a professional career. He went along grudgingly and at the time he lost his job, my father was gone. He was not challenged by my mother, and he certainly did not have the desire for a real career.

My brother's older son was still in Abilene, working for Zoltek. His younger son had three children by this time, and they moved into my mother's house.

We enjoyed watching our little niece, Marta, growing up. At our annual Thanksgiving parties, she was hanging around our friends like a little adult. She would stay up until she dropped and stayed overnight. Joan and Mary would organize annual pool parties for her birthday, which was always a fun event. During the summer, she would come over for a swim in our pool and as she got older, she would bring some of her friends along. It was always great to see her. She was our favorite niece, so she had most of Mary's attention.

By this time, Marta was in high school and doing quite well. She participated in Mute Court program and was getting to look like a better lawyer than some I hired. She decided very early to become a lawyer.

Breakthrough – Growth Years

As for Zoltek, we entered 2006 with high expectations and renewed enthusiasm. It turned out to be both our best and worst year.

Our revenue projections for the coming years were very positive. Aside from the fast-growing wind turbine business, we were starting some exciting proof-of-concept automotive projects, giving us confidence that this market would soon become the second major application for our carbon fibers. There were a number of other significant new application developments emerging, including precast concrete reinforcement and deepsea oil rig tethers and umbilical cables. Our aircraft brake business looked better than ever, and we expected a significant growth in our commercial aircraft brake business.

While we were optimistic about sales, we were still scrambling to complete the projects to build capacity and hire operational staff, including managers, engineers, and operators, to run the plants. Most of the expansion was taking place in Hungary where we should have had plenty of operators available from the discontinued product lines. However, soon we realized that most of the plant people had been doing the same job for many years and did not understand why the company had changed. They were disappointed that we had closed their old operations, and they were unwilling to change job assignments, a hangover from communism.

Many of the operators were close to retirement age. Based on age and time of service, there was a government-imposed formula for payout to employees who did not wish to change job assignment. For many employees, this lump sum payment was a significant amount of cash at the time. A number of people elected to take the money and retire. With the Abilene plant still having significant problems, the pressure was on to bring the new lines as fast as possible to full capacity. The need to hire and train a significant number of operators added unexpected pressure on the Hungarian management team, which was led by Ilona Tandi. She understood the situation and did well in making the necessary changes to build the precursor and carbon fiber capacity.

Our engineering team, led by Peter Kiss, managed the expansion projects, building new production lines in time to keep up with demand. Our production team, led by Istvan Kinter, had a lot of pressure, but managed to keep up with our customers' demands. Tim McCarthy returned to St. Louis from his European sales assignment to oversee the sales and marketing for the entire company, but his primary activity became product allocation to be sure we would keep our existing customers happy. And I took care of the aircraft brake business. The entire carbon fiber industry was watching, and this was the time for us to prove, what we had been publicly stating for years, that we could increase our capacity to meet demand by building new production lines in six months.

It was interesting to see how our primary customers reacted. Vestas worked with us on a day-to-day basis, while they also monitored our expansion process, often amazed at the rapid changes we were making. Their confidence never wavered. Several years later, after both of the original Vestas decision makers retired, I met them for dinner, and they told me that we never caused them to miss a contract commitment with their customers. Gamesa, on the other hand, required us to ship carbon fibers to SP Systems to produce prepreg, and SP cheated them and lied to them about what we shipped to them, but Gamesa always blamed Zoltek for all their wind turbine delivery problems.

The aircraft brake business was similar. Messier-Bugatti had qualified our fibers made with our own precursor for essentially all their brake programs and when the Courtaulds precursor was not available, they relied on us to supply all their requirements. I can never forget the surprise on Maurice Perrault's face when he came to visit the Hungarian plant and saw that we were actually producing carbon fibers when only equipment components had been placed on the floor during his prior visit, just two months earlier. Maurice was responsible for negotiating the supply contract, and he was gratified that we lived up to our commitments.

Goodrich, our first major customer, qualified one of our competitors because they were concerned about our financial condition. They ignored my warnings and did not extend any effort to qualify our own precursor-based fibers for all their brake programs. When Courtaulds declared bankruptcy, they offered Goodrich a final purchase of precursor, at triple the price, before the plant would be shut down. The Goodrich purchasing people intimidated me to load up on Courtaulds precursor at these extraordinary prices. We continued supplying them Courtaulds acrylic-based fibers until we used up the entire expensive inventory. At that point, they expedited qualification of the Mavilon-based fibers. This whole situation was a significant personal disappointment for me and cost Goodrich a lot of money. It took me several years to overcome this and to restore our good relationship. But we did lose part of their business.

This year was becoming our best year because what we achieved with a bare, minimum-sized team was truly remarkable. This was the first year when Zoltek became a one hundred percent carbon fiber business, including the Hungarian operation. The Hungarian team showed that they had mostly overcome the stifling government-run socialist system and had fully bought into the Zoltek carbon fiber strategy. They had become a critical part of an integral international private company. Just as important, any reservations our customers may have had about the Hungarian operation was gone after they worked together as a team and gained mutual respect for each other.

Our revenue grew sixty-seven percent to $93 million, with over ten percent operating profit. Our financial performance improved significantly, and our share price also recovered to over $39 per share, which represented approximately $700 million market valuation.

As the valuation of the company climbed, the favorite investor question became, *what patent protection do we have for our technology?* For years when I was asked this question, I would explain that the base technology dated back as early as the 1920s, and carbon fiber had been produced for military use since the early 1970s, so patenting was not the way to go. Instead I suggested we protect our knowledge by keeping our technology secret. I would try to explain what makes producing carbon fibers so difficult that no one could quickly enter the market. As soon as I would start talking technology, I lost everyone.

So finally, I started to say, "Producing carbon fibers is like sex."

This got their attention and curiosity, so I would finish with, "You can talk about it and read about it, but you never know what it is like until you try to do it. But no one would try producing carbon fibers again."

That, they understood.

An NPR reporter, in conjunction with discussion of the Iranians illegally buying carbon fibers, asked me the same question. I gave him the same answer. He loved it so much that he had actually put it on air. I received a number of calls from all over the country from friends shocked about my one and only appearance on NPR.

Although this was the best year for our business, in some ways, this year also was our worst year. Our Abilene plant continued to be a mess that cost us a lot of money trying to fix, we had to battle an unfortunate lawsuit over an ill-conceived supply contract, and we were starting to show huge non-cash costs related to the convertible financing.

The Abilene plant performance did not improve, regardless of what we tried to do. This was severely limiting our capacity. We were having difficulty keeping up with the rapidly increasing demand for our carbon fibers in the wind turbine application. Demand from Vestas was exploding, and Gamesa was starting to ramp up their carbon fiber blade production.

SP Systems tried to sell Vestas their prepreg products using a competitor's carbon fibers, but Vestas rejected this option. Vestas designed their own process to produce prepreg as part of the fabrication of their wind turbine blades. This process was developed around our carbon fibers, and Vestas had no interest in getting SP involved.

We did supply SP with all of Gamesa's requirements, but it was clear that we were having capacity problems. This was when our ill-conceived supply contract came back to haunt us. SP realized we could not supply anymore and placed a significant order in hopes of controlling our production capacity and take over the Vestas business. SP then tried to use the purchase agreement we signed four years earlier to buy and resell our fibers. Vestas wanted no part of that. They wanted to purchase our fibers directly from Zoltek.

When Vestas rejected SP's overures and continued their business with Zoltek, SP sued us. We thought it was a ridiculous lawsuit, but it turned out badly. SP people misrepresented their business, claiming that Vestas wanted to buy their prepreg products. Our attorneys were unable to effectively deal with these misrepresentations and never challenged their damage claims. It turned out to be the trial from hell, and we lost the case. This was an expensive and time-consuming diversion, at a point when we could least afford either.

We were not doing much better with our own lawsuit against the U.S. government for compensation for the use of our patented stealth technology. By that point, we had actively pursued compensation from the U.S. government for ten years.

Our patented technology was the basis for achieving superior stealth performance for several advanced aircraft and other military equipment. We zeroed in on the B-2 bomber and the F-22 fighter programs to estimate the value of our technology. These two aircraft programs cost the U.S. about $400 billion and, largely because our stealth technology, these two airplane programs were a huge success.

The U.S. Department of Justice used every legal maneuver available to delay the case. Very early in the discovery, the Northrup Grumman engineers admitted they used our technology in the B-2 design, but later, the government challenged this admission. Similarly, the F-22 stealth design was covered by our patent, but the government claimed that the materials were purchased from Japan; therefore, Zoltek was not entitled to claim damages.

Finally, the U.S. Department of Justice lawyer and a representative from the U.S. Air Force visited the Court of Federal Claims judge, personally asserting state secret privilege, blocking Zoltek's opportunity for further discovery. Our case was getting nowhere.

Working on so many issues with building Zoltek, this infringement claim was not at the top of my concerns. However, it was disturbing that if we had the opportunity to supply the carbon fibers or if we would have received reasonable compensation for these programs, our constant financial struggles could have been made much easier. Zoltek would have been a much stronger company.

This fight was not over, but it certainly became more difficult, and we realized that it would take much longer to resolve.

As we were reporting our quarterly results, showing increased revenue, and the outlook for wind energy was improving, Zoltek's share price started to climb. This, of course, was a positive development, and we enjoyed significant investor and shareholder enthusiasm. Our share price fluctuated from a low of $8.03 to $39.74 during 2006. The higher the share price went, the more non-cash losses related to the convertible financing we were required to report. By the end of the year, most of these warrants were cashed in, but these fictitious losses amounted to over $50 million.

These non-cash losses had no impact on business, but our shareholders, and more important, our customers, could not understand how that was possible.

I was called to see the BMW financial staff to explain. They kept asking me how and when we would have to pay back these losses. They just could not or would not accept any of my explanations. They just could not see how Zoltek could survive, and this concern possibly became a factor in their decision on whether or not to rely on Zoltek for a long-term partnership. There is no question in my mind that most of our existing and future potential customers were concerned about our ability to survive. Obviously, if these losses were real losses, it would have been virtually impossible to survive. This was very difficult to overcome with people inside or outside of our company.

I recognized our need for building the management team to support the expected growth of the company, but our financial reports made the recruiting process very difficult. Also, the demands on my time in dealing with immediate business issues made it impossible to concentrate on recruiting during this year. I also had to postpone dealing with the Board reorganization. For all these reasons, I considered this year to be our worst year.

As a welcome relief from business, Drew invited me again to Augusta. It had been two trips ago when Jack and I surprised him with our outfits, and I knew he would get back at me at some point. He was also concerned that I might come up with some more tricks. But by this time, I assumed all had been forgotten. Our agenda was to arrive in the morning and play a round of golf after lunch. Cocktails were followed with a great dinner in the evening, then cards, drinks, and cigars late into the night.

The next morning, we were hitting some balls on the range. I was hitting all over the place, and I noticed Drew was talking with the caddies, but I did not think anything of it. When we got to the first tee, there were a number of people standing on the tee with more coming from the clubhouse. I thought it was quite unusual, but still did not think much about it until I teed off. I did not disappoint Drew and hit a terrible drive. As I turned around, I saw the horrified look on everyone's face. That is when I realized something was up. Drew started to laugh and informed our spectators that the reason I was the Hungarian national golf champion is because I was the only golfer in Hungary. Drew had told everyone I was the Hungarian national golf champion and that is why everyone had come out to the first tee. Drew just loved it and told the story to our friends many times.

After this short diversion, I was ready to face the changing fortunes of the carbon fiber business. The demand for carbon fibers continued to grow in 2007 and so did our revenue. We were looking for another year of a sixty-plus percent sales increase, which required us to address our capacity expansion.

Less than three years after the wind turbine business emerged as our first major commercial carbon fiber market, we were running out of capacity. We had stretched our basic infrastructure to support the increased capacity to the breaking point. Anticipating that our planned expansion would be completed in 2008, the Hungarian plant would be maxed out at twenty million pounds (eleven thousand tons) capacity. This would be the largest carbon fiber plant in the world, but unless we found a way to expand beyond the Hungarian plant, our revenue potential would be limited to around $300 million.

A key component of our strategy had been to have the capacity available at the time the commercial applications developed in order to preempt competitors from establishing an early foothold in the market. As our revenue was rapidly climbing, we were getting both higher and higher demand projections from our customers and indications that other wind turbine companies were seriously considering designing longer blades using carbon fibers.

We were also getting indications of new significant automotive and deep-sea drilling applications, which would demand huge amounts of carbon fibers. If these projections were even remotely correct, we needed to further increase our capacity and, most important, we needed to increase our production infrastructure, particularly our precursor capacity.

I was already working on a plan for how to accomplish this, but I also needed to be sure to get the Board to support such an expansion. And once again, we needed to concentrate on building up our management team.

One new board member I selected was Mike Latta, a good friend and an entrepreneur who understood how small companies operate. Mike knew the other board members, and he was somewhat familiar with Zoltek. I believed his support and his fresh look at our business would be helpful.

In early 2007, I convinced George Husman to take the position of Chief Technology Officer. I had known George and worked with him on a number of development projects over several years. He was well known in the composite industry, and his joining Zoltek gave us the necessary leadership to support our carbon fibers with the application technology we needed.

George agreed to join Zoltek for two or three years, but he ended staying for seven years. His support in expanding our knowledge and application opportunities, including the revitalization of our automotive business development, was critical.

George was the right person for the technology position and also for the insider board member position, replacing John Kardos.

At the same time that I was making the changes to the Board, we also concentrated on recruiting application project managers, engineers, sales and marketing people, and general management staff. I needed to concentrate on building a leadership team to manage the significant changes that I had expected to come. I had been disappointed with earlier hires that came with experience from the carbon fiber or composite industry, but were unable to turn their experience into positive accomplishment in support of our contrarian strategy. This time I decided to look for younger people who could be trained and were anxious to learn. I also looked for people I knew well and had worked with, similar to my experience with George.

Our general manager in Hungary, Ilona (Ica) Tandi, was ready to take early retirement after leading the unpopular changes needed to re-organize the plant operations and the closing of the traditional businesses. Ica took my directions and led the transformation from the dark socialist company to a successful enterprise. She had done a great job, in spite of lack of cooperation from some of the old management members who were not willing to change. I realized it was a stressful time for her, considering the conflict with so many people she had worked with for many years and lived together in the small town where our plant was located. After she retired, she built a nice home in town, and she still lives there.

I needed to find an outsider to finish the changeover. Sándor Horváth, our maintenance manager, came from a nearby paper plant, where he was the general manager. With his management experience, his knowledge of English language, and being an outsider, he was the right person to take over as the general manager of Zoltek Zrt. Sándor was the right choice, and he became instrumental in building the Hungarian operation into a world class, and the largest, carbon fiber production facility in the world.

The only option we had to grow beyond the fully developed Hungarian plant was to locate an idle or failing textile acrylic fibers plant, which was similar to the Hungarian technology that we could convert to precursor manufacturing. We found what looked to be a perfect match, the Cydsa plant in Guadalajara, Mexico. The first young person I hired was Casey Thomas, as an assistant to the president, to assist me with researching various business projects and markets. His first assignment was to find out everything he could about this plant. Casey gained part of his MBA training in Mexico, which turned out to be very helpful.

By early 2007, we visited the facility, and everything appeared in line with our expectation that this was our best possibility for expansion.

After our success in the wind energy application and a number of visible automotive projects, coupled with the publicity of my optimistic outlook, we generated a tremendous interest in carbon fibers around the globe.

We were regularly getting inquiries for potential technical and business cooperation. One of the more intriguing inquiries came from Saudi Arabia. It seemed that the Saudi royal family had decided to create an industry and jobs for the local population based on their only resource, oil. A prince wanted to build a composite auto component manufacturing center that, of course, needed carbon fibers. He decided that the successful bidder for a major refinery project had to also build a carbon fiber plant. After investigating the carbon fiber industry, Zoltek's low-cost strategy was his preferred choice.

I met with the project manager for one of the companies bidding on the refinery project in London. Getting the commitment and a signed letter of intent to build a carbon fiber plant was the key for them to secure the project. I figured this gave us significant leverage. This project included a 200,000-ton ACN facility and 5,000-ton carbon fiber plant. The total project was several billion dollars, and the carbon fiber plant was a small but critical part. Although it was going to take several years to develop, I saw this as a great opportunity for Zoltek to potentially trade our carbon fiber technology into a joint venture for a long-term, low-cost ACN source.

Ultimately the allocation of the crude oil at the wellhead cost, which was about one dollar per barrel, was the real carrot for the successful bidder and getting that commitment from the oil ministry was not going to be easy. There were several other groups competing for it. Our potential partner seemed to be well on the way to get this approval, and they were willing to share their huge benefit with us. The preliminary joint venture concept would enhance our strategy for low-cost commercial carbon fibers and, coupled with the planned expansion in our precursor capacity, would make Zoltek the undisputed carbon fiber industry leader.

I visited Jubail, Saudi Arabia, the proposed plant site, with a stopover in Dubai. The trip was an eye-opener from several points. The purpose of my visit was to gain a first-hand understanding of the project's viability and to assess the probability of success for Zoltek. I expected to be in the desert, but the sight of nothing but sand was depressing. The extremely fine sand constantly in the air was a concern because it would be problematic for carbon fiber production.

The dichotomies in the society, the religion, and the economy were visible everywhere. Most management and technical staff were British, and the workers were from all over the world, but mostly from Asia. There were no Saudi workers, but when it came to a ceremonial lunch, there were more of them than the foreign management team. It was clear that the wellhead cost of oil is amazingly low, but the oil money supports a mostly idle population, which brings the real cost of oil up to $30 or more per barrel. This system seemed to me like modern-day slavery. The locals were the masters, and the workers were poorly paid and excluded from society.

It was difficult to see how we could work in the Saudi Arabian cultural and political environment, and I had strong doubts about our success in being part in the project. But I decided the potential benefit, if successful, was worth the effort to stay involved until the final decision was made by the Saudis.

This project also started me thinking about using a joint venture concept for our global expansion. It was fairly common in the chemical industry to sell or license technology or use the technology as the basis for establishing joint ventures. I thought this concept could accelerate the growth and the globalization of commercial carbon fibers. To this end, we developed standard designs for 5,000-ton and 10,000-ton annual production facilities that we could build anywhere in less than a year from raw land to full production.

However, our most immediate task was to deal with the acrylic fiber capacity expansion in Mexico. The acquisition was the easiest part. Converting the plant to precursor production was difficult and expensive, and building carbon fiber lines to be able to reach $1 billion in revenue would be a major undertaking. In order to achieve this lofty goal, we were looking to ultimately raise a total of $500 million in capital. Learning from our previous experience that convertible loan financing would permanently destroy our balance sheet, we knew that we needed a new approach.

Our share price was over $30 in mid-2007, and it was the right time to try to solve our long-term financing requirements. Once again, we called on Merrill Lynch to help with our dilemma. We asked them to raise money for the immediate capital needs and also to do a shelf registration for future stock sales. A shelf-registered stock sale would give us the ability to raise money as we needed in the future without the requirement of new SEC filings. This was a great idea, and Merrill Lynch was ready to go.

We completed the offering in just two weeks. It was the smoothest and fastest secondary offering we ever did. We completed the offering in August of 2007, selling 3.6 million shares at $36.53 per share, raising $132 million. In addition, we also completed the shelf registration for a $350-million future shares sale. At that point, Zoltek's market valuation was $1.05 billion. Now I was confident enough to go forward and complete the acquisition of the Cydsa acrylic fibers plant.

With the expectation of a major increase in the complexity of our company, I needed to find someone to oversee the operations, a Chief Operating Officer (COO). When I was visiting the U.S. operations of Messier Bugatti in Walton, Kentucky, I got the impression that the General Manager, Karen Bomba, was not happy with recent changes in their organization. During our dinner meeting, I confirmed my impression and started to discuss the possibility of her joining the Zoltek management team. I had worked with her for years, and I was impressed with how she managed building and developing this highly successful operation. After many discussions, we came to terms and with Messier Bugatti's approval, she joined the Zoltek management team as the COO in February 2008. At the same time, David Purcell, a sharp young man with experience with a well-known consulting firm, started with the assignment to build a professional sales organization and later, he became a Vice President.

To manage a growing company with minimum staffing, I relied on my ability to test the managers' knowledge and integrity before they could earn my confidence and trust, just as I had experienced this concept at my first job at Monsanto. For financial control, I used my ability to look at a large amount of numbers in the computer input to find outliers.

As we were completing our 2007 year-end audit, I was reviewing the data used to generate the financial reports. I found two out of place entries that stood out of the pattern: One entry for $75,000 and another for $175,000 that were in the Hungarian accounting report. After a number of requests for explanation from our CFO, Kevin Schott, he admitted to these being unauthorized and unreported payments. He instructed the Hungarian accounting manager to deposit funds in a special bank account, supposedly for the benefit of two unknown companies. After he admitted to his misconduct, he refunded the $250,000 to the company. I allowed him to resign and committed that Zoltek would not file legal action. However, ultimately the SEC fined him and barred him from future CFO positions in a public company.

The SEC regulations require the company to report any financial irregularities immediately to the shareholders, which we did.

The SEC rules also require, under such circumstances, a public company to "investigate" the financial controls. Of course, our independent accounting firm, Grant Thornton, completed their audit without finding these irregularities and had given the company a clean audit report. This "investigation" cost the company $400,000, a windfall for the accounting firm.

Shortly after this episode concluded, we received a call from the Hungarian electric supply company, demanding payment of our monthly bill, which was over $1 million. However, we had already sent this payment by wire two days prior to the call. It turned out that someone forged a letter on the electric company's stationary, instructing Zoltek to send payment to a different bank account.

Fortunately, we were able to retrieve the money when we informed the bank of the potential fraud. With the help of the Hungarian National Police, we were able to unravel what happened. They concluded it was an insider crime and suspected the accounting manager. The police set a trap to arrest the culprit when he was scheduled to pick up the cash. It appears that someone at Zoltek must have warned this person about the police trap, and he never appeared to claim the cash.

I had to clean house at the U.S. and Hungarian accounting departments and once more, I temporarily took over the CFO position. I also fired Grant Thornton as our independent auditors.

It is amazing that the CFO, along with others in the accounting department, supposedly the most trusted persons in a public company, would actually steal from the company in the middle of our financial struggle.

The Mexican Expansion

We had demonstrated that we could easily expand our carbon fiber production capacity, with our modular equipment design, fast enough that our customers would never have to be concerned about availability. However, incremental increase of our carbon fiber capacity was only possible if we had available precursor capacity. But increasing the availability of the precursor was more difficult and could not be done incrementally.

Acrylic fiber precursor production required more infrastructure and required a much higher capacity plant to be built long before the carbon fiber demand materialized. Once the basic plant was in place, the actual precursor capacity could be increased in steps to match the carbon fiber production increases. But building small incremental increases in capacity was not possible. Therefore, just as we needed to develop the significant facility in Hungary in 1996, now we needed to make a major investment in order to increase the precursor capacity to support the anticipated long-term carbon fiber production requirements. Since there were no viable acrylic plants available to acquire in the U.S., we again needed to look for a foreign acquisition.

The Cydsa plant seemed to be a perfect fit for us based on information Casey was able to find. In early 2007, we headed to Guadalajara to meet with the Cydsa management. The plant location, if it had to be outside U.S., Mexico was ideal. The plant had been shut down for over a year, and the last person in charge of shutting off the lights was Ignacio (Nacho) Nuno. He was our main contact to arrange the meeting. Pedro Reynoso, a consultant to Cydsa in charge of managing Cydsa's remaining acrylic business and the disposition of its idle assets, was there to host us and to start our discussions.

Although the plant had been idle for a long time, it looked well cared for, and the re-commissioning would be manageable in a reasonable time frame and cost. The plant was in much better shape than our Hungarian plant at the time we had acquired it. Also, the Cydsa plant was without complications of multiple business units, and this plant had five times the capacity of the Hungarian acrylic facility.

Other than security and maintenance, there were no employees, which was good news and bad news. The good news was: we could start fresh without facing major lay-offs. The bad news was: we had no existing knowledge of the plant design or experience with the local business environment. And we had no trained operations staff to manage the reconstruction or to operate this plant.

When we completed the plant tour, I asked Pedro how much money Cydsa was looking to get for the facility. Pedro was quite open and told me that the company had gone through some hard times. The plant had been used as collateral for some financing. The bank was looking for $35 million to release the property, and that was what he considered the minimum sale price. He also made it clear that the CEO, Tomas Gonzalez, would be looking for more.

I considered the price fair, but my overwhelming concern was the lack of qualified local technical and management staff. Just as important, we certainly did not have enough people within Zoltek to take on this engineering and construction project alone, and we certainly lacked the knowledge of the local customs and language. After some discussion, we identified a group of key members of the management team from the plant before it was decommissioned. Before we left Guadalajara, we had a verbal agreement that we would proceed with a deal if we could recruit the designated team and, as Pedro promised, if Cydsa's management would support us in obtaining all the permits and union contract to restart the plant. I trusted him.

For the next few weeks, we worked with Nacho and Pedro in their effort to recruit the management team while we performed the preliminary due diligence. Casey and I made several trips to meet the team and discuss our business and the plans for the Mexican facility. It all came together quickly. Obviously, we had the right people, and the most critical people were committed to returning to bring the plant back to life. They had attempted to produce carbon fiber precursor, but were not successful. So, being involved with carbon fiber production was professionally very exciting for all of them. Language proved not to be a major problem because most of the management team spoke reasonable English.

Once I felt confident about the team's being on board, it was time to visit Cydsa's headquarters in Monterrey to meet Tamas to negotiate the final deal. The entire executive staff was first class and very pleasant to work with. Tamas tried his best to get more money from me, but he was a real gentleman and agreed to the $35-million offer, which was our preliminary verbal agreement on the day we first visited the plant.

Within ninety days after my first visit to Guadalajara, on June 1, 2007, we had a binding purchase agreement, and we had agreements with the key management team. By the time we completed the offering, we were already engaged with the management team in developing the detailed plans for the rebuilding of the plant. We closed the transaction on September 1, 2007.

Ignacio Nuno did not turn off the lights, but became the plant manager. His primary initial assignment was to build the Mexican organization. We received a lot of support from the Cydsa management in organizing the proper corporate structure, which can be quite difficult and expensive if not done properly. We continued to recruit a number of the previous management and engineering staff to bring up the experience level and minimize delays in the reconstruction. Pedro worked with us all the way to make sure our project was a success.

Unions were institutional in Mexico, similar to the Hungarian system. It is a hangover of the communist influence after WW I. Proper selection of the union representative was critical. The Cydsa Human Resources manager helped us select the right union. We were able to put in place the same union as Cydsa and immediately started the recruiting process for the operations people.

Peter Kiss was responsible for the overall project, and his engineering team was responsible for installing the carbon fiber plant. The Cydsa maintenance manager, Victor Leale, came out of retirement and immediately went to work, bringing the plant back to operating condition. Ricardo Sisnett returned from teaching at the local university to coordinate the synchronization of the Hungarian and Mexican acrylic precursor fiber processes. To assist him, Barnabás Reisz from our Hungarian acrylic plant moved to Mexico with his family for a full year. Jesus Nunez was responsible for managing the operations and learning the carbon fiber process.

I spent considerable time and effort to be sure that all went smoothly, construction costs were under control, and we managed any cultural clashes that might spiral out of control. From the beginning, the Hungarian team worked well with the Mexican team. At any one time, more than ten Hungarian engineers and managers were in Mexico. The project went as smoothly as could be expected. It was wonderful to see how well the whole company worked together on such a complex project.

In the spring, the annual bank golf trip was in Scotland, which was a welcomed break. Prior to the official golf trip, Drew and I had visited Hungary. Drew was always fascinated with the history of the Austro-Hungarian Empire, and we had a relaxing time in Budapest. We also visited the Zoltek plant. Drew was quite impressed with the changes we made since the last time he saw it a few years earlier. In Scotland, we played a number of the famous golf courses for five days. To everyone's amazement, including mine, my team won the tournament.

As Zoltek's financial situation had improved so greatly, Drew followed up with his personal commitment and invited me to return to the Southwest Bank Board. By this time, the bank was actually operating as part of M&I Bank.

When it came time to start production, we needed to train operators for the carbon fiber plant. It was hard to believe, considering the free flow of illegal immigrants from Mexico, but we could not get work visas for our employees to come to Abilene for training. We finally gave up on the U.S. and sent twenty operators and foremen to Hungary for a month-long training program. This was a great idea and at a significantly lower cost. An additional benefit was that, even with the language difficulties, the Hungarian and Mexican operators and foremen established good and lasting working relationships. One of the Mexican foremen married a Hungarian girl and brought her back to Guadalajara.

But even before we completed the plant construction, the global economy was starting to show some weakness, and the U.S. Congress was vacillating about the continuation of the investment tax credit for wind power projects. Without tax credits, financing wind-farm projects would become very difficult. We started to see a definite slowdown of new wind-farm projects coming on line, and existing projects started to be delayed or were put on hold. It was becoming clear that we might again be facing another slowdown in our sales growth and the need for the Mexican plant might not be immediately necessary.

We did, however, decide to complete our Mexican project, regardless of market conditions, because it would have been prohibitively expensive to interrupt or slow down the construction. We completed the redesign and rebuilding of the acrylic fiber polymerization plant, part of the fiber spinning lines, and built a facility to house 10 million pound (5,000 ton) per year carbon fiber production facility with 5 million pound (2,500 ton) per year installed capacity. We did all this in just nine months, which was unheard of in the carbon fiber industry.

The total project cost Zoltek $100 million, but the replacement value of the acrylic plant and the installed carbon fiber lines were over $500 million. More important, we put in place the basic infrastructure to build Zoltek's capacity to support over $1 billion in annual revenue!

One other benefit from completing the plant construction was to establish a second plant for our aircraft brake business. As we were supplying upwards of eighty percent of the carbon fibers for the global commercial and military aircraft, our customers were getting concerned about potential supply interruptions with all the fibers being produced in a single facility in Hungary. As soon as we completed the initial project in Mexico, we started to build additional lines, specifically for the aircraft brake business, and we initiated the facility qualification process with our major customers. We installed enough capacity to cover our projected requirements for the next ten years.

The market for carbon fibers was again becoming unstable because the weak economy reduced demand for wind turbines, and new applications were slow to develop. However, more and more, carbon fibers were considered a strategic material, and countries around the world were aggressively looking to develop production capacity. This was a very big potential problem for Zoltek's strategy. If new carbon fiber companies emerged and capacity increased before demand, we could lose our first-mover market position. However, with the new large precursor capacity, it also presented an opportunity for globalization. With this available precursor capacity, we could offer to build joint-venture carbon fiber plants anywhere in the world and be a partner in the global capacity expansion.

I thought it would be desirable to have representation on our board from Mexico to support our major investment there. My good friend, Jim Betts, was over seventy years old and was having some health problems. It seemed that he was ready to retire. I asked Pedro Reynoso, who continued to support us in making the Mexico investment a success, to replace him.

During this period, our stealth technology patent dispute with the U.S. government was stalled. After imposing the state secret privilege and denying government liability for utilizing materials that were using our technology, but were purchased from a Japanese company for building the F-22, the court directed us to sue Lockheed Martin directly. For some unexplainable reason, our lawyers accepted this instruction and decided to move the F-22 litigation away from the government. This was a dumb move because the U.S. government encourages its contractors to violate patents to fulfill contracts, and the U.S. government would indemnify the contractor from any patent infringement damage claim.

At this point, it was clear that our attorneys were weak and helpless against the Department of Justice legal manipulation. They hired various PR firms, believing there was no legal way to win, and we needed a legislative solution, which I thought was ridiculous and a waste of money.

Lockheed Martin objected this order and appealed. I lost confidence in our lawyers and decided to engage another law firm to handle the appeal. After two years of delay, the appeals court redirected the lawsuit against the U.S. government back into the same court where we had been litigating the case before. After this unnecessary delay, as a last resort and after twelve years of litigation, the government attorneys questioned the validity of the patent.

Now we were fighting the invocation of the state secret privilege and the challenge to the validity of the patent. It seemed to me that the FBI and the Department of Justice probably had a political and a personal vendetta against Zoltek and me. Our attorneys were unable to deal with this. I realized that I needed to pay more attention to the case.

By the end of year 2008, our carbon fiber demand reduced significantly. We finished the year at a record sales level of $186 million with $25 million net profit. These were good results, but the problem was that our annual revenue growth dropped from sixty-six percent per year in the previous three years to twenty-five percent, and I was concerned what would happen to market the following year, but for once, we were in excellent financial position, and I had no concern about the future.

It seemed that our shareholders were also concerned as the wind energy tax benefits were not extended. Our share price stated to decline. As the sales slowed down, we were faced with carrying the cost of the Mexico facility, which would not be needed for a while until our sales growth recovered.

Another Setback

Early in 2009, there was an innocuous article in the financial papers about the major shareholder of BMW acquiring ten percent, which she later increased to twenty-five percent, of SGL shares. This was a serious concern, an indication of future association between the two companies.

The bad news came in spring. I received a call at seven in the morning from the BMW project manager we had worked with for several years to develop carbon fiber composite applications. He informed me that an announcement of a joint venture between BMW and SGL was being released to the press that morning. This was the only notice I received from BMW, even though we had spent millions of dollars over ten years to develop and test carbon fibers in their automobiles. We also had a signed contract that guaranteed Zoltek as its preferred carbon fiber supplier, intended to compensate Zoltek for jointly developing the use of carbon fibers in automotive applications.

It was scandalous that, in spite of our confidentiality agreement regarding our technology and the preferred supplier contract, BMW commissioned SGL to duplicate our fibers. In turn, SGL did a joint venture with Mitsubishi Chemical Co. to duplicate our precursor. It was hard for me to accept that BMW would make a deal with a company that was earlier convicted of price fixing in the graphite electrode business, and its CEO was not allowed in the U.S. until he paid a multi-million dollar fine. It just showed to me that these companies had no ethical compass and BMW was never going to be a good partner for Zoltek.

I was also convinced that this joint venture was doomed from the beginning, and I still believe it would fail. In the end, BMW locked itself into a long-term very expensive carbon fiber supply. Based on public documents, their depreciation cost alone was higher than our carbon fiber selling price would have been. Their internal transfer cost was as much as, if not more than the aerospace companies were paying for the most expensive carbon fibers.

Other than striking a serious blow to Zoltek, they put a temporary stop to the advancement of carbon fiber composite utilization for automotive applications. It is impossible to justify the use of carbon fibers in the automotive market at the high price BMW has committed to pay.

One more ironic development was that VW also invested in SGL and acquired almost ten percent of their shares. Of course, we stopped working with both BMW and VW at that point. Quite fitting, years later VW was charged with cheating on the emission testing of their vehicles. Our experience was not exactly a positive indication of the German industry's collective ethics. They were not the companies with whom I would ever like to partner. As an instance of poetic justice, the SGL shares lost about seventy percent of their value after the BMW shareholders and VW invested in SGL.

BMW's dishonesty and poor judgement was not limited to their carbon fiber supplier. They were misrepresenting that the i3 model was a carbon fiber car and a green car because it was produced with green energy. However, it turned out to be an aluminum car with some carbon fiber component. Although the carbon fiber plant electricity was provided from a hydro-electric generator in the state of Washington, the rest of the production, including the precursor production in Japan, was based on fossil fuel energy.

All said, it was quite a blow to Zoltek and to me personally.

I just regret that we had spent so much effort and resources to support the BMW development work while we could have done more productive work by advancing our composite intermediate products.

The only good that came from this relationship was that we successfully demonstrated the feasibility and the economic benefits of commercial-grade carbon fibers in automobiles.

Once the reality of this loss set in, we looked to find a new automotive company that could become the leader in introducing the large-scale use of carbon fibers. We decided that Daimler/Mercedes would be the most likely company to be energized by the BMW move. We reestablished our relationship with their engineering team and initiated a number of projects.

We also looked more seriously for opportunities with the U.S. auto companies that had been slow to embrace carbon fiber composite technology. We also looked for composite part suppliers to the auto industry to establish new partnerships.

A few years earlier, I had visited the largest VW plant. In this plant, the production of the metal body components started with rolls of steel and ended with a finished part and continued to a full car body. My host commented that until carbon fibers could be processed in a similar fashion, utilizing carbon fibers would be limited to special purpose uses. This might have been an overstatement, but this idea stuck in my mind. Certainly trying to make this idea a reality would have been a better use of our time and resources.

We initiated several internal projects and forged agreements with innovative companies, using our carbon fibers to develop new product formats, design concepts, and fabrication methods to build car components.

The biggest obstacle for the automotive application was no longer the carbon fiber cost, thanks to Zoltek, but rather the application methods, which were way too expensive. The BMW i3 was a good example. It started to be a primary carbon fiber car, but it turned out to be carbon fiber hype rather than a cost-effective lightweight, high-performance car. Another example was the Tesla's roadster, which was made with Zoltek carbon fiber woven fabric, but the process to produce the parts was so expensive that when Tesla designed its sedan, they could not commit to carbon fibers and went back to using aluminum.

Unfortunately, nothing in the automobile design happens fast, and it was not going to be easy to make up the time we had wasted working with BMW. While we had high degree of confidence in our leadership in the commercial carbon fiber concept, after this loss and the general slowness of expanding demand, our leadership position was questioned by our shareholders. Our share price fell back to the ten-dollar range and stayed there for over three years.

The automotive industry was a major disappointment and that left the wind turbine business as the largest imminent revenue potential. The overall wind turbine business was uncertain to recover anytime soon, but potential new wind turbine customers were emerging globally. A number of them were interested in using carbon fibers in the turbine blades because they saw the overwhelming success of Vestas. Our optimism was also fueled in a significant way by GE adopting carbon fibers in a line of its wind turbines.

Earlier I had added Phil Schell to our management team to handle the wind turbine business. In addition to GE, he started to work with several Chinese companies. The Chinese wind turbine business was booming relative to the U.S., and the in-China companies were the favored blade suppliers. Our development group went to work on capturing GE's business, which we recognized as the most promising potential new adopter of carbon fibers in wind turbine blades. We had worked on this project for nearly a year, and our customer support group assured me that the project was going very well.

GE had its turbine blades fabricated in Brazil with a very difficult and expensive method. We were developing a low-cost prepreg process and a very efficient application system that would reduce the turbine blade fabrication process to a fraction of their prevailing cost. All of the demonstration work was done in Brazil, but GE was trying to establish a blade fabricator in the U.S. We were designated to be the supplier to this company. Our first shipment had some unexplainable problems that we were not able to resolve immediately.

I was called by GE while I was in Hawaii on my annual vacation. As I was trying to recover the order over the phone, it became clear that our people did not communicate well with the GE engineers during the trials, and the problem could have been anticipated and solved during our Brazil trials.

This incident was a troubling one, shaking my confidence in our team, and caused serious doubts in my mind. We were unable to retain GE's business, and GE decided to convert the U.S. supplier to glass fiber blade production, and we lost this order and this opportunity. The result of this incident was not only the loss of a lot of business for Zoltek, but GE ultimately cut back on the use of carbon fibers because their manufacturing method cost was excessive, and the fabrication method was unreliable. Clearly this was another blow to expediting the adaptation of carbon fibers.

This all happened while I was trying to build a congenial management team and develop a succession plan. It was disturbing that no one took responsibility for this failure. After I overcame my disappointment, we organized a two-day management meeting with twenty-five of our senior managers from all operations around the world. It was my intention to restate our strategy and, together as a group, set goals for the organization. Once we set the goals, we were planning to initiate a performance-based compensation plan.

The process did not go nearly as well as I hoped. Two things concerned me. Most of the managers were clearly trying to set very minimal goals to be sure everyone would be eligible for a bonus, rather than accepting the challenge of the commercial carbon fiber concept Zoltek was built around. However, even more concerning to me, there were signs that some managers started to worry about internal politics more than the achievement of our business objectives. I found this very disturbing.

Meanwhile, our 2009 performance was turning out to be even more disappointing than I expected. Our revenue dropped by twenty-five percent and once more, Zoltek recorded a loss. Lower revenue had mostly resulted from a serious setback in the wind turbine business, and there had been no new application to take its place. Our losses were primarily the result of the carrying charges of the Mexico plant. We continued to be optimistic about the applications we were pursuing and put new development agreements in place with a variety of partners.

I decided to give it some time and see how various members of the management team would handle their assignments. I also realized that I needed to spend more social time with the core management group to get them to work together more effectively.

In spite of all the effort I made to get the management team together socially and have them participate in the quarterly board meetings, they were still not working well together. I thought that by giving them more autonomy, they would become more responsive. But that did not happen. There were examples of excellent individual performances, but not an effective and supporting management performance. It became more and more problematic to have constructive discussions about the business. Discussions might identify problems, but not solutions. Projects were claimed to be going well, but results were not clear. Projections were made, but not achieved.

This was evident at board meetings as well. For some reason, the board did not ask any hard questions of the managers. If the results were not acceptable, they were asking me the questions in the closed board meetings that they should have asked the managers. I accepted their criticism, but this was not helpful for me or for the management team.

Our share price was chronically below ten dollars; Zoltek's market value was close to our book value, making us vulnerable for an unwelcome takeover bid. At the same time, more and more large companies were entering the market in support of our competitors. I felt that maintaining our independence was in serious jeopardy.

I received two serious merger inquiries, first from GrafTech and later from Solutia (the specialty chemical part of the old Monsanto), resulting in preliminary discussions. Interestingly, both companies were looking for a new product line as a platform for growth, but both were valuing Zoltek based on historic financial performance and not based on future growth opportunities and/or the value of our existing infrastructure and capabilities. Although I took these discussions seriously, they both broke down for the same reason, neither company made a serious effort to understand our strategic objectives and the value of the installed capacity.

The first half of the year 2010 continued to be disappointing, and frustration started to set in. We started to lose some of the management, and our Chief Operating Officer resigned to return to Messier Bugatti. We were back to having all the top management reporting directly to me, which was disappointing at this critical time. The second half of the year started to show improvement, but for the full year, revenue was 7.5 percent lower than prior year. However, the tax credit for wind energy was approved by Congress, giving us reason for optimism.

A positive development came when Vestas decided to change their turbine blade manufacturing technology. They requested me to assist them in finding pultrusion companies that could produce enough and competitively priced products to enable Vestas to change its primary turbine blade fabrication from prepreg to pultruded profiles. (Pultrusion is the opposite of extrusion. The process is pulling the fiber through a resin impregnation bath and a through heated die just long enough to cure the resin.) I suppose they expected me to jump on this opportunity, so they assured me that they were not asking Zoltek to get into the pultrusion business, but just for our recommendation.

However, we had already targeted pultrusion as a core competency because this process was a very effective way to produce intermediate or finished composite parts in a single step by combining carbon fibers with resins. This process was very efficient, but extremely slow. Our objective was to develop a process that would dramatically increase the production rate. We had already hired some experts, and we were working on installing trial equipment.

There was no existing company that effectively and competitively worked with carbon fibers for large-volume applications. Once I was convinced we could produce the required product Vestas was looking for, we were able to convince Vestas we were their best option. With everyone working together, Zoltek soon became their primary supplier. In one year, we went from no pultrusion business to being the largest carbon fiber pultrusion company in the world.

With the recovery of the wind turbine business, our revenue started to improve in 2011, increasing twenty percent to over $150 million, but our share price did not move. I continued to be concerned about maintaining our independence not only from the potential stock market interference, but from internal weakness.

Unfortunately, as our business outlook was improving, another serious setback occurred in my personal life. In February, Drew suddenly died of a heart attack. True to his character, as he was wheeled into the emergency room, he was asked if he was allergic to anything. His response was that he was allergic to cheap whiskey. His death was a shock to me and to all his many friends. He was a very important person in many of our lives and particularly in my life. He was instrumental in my ability to survive the financial difficulties that my business encountered in the early years.

He was a true friend. He introduced me to his friends and supported me in joining social organizations and clubs. A number of his friends also became my friends. He helped to make my life in St. Louis much better. Over our twenty-year friendship, we had wonderful times together, many golf trips all over the world, trips to Augusta National, trips together to Hungary, Cardinal baseball games, and many fun events in St. Louis. All of us miss him and think of him often as we tell stories about all he did for many of us and our businesses, not to speak of all the good times we enjoyed together.

Early trade show with Zoltek sales group

One of our many social event with our Zoltek employees

First Zoltek employee, Roger   Terry Hickey and Bill Pfitzinger who acquired the early Zoltek business

Hungarian plant at the time of acquisition, 1996

George Bakos and George Pászty with me-were key to the Hungarian acquisition

Hungarian management team-meeting at the Waldorf, NY

Ilona Tandi and George Pászty at celebration of the Hungarian acquisition

Ongoing educating management on socialism vs. free enterprise

Socializing with management—cooking gulyás and discussing the future

Aerial view of Hungarian plant after carbon fiber facility was installed

Hungary management group, 2011

George Husman and I in front of 50 meter wind turbine blade

Board of Directors meeting and carbon fiber plant visit

Aerial photo - Part of Mexico plant

The original Mexico management team and I—Jesus Nunez,
Jose Fuentes, Ricardo Sisnett and Ignacio Nuno (missing Victor Leal)

Zoltek employees in Mexico, 2012

Messier—Bugatti twenty year contract signing after the Mexico plant qualification

Tibor Ledvényi, Sándor Horváth, Péter Kiss and I at the
first of my many retirement parties with maquette of the constable

Zoltek management team at the St. Louis Club after sale of Zoltek, 2016
Eiji Fujioka, John White, Hidetaka Matsumae, Dave Purcell, Hiroshi Matsuo,
Mark Kawamura, Phil Schell, Mike Westcott and Duke Aihara

Sidestep – Globalization Attempt

There were many difficulties with building our business around a new concept in material technology. The short summary was that we needed to develop the demand and at the same time, build the product availability, usually long before demand justified it. With the disappointments in the two most important future markets, the automotive and wind turbine markets, I was trying to develop a plan to improve our competitive position.

Once again, we were in the position that our business was stagnant, but our outlook was improving; we needed to plan for expansion. We had a significant untapped precursor capacity that could support a significant increase in carbon fiber production capacity. Our share price continued to be depressed and financing additional capacity of our own would significantly dilute our shareholders. We just did not have the horsepower in our organization, and our future success was not as convincing as it should have been.

We were getting a steady stream of inquiries from all over the world to establish relationships with Zoltek and establish carbon fiber manufacturing in a number of countries. I wanted to investigate these possibilities and see how we might put together a globalization strategy that would support the global market development and establish a world-wide production network, all financed in the most part by joint venture partners. Zoltek would provide the technology, the plant design and construction, and the precursor supply from Mexico.

This project required a lot of travel and a significant part of my time. I was concerned about this diversion, but it was necessary. I also thought my absence would provide the opportunity for our management to form a cohesive team and to demonstrate that they could handle our existing business together.

China represented the largest potential competitive threat as well as the most significant opportunity. For several years, we had been active in the China market, and our Chinese business was becoming significant. China was also considered to be potentially the largest wind energy market in the world, and their political system significantly favored companies located in China to build the turbines. We started to work with several wind turbine companies to introduce the carbon fiber technology needed to manufacture very long wind-turbine blades. Vestas realized that if they wanted to be the market leader, they had to establish a major presence in China, which they did. We were starting to ship significant quantities of carbon fibers to China from our Mexico facility.

The Chinese government decided to target carbon fiber technology as a critical national objective. Suddenly there were thirty companies in China officially pursuing the development of carbon fiber technology. The centralized government was starting to break up and privatization started. The government offered incentives to develop the carbon fiber technology, resulting in no fewer than thirty companies announcing their interest, and a number of them contacting us to assist them. After preliminary screening, we zeroed in on two likely possibilities. I spent much time on this project and traveled to China to personally meet the key people involved. It was not a pleasant experience.

The top management people in the companies I visited were no more entrepreneurs than Mao Zedong. It was my conclusion that they all were part of the communist hierarchy who had always lived like royalty, and the change from the communist system was just like in Russia: the old regime was able to convert the country's productive assets and cash into their personal wealth. I was not as familiar with the Chinese system as I was with Russia, but it was clear that, in China, obtaining real estate was a very important and complex process. One way to get control of real estate was to participate in the government's carbon fiber development objective. It seemed that an agreement with Zoltek would assure favorable treatment from the government for land acquisition and possible financial support.

One of the two companies, a chemicals manufacturer we thought was a viable prospect for a joint venture, actually had lower level management and technical staff who were sincerely interested in carbon fibers. There were two engineers who had some knowledge about the carbon fiber process. They were nice young people who were excited about the possibility of being part of this project. It was also interesting to learn about their personal lives. Both were from small towns and commuted to work in Hangzhou and lived in a company dormitory. They were allowed to visit their wives and kids once a month for a weekend. Incredibly, there were many thousands of brand-new apartments and condominiums empty for years because nobody could afford to rent or buy them.

We were making progress in our discussions with the operations and technical people and then it came time to meet the Chairman. They arranged a very nice dinner party in the most expensive part of the city. It was an elegant event with a dozen company people and assistants. The Chairman was a typical old communist demagogue. He was bragging about his newly acquired wealth and his new multi-million dollar house, right in front of the two young engineers who could not afford to live with their families in the city where they worked. It was difficult to take his entire dialog, but for the endless bottles of

Lafitte Rothschild, 1982 valued at over $1,500 per bottle, served with dinner. Ultimately our discussions broke down when we realized that the Chinese contribution to a joint venture was limited to the real estate that they actually would receive from the government for free.

The other company with which we had serious discussions was a wind turbine manufacturer. They were planning to adopt carbon fiber technology to their offshore wind turbine blades. This company was actually listed on the New York Stock Exchange and had some American-Chinese technical staff. We thought the negotiations would be different, but they ended up the same way as others had. On my visit to their headquarters, I was shown the plant location they had designated for the carbon fiber plant, and they paraded me to the regional government and press conference to talk about Zoltek's interest in developing a joint venture in China. After all that, it became clear that they were not making any real effort to design a carbon fiber-reinforced turbine blade. They were clearly spending a lot of money, but were not willing to spend any of it on the carbon fiber project. Finally, I decided there was nothing of value for Zoltek in getting directly involved in a Chinese joint venture.

The Chinese companies were looking for established technologies with predictable demand where the low cost in China would be their advantage. New application and market development, along with risky investment, was of no interest for them, unless the joint venture partner was willing to handle that burden.

ChemChina, the government-owned chemical company with acrylic fiber operation, was an interesting and puzzling story. They entered into the carbon fiber race by acquiring the old Courtaulds acrylic facility in Grimsby, UK, from the second bankruptcy. After two years of effort to restart their precursor production, they installed an experimental carbon fiber production line. Another two years later, with no real progress, they finally closed the plant. They then reappeared in

Lanzhou, China, with a group of Courtaulds experts to start the Chinese carbon fiber plant. After five more years of effort, and reportedly, a $500-million investment, the Chinese carbon fiber plant produced no credible product.

While the China situation was starting to look like a lost cause, the Korean government officially targeted carbon fiber technology as a strategic material and challenged the Korean industry to become a world-class producer as they had done with ships and automobiles. Immediately six companies responded to the challenge, and we were getting inquiries. I visited all of these companies and selected one of the largest Korean companies as our potential partner.

We spent a lot of time developing a joint venture concept, and it looked like a viable option for a while. Although it was a huge financially powerful company, one of the requirements for the joint venture they insisted on was that Zoltek would be responsible to generate and guarantee the revenue of the joint venture. As we were doing the financial projections, it became clear that they had assigned no value to our technology, and their expectations were that Zoltek would take all the financial risk. However, if the venture was successful, they would be able to force Zoltek out of the venture by requiring Zoltek to make additional investments to maintain its share at much higher valuation levels. Finally, things really started to fall apart when we learned of several carbon fiber opportunities within other divisions of the company, but we could not get any help from our potential partner to capture this business. We had to walk away from this transaction.

Phil Shell introduced me to a businessman from India at an AWEA (wind energy) conference in Chicago, who built a composite business in Vadodara, India. He was doing business with several U.S. companies and wanted to enter the carbon fiber business. His company was selected by the Indian government to produce carbon fibers for the Indian military. I had to see what this company was all about and accepted his invitation to visit his facility. I was quite impressed with his vision, the manufacturing facility, and the composite design capabilities he had built.

They were actually trying to develop new markets in India. This company was by far the best potential partner I had encountered. We immediately engaged in a discussion about building a carbon fiber plant together. Our discussions proceeded quickly and all seemed to be going well. We agreed on almost everything until we got to the financial part. Quite contrary to my previous joint venture discussions, we had no issues with the value of our technology or with who would pay for the carbon fiber lines.

His only request was that I send a proposal for $10 million more than the actual project cost, then the company would get financing for the entire amount and he and I, personally, would split the extra $10 million. I had difficulty accepting what I heard and immediately refused to go along with such proposal. After a number of meetings, we finally met in Budapest with his top financial person and board member. They plainly stated that this was the way business was done in India, and if I wanted to do business, this was the only way. I told them that a partnership that starts with a bank fraud just does not work for me. Not surprisingly, the company has since defaulted on their financing and has been in serious legal and financial problems and at least for a while, it was closed.

As new potential carbon fiber applications, such as longer wind turbines, utility towers, and electric cable reinforcement emerged in India, I was called by one of India's premier textile companies. They actually had an idle DuPont acrylic plant that was identical to one in our plant in Hungary and had done business with us, selling spare parts. Their acrylic fibers plant in Vadodara had been shut down for several years. It was located close to the composite company we initially considered for the joint venture. The plant was in an acceptable condition to rebuild at a reasonable cost. If the precursor facility was combined with the carbon fiber and composite facility, it would have made an excellent, integrated company. I suspected that at one point they were considering this combination, but by this time, the composite company was in trouble. I believed this company easily could have funded such a business venture, but like the other potential Asian partners, they were interested in restarting their acrylic plant to produce precursor and build a carbon fiber plant, but were not willing to make the necessary investment.

The part of the Saudi project that included the carbon fiber facility was awarded to SABIC (Saudi Basic Industries), and they were unwilling to enter into a long-term and low-cost ACN supply agreement, which was a pre-requisite for Zoltek. We did discuss the carbon fiber plant separate from the ACN supply agreement, but the terms were not acceptable. They also verbally proposed to acquire Zoltek after they acquired GE's plastics business. Once we rejected their offer, they signed a contract with an acrylic fibers company that has never produced carbon fibers and probably never will.

Over a two-year period, I traveled all over the world promoting our carbon fiber concept, looking for ways to expand and globalize our concept. In addition to the examples above, I visited companies and had serious joint venture discussions in Argentina, Brazil, and Iceland. We also talked with companies in Australia and Malaysia. Each company and country had something to offer in producing carbon fibers economically and supporting certain existing local markets, but we found no companies that were willing to spend time and resources to make the necessary investment or devote resources to develop new applications to grow demand.

My conclusion was that the companies we considered for joint venture were only interested in becoming a manufacturer of carbon fibers not to build a carbon fiber business. They were looking for the U.S. partner to invest in a facility in their country, believing that they could not lose on the transaction because the facility, once built, could never be removed. If the venture were to become successful, they could systematically increase their ownership share of the joint venture and ultimately gain control of the technology for minimum investment. On the other hand, if the joint venture did not work, they could abandon it and lose nothing.

This was totally contrary to what we wanted, which was local investment to build the manufacturing facility and a fifty-percent ownership share for the contribution of our technology. This was the minimum, and we were also looking for our partner to work on application development, at least in their own country, in cooperation with our own market development effort.

At the same time, our management development was not going well. Instead of becoming more cohesive, our management evolved into competing factions. And competing internally, which was very unhealthy and counterproductive. It was time for me to return to try to fix it.

Finally, We Made It

In 2012, our revenue continued to recover, and the future looked better than ever. Once more we were in a position that required us to make a decision how to supply an unpredictable demand. As the industry leader, if we did not demonstrate that we had production capacity, the market may not develop or if the market did develop and we had no capacity, we could lose our edge over our competitors. The Mexican expansion was a good example; it took four years for demand to begin to catch up to our capacity expansion. This has been our challenge throughout our history. Globalization strategy proved not to be a realistic option.

By this time, the Mexican facility was running well, but the Abilene plant had been shut down for some time. Restarting Abilene would have been expensive, and I saw no improvement in the local situation to give me optimism for a better outcome. We decided our best option was to move the Abilene carbon fiber lines to Mexico.

We also added the new lines in the Mexican plant to produce fibers for the aircraft brake market, both to add capacity and to establish a second facility needed for eliminating the long-term supply interruption risk for our customers. The qualification of the plant and the fibers produced there would take at least a year, but without the demonstration of this capability, the qualification process would not start. We were rewarded for this decision by receiving a twenty-year, ninety percent supply contract from Messier Bugatti.

We had already succeeded in the development of the commercial carbon fiber concept, and our 2012 financial performance demonstrated that our low-cost concept was also economically viable, proving that our business could continue to grow profitably. Our challenge continued to be to make the use of carbon fibers easier and more cost-effective, making the finished composite parts affordable. To this end, we acquired a facility and built a new plant in St. Peters, Missouri, where we installed our prepreg and the pultrusion operations. We also directed Entec, our equipment company in Salt Lake City, to support this strategy and design fiber handling equipment that could supplement our customers' process equipment.

We concentrated on developing intermediate products that combined resins, thermoset or thermo-plastic with carbon fibers that could reduce the number of production steps and be easily fabricated into finished products. The ultimate desired outcome was to develop carbon fiber intermediate formats that would facilitate a single-step process to produce finished composite products. Entec was the leading filament winding equipment designer and had the only process at the time within Zoltek that met these criteria. We spent a lot of time and money on development of other equipment to reduce the cost of intermediate products.

Zoltek became a truly global company with multiple operations in the U.S., major manufacturing facilities in Hungary and Mexico, and sales offices around the globe. In all, we had over 1,500 employees, but our organization was very flat, in most segments only three deep. We needed more talent to accomplish these application projects by ourselves. We looked to complement our own effort with development partners with limited success.

A good example was our development agreement with Magna Automotive that was initiated by George Husman. We agreed to develop the production of SMC (sheet molding compound) products and the press molding process for automotive parts.

We had high hopes for SMC production and resulting composite parts production, which combined short carbon fibers with resin in a thick sheet form that could be molded into finished parts. This agreement turned out to be a total disappointment. Magna decided to sell their SMC production facility, but our agreement prevented us from entering production on our own. We had much less optimism about the press molding process for prepreg, but that led to the successful introduction of Cadillac hoods, and it went into full production.

The boating industry was the defining commercial application for glass fibers, and this application also offered opportunities for carbon fibers. However, only high-cost yachts and racing sailboats, where cost was not an issue, were using carbon fibers. The snobbishness of this part of the boating industry prided themselves on the use of aerospace carbon fibers and selling the low-cost commercial concept was not gaining any traction. Surprisingly, because Lake Balaton is the largest fresh water lake in Europe, Hungary has an active sailing community and robust boat building industry.

Peter Kiss, mostly out of personal interest, maintained contact with the people in the sport and the boat builders. Through him we received an inquiry from Nándor Fa, who wanted to enter the 2016-2017 Vandée Globe races, a sailboat race around the globe by a single person. He was going to design and build his boat and be the captain in the race. He needed carbon fibers, but he had no money and asked Zoltek to help. Peter was all for it, but I saw significant cost and risk going along with the possibility of a successful demonstration of our carbon fibers. If Nándor failed, it would more than likely be blamed on our fibers, but he convinced me that his commitment and conviction for this project was strong enough to succeed.

For the previous five years, we spent over $8 million annually for application development. This was a lot of money for Zoltek, but it was just not enough to accomplish what we needed to do.

During 2012, our financial performance was the best in Zoltek history. Our revenue recovered beyond 2008 levels to $190 million, the highest ever. We were beyond all the ridiculous non-cash accounting losses, and our net profit was $23 million. But it was a bad year for our shareholders, as our share price steadily declined all year. Our shares were trading as low as $6 when we had validated our commercial-carbon-fiber concept and our production facilities had an economic or replacement value of over $35 per share.

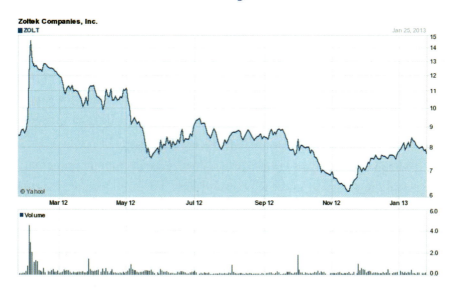

This, of course, was a serious concern for me. The best I could figure was that there were four reasons why we lost the investors' confidence:

one, we underestimated the time it would take for new applications to develop; two, Zoltek was perceived as only a wind energy company; three, visible progress outside of wind energy had been slow to show up in our revenue; and four, the development of our expansion projects before visible proof of demand was misunderstood to be an error in judgement. It seemed our shareholders had lost confidence in our strategy and after too many reversals, no longer saw value in the unstoppable progress that was taking place in our numerous demonstration projects.

Beyond the shareholder disappointment, I was concerned that, for the first time, we significantly outperformed market valuation of our company. Based on our identified growth potential, the intrinsic value of our company was far higher than our share price. This is an uncomfortable position that attracts corporate raiders and private equity funds.

To take the company to the next level required a focused management team, but after years of trying to build the team to be responsive and cohesive, we had made little progress. While we had smart and talented people, our management team was still not functioning effectively and accepted mediocre performance. I just did not feel they were ready to take over if something happened to me.

I started to more seriously consider selling the company, but the process to sell a company was quite complicated and time consuming, and I just could not get myself to start the process.

Cytec decided the commercial carbon fiber business offered more opportunity for growth than their relatively stagnant aerospace business and approached me to discuss a merger. We had several meetings, and I looked at the possibility seriously. Timing was not the best because we were too busy to deal with the many opportunities we were facing and again, their initial valuation was based on the past, not on the future opportunities. We continued our discussions to see where we could develop value together, but our discussions with Cytec went nowhere, and we concluded to go in different directions.

Almost immediately, Hexcel showed interest in discussing possible cooperation. There was a good potential fit between our companies, and we had worked together in the past on some projects. Hexcel was active in aerospace and also had significant commercial business, including supplying fiberglass prepreg to Vestas. Adding our commercial carbon fibers would have given Hexcel more opportunity for growth, and a merger with Hexcel shares would have been a great financial outcome for our shareholders.

Section 7
End of My Carbon Fiber Story

Attacked

The year 2013 started out routinely, except that I had turned seventy years old. I was just as enthusiastic about Zoltek, and I was confident because we had clearly proven our concept, but we had a way to go to fully execute on our strategy. The rest of the journey was not going to be easy. Being able to assure our stakeholders that we would get there was now my number one concern.

The sale or merger of the company was not gaining momentum. GrafTech decided to do a disastrous acquisition of a raw material source for their graphite electrode products and seemed to have abandoned their growth strategy. Solutia was acquired by Eastman Chemical. So both companies were out of consideration. However, our discussion continued with Hexcel.

I was also contacted by Jeff Quinn, the ex-CEO of Solutia, to discuss "some ideas." He told me that he was trying to put together a materials company through acquisitions, and he wanted to return to discussions with Zoltek. He was not clear on what he really wanted to do, other than that he wanted Zoltek to be involved, and as I interpreted it, he wanted Zoltek to be the core acquisition. He asked me if I was interested, and I told him if his ultimate business plan made sense and if it would be beneficial to Zoltek shareholders, I would be interested. I asked for more details, and I suggested meeting again when his plans were more defined, and he was ready to discuss financial terms.

When we met again, he told me about potential acquisitions, which I did not find complementary to Zoltek, and therefore, made no sense to me. What was really disturbing, however, was his idea for some complex financial engineering. He and his investor group would offer a cash dividend to Zoltek shareholders and, using part of the SEC shelf registration for $350 million, issue a significant number of new shares to pay for the dividend. In other words, the dividend would be funded by Zoltek's own cash. The rest of the $350 million would provide the cash for the other acquisitions. The resulting dilution would destroy the existing Zoltek shareholders' value. He basically wanted to take over Zoltek at the expense of the existing shareholders, so he and his investor friends would end up with the majority of Zoltek shares. I just could not see any value in his proposal for Zoltek, and I walked away from any further discussions.

Within a few days, he wrote a letter to our directors, reiterating his proposal. He got the same response officially from the directors. On March 4, 2013, we received a notice of an SEC 13-G filing, which notified Zoltek that a group of investors, headed by Jeff Quinn, had acquired ten percent of Zoltek's outstanding shares and that they were taking steps to acquire all of the outstanding shares. In other words, they were initiating a hostile takeover at a ridiculously low price. The fact that I personally owned twenty percent of the company made the possibility of a successful hostile takeover virtually impossible.

The process to fight a hostile takeover is very expensive and ugly, with generally a destructive outcome. Within days, derogatory articles and press releases appeared in the local newspapers, questioning our director's integrity and competence. This was just the beginning, and things were going to get worse. We needed to hire legal and public relations experts and gear up for a proxy fight. We were sure we would win this battle, but it was a totally unwelcome distraction from much more important activities.

While we were preparing for the proxy fight, I started to consider the impact on our directors and management, our employees and our customers, and, of course, our shareholders. My conclusion was that it would be highly negative to all and interfere with our business for at least twelve months at this most critical time. The question I could not answer was how we could recover and maintain our energy and enthusiasm to continue the difficult work ahead of us during and after this distracting process.

Just going back to business as usual did not seem possible. When large companies went through such an event, most employees were so far removed from the battle that they would be immune to it. In our case, the whole company would be involved and concerned and would speculate about the potential outcome. Many would even take the whole thing personally. It looked all negative, and I just could not see anything positive coming out of it, win or lose. There was a slim possibility that the battle would unify our management team, but I was not ready to take that chance.

I again started to concentrate on the option to sell the company, hopefully to a company that shared Zoltek's strategy and business plan, but with significantly more financial, technological, and management resources. Personally, I felt comfortable that I had accomplished my objective to demonstrate the viability of the low-cost commercial carbon fiber technology and business concept. I certainly wished that we were further along in turning the concept to the size of business that I always felt it could be. But it had taken twenty-five years to get to this point, and it would take significantly more time to reach our ultimate goals. There were more and more substantial companies entering our markets, raising questions of our ultimate ability to succeed as an independent company. I also wished for better timing, when Zoltek's share price would more closely reflect its true value, but the timing for this was certainly unpredictable.

The overwhelming argument, however, was that the process to fight a hostile takeover started with the valuation for the company, which is the same first step for the sales process. If the valuation would be above the takeover offer, then there would be no proxy fight, and the hostile takeover would be done. By committing to the sale option, much of the disruption, legal wrangling, and shareholder vote solicitation came to a halt. If the valuation approached a reasonable value and the share price was acceptable to the shareholders, a successful sale of the company could be completed. So, after much thinking and evaluation of alternatives, I decided to take this opportunity to actually go for the sale.

While it was an emotional decision to sell the company that I started and built for nearly forty years, I was convinced it was the right thing to do. I never felt the overwhelming emotions, as so many people thought that I would, compare it to the loss of "my child" or any other emotion nearly that strong.

We had selected J.P. Morgan to handle the valuation work for the proxy fight, but we needed to review more options for selecting an investment banker for the sale.

Selling Zoltek

Once we initiated the sale process, the proxy fight was discontinued. But before we were fully engaged, Hexcel asked for a meeting. They were following up on earlier discussions to see if we would consider a pre-emptive proposal before other potential buyers would be invited to make a bid. This was interesting and if the offer was actually pre-emptive in value, it might have been worth the legal battle that was sure to follow from the Quinn Group. But the proposal was low and not stock-based, so we invited Hexcel to stay in the auction process to see how that would turn out.

Our first step was to interview investment bankers and select the one we thought might be the best qualified to conduct the most successful auction. We interviewed five of the largest investment banks, including Stifel Nicolaus, the local investment bank. They were all quite interested because there would be a large fee involved if the auction were successful. After we revised all the proposals, we were convinced J.P. Morgan was the most knowledgeable about our business and familiar with potential companies interested in Zoltek, so we selected them. Once we made our selection, the next step was to prepare a presentation, with the help of J.P. Morgan, about Zoltek.

Concurrent with our management team preparing the presentation, our bankers were soliciting companies that would be interested in reviewing our offering documents. We had over a dozen interested companies requesting further information and finally, we selected six, including the group led by Jeff Quinn. Our entire upper management team made individual presentations to each of the finalist companies.

These meetings were usually followed with dinner and open discussions. Considering that some of the interested parties were competitors, these meetings were quite intriguing. Jeff Quinn showed up with just about all the composite industry consultants, who generally were not complimentary of Zoltek. We did our best not to be cynical with this group, but we did not have dinner with them.

Once the presentations were over, several companies visited our plants. All this was time consuming and disruptive to our business. When all the meetings and visits were complete, we all agreed that Toray best understood what Zoltek was all about and personalities seemed to mesh the best. Quinn's final offer was not even close, but still tried to disrupt the orderly sales process. In the end, Quinn could not get financing for a competitive cash offer, and there was no opportunity for creative financial engineering in an orderly process.

I was not surprised because I had previously met with Toray management, particularly Moriyuki Onishi and Masahiko Kawamura, several times to discuss possible cooperation. We provided samples of our products that Toray had tested. Although Toray was the leading carbon fiber supplier to the aerospace industry, they seemed to have a clear understanding that they could not be competitive with their own products in the commercial applications market, and much of the potential commercial applications might never develop unless carbon fiber prices dropped significantly. Toray had, in the past, met our prices, but they lost money by doing so and seem to understand the difference between the commercial and the aerospace carbon fiber markets.

Significant due diligence by several companies continued to dominate much of our management's and staff's time. Between their financial offer and our confidence that Zoltek would continue to be a factor in the carbon fiber market, we zeroed in on executing a transaction with Toray. We arrived at a proposed share price that had to be evaluated for fairness and approved by the directors. The entire process took over six months and finally, on September 27, 2013, we signed a merger agreement with Toray Industries, Inc. at $16.75 per share, which represented an approximately $600 million value for the company. With the Zoltek acquisition, Toray became the industry leader in all carbon fiber markets.

After we finalized the agreement, Toray asked me to go to Tokyo for a press conference and the ceremonial signing. After I checked in for the flight, I received a call telling me not to go because J.P. Morgan had some unfinished issues that needed resolution. I cancelled my flight, went home, and planned a nice dinner with Mary. As I was about to put the steaks on the grill, I received a call from Moriyuki Onishi, asking me where I was. It seems the issue was resolved with a small increase in the share price. When he realized that I was still in St. Louis, he was disappointed and asked me to resume my Tokyo trip as soon as possible.

I took the next flight, and I arrived at Toray headquarters about a half hour prior to the scheduled press conference. I had fifteen minutes to get ready.

The press conference was very interesting, and it was obvious that Toray was a very significant Japanese company. There were about fifty reporters and clearly, they knew all about Toray's carbon fiber business and why Zoltek was important for Toray. There were many questions regarding the justification for this transaction. The consistent message was that the combination of our two companies would make Toray the undisputed overall leader of the carbon fiber business, capturing well over sixty percent of the global carbon fiber market.

When I arrived at Toray headquarters in Tokyo, I met a number of people in their carbon fiber business and witnessed how so many Toray people had a high respect for Zoltek and what we were able to accomplish.

They were clearly excited about the merger. I learned that Zoltek was the largest acquisition Toray, a $20-billion revenue company, had ever made. I also had the opportunity for the first time to meet the man who ultimately approved the merger, Akihiro Nikkaku, the President of Toray.

There was a lot to be done after we completed the merger agreement, but before the transaction would be completed. Several U.S. and E.U. government approvals were required and, after the announcement of the merger agreement, no fewer than nine shareholder lawsuits were initiated that needed to be defeated.

The $16.75 share price was disappointing for me since the replacement value for the company's installed productive assets was more than twice that value. However, this price was twice the price of the shares when we started the proxy fight. At this point, Zoltek's independence was effectively over.

The agreement defined both conditions, under what circumstances and at what penalty Toray could walk away from the merger. The agreement also defined the operating limits under which Zoltek management could continue to operate the company until the transaction closed. Fortunately, all the parameters were well within Zoltek's normal operations and represented no limitations. Zoltek continued to operate as if nothing had happened. Finally, the transaction closed at the end of March 2014, and all the shareholders were paid cash for their shares.

One open item remained after the merger was closed: the settlement of claims against the U.S government for the stealth patent infringement. When Zoltek went public, only fifty percent interest in this patent was included, and the other fifty percent was retained by me, personally. Now we needed to determine the value of the patent and to make payment for my fifty percent ownership.

The valuation depended on the result of a successful settlement with the U.S. government. At the time we signed the merger agreement, we were just about to start the trial in which the U.S. Justice Department was attempting to have our patent declared invalid. If they succeeded, the lawsuit would be over. There was no value ever assigned to the patent on our financial statements, so there were no issues about the financial valuation of Zoltek at the time of the merger.

The invalidation trial was completed in November 2013, and I was Zoltek's only witness. During the trial it became clear that our attorneys did not know the technology and were making claims against a prior art technology. They did not share information with me because they interpreted the confidential status of the case so that I was not entitled to information they received through depositions. The Court of Federal Claims judge committed that he would publish his decision by the end of December of that year. We waited, but his decision did not come until March 31, 2014, almost simultaneously with the closing of the merger transaction. The decision was negative and clearly faulty. We immediately began the lengthy appeal process.

Toray wanted to terminate all our legal actions, including this one. I asked Onishi-san to wait until our appeal was completed. If we lost the appeal, all was over, but if we won, which I was sure we would, we could decide how to proceed at that time to determine the value and the compensation for my share of the settlement.

Soon after the transaction closed, we found out that the Toray management team had been selected, but they would not arrive in St. Louis until after they received their visas in June or July. We had occasional visits by the upper management of Toray's carbon fiber unit, but we continued to operate Zoltek totally independently. It was amazing that they had total trust in us to allow this to happen. I do not know of another such example because it is typical for most companies to make sure they take control immediately. Under our management, Zoltek's business continued to grow and generate substantial profits and very positive cash flow.

At the end of June, the Japanese managers arrived. Three arrived in St. Louis and two in our Hungarian facility. During the first month, they spent time to settle in and only took direct operating responsibility in late July. Masahiko Kawamura, who had been promoting the cooperation with Zoltek for several years, was appointed as the new CEO.

After the Sale

Before Toray made its final decision and offer, I met with Onishi-san, the head of the Toray carbon fiber business and Yoshinaga-san, the director of research and development, for dinner in St. Louis. The due diligence visit to Mexico had a few open items, and they left a negative impression with the Toray team about the facility. We enjoyed a very nice dinner and had an opportunity to discuss the Mexican facility and any concerns they had. The discussions ended positively and to eliminate any remaining concerns, I offered to stay around and work with Toray to make sure the transition would be a success. My commitment was open ended, and I did not expect or ask for an employment contract.

By this time, most of my friends had been retired for years and many of them spent the winter in Florida. Mary and I decided that it was time for us to look at doing the same. In December 2013, we took a week to investigate the possibilities. We found a place we liked, fairly central to a number of our friends from St. Louis. We later realized that other old friends from our past, the Bettses and the Sandals, were also living close by. We bought a house and started to remodel it. The house was completed by mid-2014, and we spent our first winter there that year.

For the first month after the Toray management team arrived, I continued to run our weekly management meetings and turned it over to Kawamura-san when it was clear he wanted to take over. Soon after, I no longer attended the weekly management meetings. George Husman, our CTO, has stayed with Zoltek for a lot longer than he planned, and he was ready to retire and move to Florida. I continued my full-time schedule until September 2014, just three months after the Toray management arrived in St. Louis.

It is a normal thing for the new management to take control as soon as possible, and that was what happened at Zoltek. Dual management never works, and it could not work for Zoltek either. Zoltek managers came to me to ask a question and when they did not like my answer, they would go to the Toray CEO, Kawamura-san, without telling him my response. Obviously this situation could not go on, and I believed it was time for me to back off. I continued to lead some customer contacts and the aircraft brake business until I was able to turn these over Dave Purcell and Mike Westcott.

However, after two years, I am no longer current on the pressing business issues, but I was asked to continue as a member of Zoltek Board. I also continue to be available to answer any questions or provide technical support when needed. I think my availability offers Toray management some comfort in case something goes wrong. This looks to be a standard process for Japanese companies.

I believe it is important for me to continue to remind everyone about the concept behind the continued expansion of the commercial carbon fiber business.

I hosted Nikkaku-san, the President of Toray, on his first visit to the Mexican facility. While the initial impression of the due diligence group was negative for unknown reasons, this visit was very positive. Based on his positive impression, Nikkaku-san approved the installation of a thermoplastic compounding facility and sometime later, an automobile airbag sewing facility at our Mexican plant.

I also hosted Nikkaku-san when he visited our Hungarian facility for the first time. He was even more impressed with the people and that facility.

He has returned to Hungary since and has committed to very significant expansion for carbon fiber and composite intermediates. I liked Nikkaku-san and was glad to see he has been pleased with the Zoltek acquisition.

Zoltek is running at full capacity with reduced production rate. Mostly from the growth of demand by our pre-merger customer base, sales have steadily increased, producing significant profits and cash flow. Everyone agrees that Zoltek has been a financial success.

In retrospect, it was difficult to believe that a small team with no prior experience with carbon fibers was able to successfully develop the commercial-carbon fiber concept and build the world's largest fully integrated carbon fiber plant while several companies with huge financial and technological resources failed. This was the reason, I believe, why Toray acquired Zoltek. I am hopeful that our concept will not be abandoned, and Toray will understand that our fibers are the most economical and well suited for all the commercial applications, and that there is no reason to change our base technology and certainly not lose our cost advantage.

In the past, I have told many customers that even if we gave them our carbon fibers free, they would not be able to produce their products at a competitive cost unless they improve their own manufacturing process. We needed to develop and sell more functional intermediate products to help our customers achieve reasonable finished product cost.

A significant reason why we sold Zoltek was that I felt we needed more technical and financial strength to alter the commercial composite product design and develop new products and processes. If we could not do that, we would potentially lose our industry leadership. I believe Toray recognizes this need and will expand their activities and investments in these areas around Zoltek's carbon fibers. I continue to hope that Zoltek will accomplish the long-term objectives and importance in the composite world that we had worked so hard to achieve.

The last open item, the stealth technology patent valuation, was resolved over two years after the merger was completed. On February

19, 2016, the U.S. Court of Appeals overturned the Court of Federal Claims decision to invalidate our patent and mandated the lower court to deal with infringement and compensation. This was good news. However, we were in no position to perform any form of discovery because the state secret privilege was still in force.

Again, for the second critical time, our attorneys did not know what to do next. Again, they were looking for legislative help as if any congressman or senator would introduce legislative action to pay Zoltek's damages. They were asking me to approve hiring public relations consultants to generate publicity that would compel the U.S. Air Force or some politician to support our claim. The attorneys also believed that they were the owners of the case, not Zoltek! We were going nowhere.

So, again, for the second time over the twenty-year litigation and for the same reason, I decided we need to change the legal team to bring an end to this legal action. I was handling the entire legal battle for the company because Toray really does not like lawsuits, and Toray asked me to take over the entire case.

To do this, the ownership had to be officially transferred from Zoltek to me since our attorneys mishandled the case from the beginning and did not file the original lawsuit on a joint ownership basis. There are rules against transferring claims against the U.S. government, but there is an exception in the case of transfer of company ownership. While my new attorney expected the government lawyers would oppose this move, resulting in as much as two-year delay, he was confident we would not have a problem with this transfer. Toray was in full agreement for us to proceed with the process.

However, almost exactly two years after his arrival, Kawamura-san was transferred and a new CEO, Yoshihiro Takeuchi, was appointed. After he received an unethical and threatening letter from our fired attorneys, he became concerned and decided to hire a law firm to advise him how to proceed. At these attorneys' recommendation, he decided that Toray should stay involved with the patent lawsuit.

By that time, the attorney I engaged, Mark (Thor) Hearne had taken over the case. To expedite matters, he continued to head up the litigation in the name of Zoltek, and he effectively represented my interest as well. Thor was well known in the Court of Federal Claims, and he was able to quickly move the case forward. He reached an agreement with the government attorneys to begin the mediation process.

Based on information from earlier deposition that I finally received and knowledge of this technology, we arrived at an estimate of $125 million value for our technology plus interest. There was no way to better define a reasonable valuation because the secret privilege would hold us from finding out details of the actual construction of the airplanes. With Toray staying in the case and looking for quick resolution and a final disposition of this lawsuit, our negotiating position, with the state secret privilege in effect and blocking Zoltek from further discovery, was hopeless to arrive at a settlement representing a fair value for our technology.

On October 13, 2016, we entered into settlement discussions. Finally, we were bringing this last open issue to close. We agreed to settle for $20 million. This was a disappointing amount, but considering the alternatives, it was the right thing to do. We received the settlement payment at the end of May 2017. This being the last open item in the transaction, it concluded my financial interest in Zoltek.

The 2016-2017 Vandée Globe races were completed in February 2017. Fa Nándor and his boat, *Spirit of Hungary*, finished in eighth place. There were thirty boats that entered, and only fourteen completed the race. This was a fantastic accomplishment and completely proved that our carbon fibers should become the standard for the boat industry.

While these business events were unraveling, Marta graduated from University of Mississippi and continued on to law school. She became a lawyer in 2014.

Mary's mother died in 2015 after several years of poor health. As usual, families get close or fall apart at these sad times. In our case, during her funeral, we met and reunited with Mary's brother's children after many years of minimum or no contact. This is something Mary wanted to happen because she missed seeing them growing up.

Once my role diminished at Zoltek, I started to think of the future. I have spent significant time writing this book, and now I am looking to see what I can do to help others. I have completed and endowed a project to establish a Chemical Engineering and Biomedical Engineering student exchange between the University of Minnesota, where I went to school, and the Budapest Technical University, where I would have gone to school if I stayed in Hungary. My hope is that the two universities will develop a long-term relationship, and the participating students will enrich their scholastic and social experiences. I continue to look for other projects that would improve life for others.

In my spare time, I am practicing how to play golf and try to live up to the standard of the Hungarian national golf champion!

Picture by Mary – Hole #8 on the Hills Course of Jupiter Hills Club, Florida

Epilogue

Looking back at my life, I lived both under an oppressive dictatorial government and in almost total freedom as I progressed from poverty to financial success. I can say without any reservation that freedom and prosperity is far better than oppression and poverty. So, why is it that most people of the world live under oppressive and dictatorial government and in poverty?

For thousands of years, the economy revolved around agriculture and ownership of land. Other than the land owners and elite classes, most people lived as surfs, slaves, or soldiers. Very little had changed until the eighteenth century, starting with the agricultural revolution and followed by the industrial revolution. The agricultural revolution improved productivity and significantly increased the quantity of food production. This led to significant population growth and migration to towns and cities Along with this change came huge demand for manufactured goods that led to the industrial revolution in the nineteenth century

In an industrial economy, individuals could create wealth by innovation and mass production. As the industrial revolution spread around, the globe and rapidly progressed through the nineteenth century, the need for laborers and raw materials further changed the economics. One outcome was the introduction of socialism. The objective of socialism was to prevent the development of a new wealthy class and to share the riches among the working class. But changing the entrenched system was not easy. Several European revolutions and wars broke out as the social unrest and political instability in Europe escalated, ultimately leading to the outbreak of the First World War. Finally, communism was brought upon the world in the middle of the world war by the Bolshevik Revolution of 1917 in Russia.

The First World War was considered the war to end all wars and the establishment of a "New World Order." But, of course, it did not. On the contrary, in my opinion, this war was the beginning of the second Hundred Year's War of the civilized world. Almost immediately this new world order paved the way to the formation of new dictatorships around the world and in just twenty years, the Second World War that spread the conflict around the globe commenced.

After nearly 100 million people were killed, the primary conflicts ended with the defeat of Germany and after two nuclear bombs, the surrender of Japan. However, some minor conflicts never ended and almost immediately new ones started. All of the global conflicts, including the current Middle East wars and terrorism that followed the official end of the Second World War, can be traced to the unreasonable and short-sighted agreements and treaties.

With the Allies' support and the agreements at the Yalta Conference, after WW II, all of Central and Eastern Europe was handed over to the Soviets who then imposed the communist political system and socialist economy on the countries taken over by them. The Yalta Agreement was between Roosevelt, who thought Stalin was a nice guy and referred to him as "Uncle Joe;" Churchill, who was willing to make a deal with the devil to save England, which he did; and Stalin, the mass murderer. Before Roosevelt died, he realized who Stalin really was, but forgot to tell Truman, and Churchill made his Iron Curtain speech, marking the beginning of the Cold War at Westminster

University in Missouri in March of 1946, less than one year after the end of WW II.

England and France, once again, led the way to create another "New World Order" by establishing new borders for many countries and establishing new countries, many in the Mideast, without consideration for historical precedence or ethnic compatibility. Communism spread from Europe to Asia, with China leading the way, and to South America. Almost immediately, new wars to defeat communism commenced. The most notable wars were the Korean and the Vietnam wars. Even before these wars ended, conflict between Israel and its surrounding Muslim countries started, which was followed by the re-emergence of Muslim radicalism.

When the two largest communist governments, the Russian and Chinese communist systems, collapsed, communism was almost completely erradicated around the world with few notable exceptions, like North Korea. It is interesting that after the communist systems collapsed, the countries' productive assets and treasury were looted by the communist thugs for their personal accounts. It is also interesting and revealing that mostly the old communists are still in control, but they no longer spew the socialist rhetoric. This gave rise to new type of dictators, like Vladimir Putin and other filthy rich criminals. But most people who suffered under the communist system for decades are just as poor and continue to suffer, while the global conflicts just continue. And the majority of the world's population continues to live under oppressive governments and in poverty.

If I am right about the Second Hundred Years' War, we should now be nearing the end. But the world is still under as much tension as ever, and it is not clear how will it end.

The 1956 Hungarian Revolution was the first armed conflict that was televised live, leaving a lasting impression on the world and helping to discredit the Soviet communist dictatorship. It took more than thirty more years for the communist system to be rejected globally.

I lived under the oppressive communist system and escaped from that world to the USA where I experienced freedom for the first time. Since then, the American people had been losing more and more of this freedom. It seems that many people in the U.S. have been embracing the spread of global socialism, as the rest of the world that had experienced it, has rejected it. It is great concern to me that the progressives in U.S. are trying to revive it again.

Asked by Chris Matthews of MSNBC, "What is the difference between a democrat and a socialist?" Debbie Wasserman Schultz, the then-chairman of the Democratic National Committee, who I consider to be a progressive zealot, could not answer. No doubt she would have had an even harder time trying to explain the difference between a progressivist and a communist. So, let me offer my definition.

"Communism" and "progressivism" are political terms that define how to destroy an existing socio-economic system characterized by individual liberty and free exchange and drive it to socialism, which has as its ultimate objective the equal sharing of poverty and misery for everyone, except for the ruling class of government officials, who live like royalty. (Washington, DC is the city with the third highest per capita income in the U.S.; we are getting there!)

The fundamental difference between communism and progressivism is the rate at which socialism is achieved. In Russia after the 1917 revolution, Stalin was responsible for murdering more than 20 million Russians. In China, after 1945, Mao Zedong was responsible for murdering over 40 million Chinese people and an additional 20 million people to die from starvation caused by the socialist economy. These are the two worst examples from many of how communist dictators eliminate entire cultural, intellectual, and economic classes standing in the way of the living hell of a socialist "paradise."

Stalin believed that people are incapable of comprehending this level of death inflicted by dictators. He stated that a single death is a tragedy, but millions of deaths is a statistic.

Progressivism is a slower process, but leads to the same end. Once socialism is getting close to fruition, three important things happen: first, the population is stripped of all weapons and criminals become the enforcers of the socialist ideology; second, free speech is eliminated, speech is controlled, and overtaken by propaganda; and third, the population is encouraged to spy on each other to destroy and eliminate all the remaining opposition against the change. There are clear signs in the U.S. that these forces are beginning to gain strength. It is incomprehensible to me how anyone can ignore history and embrace the change to socialism.

The United States of America, over its near 250-year history, has become the wealthiest, freest, most diverse, and open society and the strongest country in the world. It is fortunate for anyone, natural born or immigrant, to be a citizen of the U.S. Not surprisingly, many rogue nations want to take what we have and illegal immigrants want to come and take advantage of our system. The best way to respond to these threats is to provide the example for the rest of the world to follow and to defend our country, its sovereignty, and its values. However, alarmingly, we have been apologizing for our success and doing things to destroy our own economy to be just as miserable as the rest of the world, calling it globalization.

The public service unions are driving the size and cost of government higher and higher without any controls because the management (made up of politicians) does not properly represent the taxpayer's interest. Not surprisingly, non-productive government jobs have become higher paying with better benefits and more stability than jobs in the private sector. This problem is compounded by lack of accountability or reasonable performance standards for government employees or for the quality of education for teachers. If we include the employees working for the government contractors, almost half of the population is either actually working for or lives off the government.

Unfortunately, public schools and liberal colleges, under the protection of teacher unions and tenure system, have become centers of socialist propaganda, not centers of quality education. One of the worst examples is the induced fear of global warming propagated by the politically motivated scientists. The existence of global warming is not at all certain and therefore, now it has been renamed climate change. However, all the proposed solutions result in global redistribution of wealth, which is the real objective.

There are now proposals that would make expressing any doubt about global warming illegal. This idea is the same as it was over 2000 years ago, when it was illegal, punishable by death, to question the notion that the earth was flat.

In my experience when trying to start joint ventures to produce carbon fibers around the world, it became clear that most countries expect the U.S. companies to finance the ventures, to provide the technology, and to be responsible for the sales. The result is that our capital moves to other countries and U.S. workers move out of the workforce, which continues to significantly increase the number of people depending on entitlements from the government. The invested capital, technology, and the manufacturing profits stay in the foreign countries while our government borrows money, from the very same foreign countries, to pay for the entitlements.

Once the investment is made and the technology is shared, the recipient countries correctly believe that they are in control. In the end, we become a consumer nation with diminished productive assets, and the other countries become self-sufficient. The "new world order" will result in the world economy turning upside down, giving way for global socialism.

It has been my observation that most Americans believe that our way of life and political system is stable and can survive just about any affront against it. This confidence comes from American's naiveté and never having experienced a sudden and complete deterioration of our way of life. While it would not be easy to completely destroy the American system, if only for its size, the deterioration has been happening slowly and steadily. However, once the deterioration goes over the tipping point, the process will accelerate.

The election of Donald Trump as the president has restored my faith in the American voters, and I hope the new government can turn our progressive trend around and restore a more positive and successful attitude and national pride and, once again, open the way to expanded opportunities for all the citizens and legal immigrants.

I realize my view of the world and my historical perspective is not shared by many Americans and certainly not by most of the younger generations. The lack of proper education in history of the world, and specifically America's role in it, along with the never-ending propaganda, has done the damage. I hope this will reverse before it is too late. The idea of changing the U.S. to socialism so that it can suffer along with the rest of the world would actually make life worse, not better, for everyone. And, in the process, removing the shining beacon that the U.S. has been will destroy whatever little hope is left for the oppressed people in the world.

I believe it is a universal truth that, while money does not buy happiness, it is easier to be happy with money than without, but not everyone has the same potential to accumulate an equal level of wealth. It is most important to have a realistic expectation that matches one's ability and willingness to do what is necessary to achieve his or her goals.

Even in the best of times, success in America is not guaranteed. However, there is no other country in the world that offers more opportunity to succeed than the United States of America, and I am one of the fortunate individuals to have experienced it.

Success is most often expressed in financial terms, but, of course, success may be expressed through the achievement of individual goals that give people their own desired pride and happiness. In any free society that rewards achievement and provides the opportunity to set one's own goals, there will be a hierarchy from the less fortunate to the wealthy, but there must always be a free path to move upward. Equally, people who wish to maintain a simple life and not get into the race for glory should be accepted and their way of life respected.

I decided very quickly after I arrived in America that I wanted to achieve financial success. First, I pursued my goal in the corporate world and later in my own business. Without a legacy, my goals were quite general on how to achieve my overall objectives. Nonetheless, I became part of the group representing the richest 0.1 percent of Americans. On top of a lot of tireless work, getting to this level took acquired skills, strong and consistent determination, never-wavering commitment, and some luck and support from family and friends. Every success story is unique in its own way, but there are a few principles that I practiced and believe are necessary and common to all.

Starting a business is not like starting a new job, it is life changing journey. It demands a high degree of confidence, based on experience and/or unique knowledge to start a successful business, and not on an abstract idea developed in vacuum.

In my case, after nine years of an unsatisfactory corporate career, I gained the confidence to move on and try to make it on my own. I was 33 years old, I was frustrated and impatient. Other people arrive at this crossroad in their lives at different times and under different circumstances. There are many stories of people skipping higher education to start their business, many of them in the world of information technology, and there are examples of arriving at this level late in life. For example, Colonel Sanders at age of 62 founded Kentucky Fried Chicken restaurants.

Although my comments are directed at entrepreneurs who start their own business, many businesses are launched by a group that can work together, rather than by a single individual. In this model, each member contributes to the enterprise's success. In general, it is important to have one leader who represents the company, but in most successful companies there are a number of leading managers who make the company productive and offer these leaders recognition and exceptional rewards for their contribution. A good example is Andrew Grove of Intel. He was the third employee hired by the company and worked for Intel for almost his entire working career. His name became synonymous with the company, and he became the long-term Chairman and CEO. At Zoltek, I achieved financial success beyond my original expectations, and also, in the process, about twenty-five people at Zoltek also became millionaires.

A business must have a vision and clearly articulate through its mission what products or services it will provide. These may change along the way, but without a vision, the business cannot focus. It is also important to have a realistic expectation of what size the business will become. Once the vision is identified and clearly communicated, this expectation will serve as the guide for managing risk. If the expectation is too low, it is easy to miss opportunities and accept mediocre performance and if the expectation is too high, it can result in taking unacceptable risks that could put the viability of the enterprise in jeopardy.

Initially Zoltek was a manufacturers-representative business. This decision was based on my experience in working with the Monsanto sales representatives and building a good reputation with them. At one point, I had gained enough confidence and thought I was ready to become one. At that point, I had a lot of help in finding good companies to represent in the St. Louis territory. This business also did not require significant investment, and it was a business that could work with only one person. My business eventually evolved from the manufacturer's representative business, to an industrial distributor business, to engineering and construction service and finally, to revolutionizing the carbon fiber industry as a capital-intensive manufacturing business.

Without a plan, it is impossible to build anything, and this applies to businesses as well. While it is important to have a strategic business plan, it is also important to have flexibility. Almost immediately after the business plan is completed, something could happen that makes part or the entire business plan obsolete, and the plan needs to be modified. Executing a business plan needs commitment, but also requires constant review and flexibility to respond to changes in the business climate. Not many companies go from start to success without encountering some serious setbacks or discovering new opportunities that require a change in direction.

For Zoltek, this need for major change manifested very early. My entry into carbon fibers was to complement our flexible graphite sealing business but, within a year, it took on a whole new life and ultimately resulted in a total overhaul of the company. This change in my business plan distinguished Zoltek in the carbon fiber business, and it was the root of the significant growth in value of Zoltek.

All businesses need capital and unfortunately, often when things do not look promising. Most entrepreneurs need to find funds from others to start their businesses. The amount of money needed is defined by the business plan. Often people try to get financing just because they need money and before considering how they will make sure they will be able to pay it back. People give, lend, or invest money because they believe and trust the people they support. In some of my private investments, I experienced that some business owners actually believed that it is not fair for investors to profit from the company's success because they did not work for it. Once this attitude becomes evident, financing opportunities evaporate.

I always looked at financing as a serious personal commitment. Relaying this commitment to investors was root of achieving success in obtaining financing. Although my original business was based on low capital requirements, it became a highly capital-intensive business. The start-up capital came from re-mortgaging our home and ultimately becoming a public company, relying on investments by shareholders from individuals and professional investors. My philosophy was always to look out for the investors' and lenders' interests, and I would only look for funding when I totally believed that I would be able to repay the loan or be sure the investors would have a reasonable return.

Unfortunately, following these principles is not enough to guarantee success. In addition, there are some basic business realities that also need to be followed, and these are developed by individuals to fit their own personalities and ambition. When things are going badly, the easiest thing to do is to give up. There are many reasonable excuses to justify it and there are lot of sympathetic friends and family to make you feel good, but giving up is just admitting failure.

All of this does not substitute for the commitment, hard work, and long hours it takes to lead an organization to success. One more time, I have to say, "Only in America!"

Index

A
Abilene plant, 274, 279, 294, 307–309, 318, 321, 337, 365
Advanced Research Projects Agency (DARPA or ARPA), 231–33
American Cyanamid (later Cytec), 235
Amundson, Dr. Neal, 90–91
Anneliese (caretaker's daughter), 58, 59
Árvai, Lajos, 278
Austro-Hungarian Empire, 55

B
Baker, Des, 153–54, 163
Bakos, George (György), 236, 240, 245, 252, 254, 263
Baraccani, Alfonzo, 120, 121–22, 128–29
Barta, Ferenc, 240–41, 249
Baur, Andrew N. (Drew), xxii, 188, 190, 194, 296, 337, 348–49
Bealke, Linn, xxii, 188, 200–201, 296, 301
Bendix (later Allied-Signal, Honeywell), 184, 222–23
Bernstein, Bruce, 309
Betts, Jim, 200, 339
Betts family, 120, 383
BMW, 274, 294, 297, 341–43, 344
Boehm, Elmer, 108–109
Bomba, Karen, 330, 347
Brennan, Father Gene, 159
Brennan, Father George, 159, 276
Budapest
   history, 3–4
   in WW II, 12–13
   postwar, 15–17
Burke, Tom, 164–65, 167

C

carbon fibers in aircraft brakes
    carbon/carbon composite, 173
    developing the aircraft brake market, 222

carbon fibers in everyday commercial products
    commercialization concept, 227–30
    applications, 174–77
    developing commercial market, 281–91
    in wind turbines, 297, 305–308, 338, 344–45, 347–48, 358
    in automobiles, 297, 341–44, 367
    in golf club shafts, 283
    manufacturing process, 172–74
    Zoltek plan to revolutionize industry, 179–81

Carbon Industrie (Messier Bugatti, Safran) 175, 183

CIB Bank, 239, 249

communism
    author's comments on, 87–88, 389–95
    break-up of communism, 236
    in Russia, 247–48

Courtaulds, 184, 197, 199, 228–29, 295, 311

Cydsa, 327, 330, 333–36

Cytec, 369

D

Daimler/Mercedes, 297, 343
Demendi, Joe, 171
DeSchutter, Dick, 112–3
Diamond Fibers, 241–42
Dill, Charlie, 200–201, 296
Dole, Tom, 168
Dorr, Jim, 200
Dresser Industries, 156
Duffy, Mike, 117, 147
DuPont acrylic fibers, process, plant, 185, 236–37

E

Ede (Édi) (uncle), xvi, 9, 30, 46, 60, 255
Esztergom, 55
Eszterházy, Dániel, 54
Eszterházy, House of, 53

F

Fa, Nándor, 367, 387
Finholt, Rick, 191–92
Flexigraf, 165, 218

Föz, Miklos, 66, 76, 78
Frasier, Tom, 150–51

G
Gallagher family, 116, 212–13
Gallagher, Joan (Marta's mother), 117, 182
Gallagher, Mary Catherine (Mary Rumy), xi, 115–18, 133
Gamesa, 307, 310, 319, 321
General Electric, xviii, 345–46
Gonzalez, Tomas, 334
Goodrich, 184, 185, 201, 220, 295, 319
Grafoil (Union Carbide), 153–54
Grant Thornton, 331
Green Cross (Rockefeller Institute), 7
Griesedieck, Chris, 156, 158

H
Habsburg, Archduke Franz Ferdinand, 4
Habsburgs (House of Habsburg, Austria), 52–54
Hearne, Mark, 387
Hercules Chemical Company, xxi, 186
Hexcel, 370, 373, 377
Hickey, Terry, 218
Hirst, Samuel, 26
Hirst, Theodore, 26
Horthy, Miklós (Adm.), 6
Horváth, Sándor, 326
Hungarian plant (see Magyar Viscosa), 324–27, 330–32
Hungarian Revolution, 39–47
Hungary
    history, 3–4
    Treaty of Trianon, 4–6, 11
    German occupation begins, 11–12
    after Munich Agreement, 10
    hyperinflation, 16
    under communist rule, 16–17, 30–31
    Revolution, 39–47
Huntington, Arnie, 168, 220
Husman, George, 325–26, 367, 384

I
ICD (agent for Nitron), 245, 252–53
Imre (school friend), 58, 59
Industrial Development Authority Board, 161–62

J
JP Morgan, 376, 377
Jacobsen, Ole Barup, 304
Jet Propulsion Laboratory (JPL), 176
Jobbágy, Domokos (Domi), 60, 66, 76, 89–90

K
Kardos, John, 200, 326
Kawamura, Masahiko, 378, 382, 384
Keiser Industries, 241
Kinter, Istvan, 318
Kiphart, Orel, 220–22, 264, 266, 268
Kiss, Peter, 160, 185–86, 219–20, 226, 263, 270, 318, 367
Kodály, Zoltán, 31-3
Korányi, Dr. László (Laci), 27, 123, 160
Kristensen, Ole, 307
Kun, Béla, 5–6

L
Laci (cousin), 40
Latta, Mike, 325
Leale, Victor, 336
Ledvényi, Tibor, 308
Litz, Tom, xxiii,199, 200
Lowell plant, 167, 177, 192–93

M
Magyar Viscosa Rt. (Hungarian Rayon Corp.), 185–86, 236–40
Malassine, Bernard, 224
Manci (Margit) (aunt), 24, 40
McCarthy, Tim, 298, 306, 318
McDonnell, John, 200–201, 280, 296
McMurry, Dick, 184, 201, 220–21
Merrill Lynch, 266, 329
Messier-Bugatti (Carbon Industrie), 183, 185, 224, 273–74, 295, 319
Mindszenty (Cardinal), 23, 44, 46, 124–25
Missouri Research Park, 190–91
Mitsubishi Chemical, 199, 341
Monsanto, 235
    WG Krummrich plant, 95, 107
    Enviro-Chem Division, xix–xx, 143, 147–49, 163

N
Nagy, Imre, 39, 44
Nikkaku, Akihiro, 380, 384–85

Nitron, 249
Nobel, Iván, 31, 36
Nunez, Jesus, 336
Nuno, Ignacio (Nacho), 334, 335–36

O
O'Brien, Father Joe, 117, 138, 143, 159, 219, 276
Omicron Capital, 309
Onishi, Moriyuki, 383
Orlon (DuPont acrylic fibers), 185
Owens Corning, 284–85

P
Panex (Zoltek carbon fibers), 178
Pászty, George (György), 236, 240, 252, 254, 255, 265, 277–78
Pauli, Chris, 196
Pauli & Co., 196
Perrault, Maurice, 319
Pfitzinger, Bill, 218
Power Dynamics, Inc., 147–50
Pratt-Whitney, 287
Purcell, David, 330, 384
Pyron (Zoltek oxidized PAN fibers), 178

Q
Quinn, Jeff, 373–74, 377–78

R
Reisz, Barnabás, 336
Rene, Cheryl, 193, 194–95, 203, 264–65
Research Park, University of Missouri, 190–91
Reynoso, Pedro, 334, 335, 339
RK Textiles (later RK Carbon, SGL), 175, 184
Rumy, Árpád (brother), 25–26, 33–34, 74, 146, 166, 181–82, 313–314
Rumy, Árpád (father), 3, 7
    marriage, 7–8
    politics, 9
    military career, 8, 12–13
    as POW, 13
    return from Russia, 19-20
    arrested by AVO, 21–22, 24–25
    works on farm, 32–33, 35
    early death, 137–38
Rumy, Árpád (nephew), 182
Rumy, Károly György, 54–55

Rumy, Ilona Tones (mother), 3, 7-8, 26, 28-30, 72, 138, 314
    marriage, 7
    being alone, 17-18, 25-26, 138, 314
    professional career, 7, 17-18, 73
Rumy, Lajos, 8, 11, 12, 55
Rumy, Mary Gallagher, 115–18, 133, 147, 148–49, 152–53, 163, 165, 182, 186–87, 300
Rumy, Zsolt
    board memberships, 161–63, 262, 297, 337
    childhood life, 17–21, 23–38, 56-58
    early life in America, 65–69, 71–73, 75–78, 81-83
    childhood/summer/part-time jobs, xii, xvii, 71–72, 76–77, 79, 80–81, 83, 88–89, 93, 131–32
    on communism, 87–88, 389–95
    at General Electric, 132–37
    golfing, xxii, 89, 159–60, 190, 221, 276, 288–89, 300–301, 323–24, 337, 388
    government secret clearance, 186–87
    joins Psi Upsilon, xv–xvii
    MBA, 126, 133
    meets Mary, 115–118
    Mary's first visit to Hungary, 122–24
    at Monsanto, 95, 107–115, 136, 139–42
    selling shares of Zoltek, 276
    on socialism, 87–88, 389–95
    thyroid cancer, 158–159
    at University of Minnesota, 82, 86–88, 90, 91–92, 93-94, 388
    visits Russia, 242–48
    at W. R. Grace & Co., xviii,114, 119–22, 125–31
Rumy family
    under communist rule, 15–47
    historical background, 50–56
    going to America, 58
    as immigrants in the U.S., 65–83
    life in Minneapolis, 69–70, 74
    US citizenship, 85–86

S

Schell, Phil, 344, 361–62
Seers, Roger, 148
SGL, 175, 273, 295, 341–42
Smallholders Party, 44
Solutia find, 373
Soos, István (Pista) (school friend), 58, 59
Sopron, 3,15, 49
Southwest Bank, 194–96, 200, 262, 296–97, 337
SP Systems, (Structural Polymers) 287, 289–90, 321
St. Louis County Economic Council, 160–63
St. Louis Sister City program, 163

St. Louis University, 133
Stackpole Fibers, Inc., xx, 165, 167–72, 176
Standal, John, xv, xvi, xvi, 73, 117, 383
Stealth (radar absorbing carbon fiber) patent, 176–77, 260–61, 322, 339–40, 381, 385–86
Svendsen, Arne, xv, 73, 77

T
TRW, 225
Takeuchi, Yoshihiro, 386–87
Tandi, Ilona, 295, 318, 326
Technical University student demands, 36–37
Tesla, x, 344
Thomas, Casey, 327, 335
Tones, Ilona (mother's maiden name), 3
Tömör (Tones) Ede (Uncle Édi), xvi, 9, 30, 46, 60, 255
Toczylowski, Marta, 182, 315, 387
Toray Industries, Inc., 368–82
Toyo Tanso, 164–65
Treaty of Trianon, 5, 56

V
Vestas Wind Systems, 300, 306–08, 310, 318–9, 321, 347–48, 358
Volkswagen AG, 342, 343

W
Waraksa, Bob, 200, 219
Welch, Jack, 134, 135, 136–37
Westcott, Mike, 263, 384
Wilson, Andy, 205
Wilson, Woodrow, 5
wind turbine industry, 297, 305–08, 338, 344–45, 347–48, 358
Witterschein, Bob, xxii,188, 190, 194–95
World War II
    Battle of Stalingrad, 11
    Budapest during, 12–13
    ends, 13–14
    Horthy government in, 10–11, 12
World War I, 4–6, 11

Y
Yalta Conference, 15
Yoshinaga, Ninoru, 383

Z
Zoltek Companies, Inc.

aircraft brakes business, 183–87, 338
attempts at globalization, 357–64
automobile airbag applications, 225–26
Baur investment group, 296
buys Stackpole Fibers, 167–72
commercial carbon fiber applications, 227–31
Composite Intermediates unit, 288
considerations in selling, 375–76
Equipment and Services Division, 217–18
financing, 151, 154–55, 156, 158, 188–91, 194–95, 249–52, 264–68, 299, 309–10
founded, 150
globalization strategy, 357–64
government contracts and, xxi–xxii, 175–76, 186, 261
headquarters building, 158
hostile takeover effort, 374–76
Hungarian acquisition, 55, 236–41, 249–55
Indonesian agent, 164
Initial steps to become an entrepreneur, 147-50
initial public offering (IPO), 195–97, 204–05, 207
inquiry from Saudi Arabia, 327–29
Lowell plant, 177–78, 192–94
management team issues, 345–348, 369
meeting with SEC, xxiii–xxv
Mexican plant, 329, 333–40, 365–66
Panex, 178
performance-based compensation plan, 345–346
plan to revolutionize carbon fibers industry, 179–81
proposal to Indian company, 361–63
Pyron, 178, 179, 184
record financial performance, 368
shelf-registered stock sale, 329–30
stealth patent, 176-77, 260–61, 385–86
stock splits, 233–34, 265
succession plan, 313
Toray merger, x–xi, 378–82
US government patent infringement claim, 322, 339–40, 387
ZOLTEK-2000, 257–60
Zoltek Zrt, 270–275